외신으로
본
대한민국의
VOCA
BULARY

지금까지 이런 영어 단어 퍼레이드는 없었다!
영어 공부에 진심인 학습자를 위한 책

외신으로 본 대한민국의 VOCABULARY 1

최홍수 지음

사설닷컴

추천사

영어는 가장 세계적인 언어요, 과학·기술·정치·문화를 가리지 않고 공통어가 됐다는 것은 주지의 사실입니다. 157개국의 항공사에서 영어로 안내 방송을 합니다. 인도(India)만 해도 영어신문이 3,000종입니다. 유럽자유무역연합(EFTA : European Free Trade Association) 소속 6개국이 영어로 업무를 처리하지만 그중 영어가 공용어인 나라는 없습니다. 이런 현실은 우리나라도 별반 다르지 않다고 생각합니다.

흔히 영어와 다른 언어의 가장 큰 차이점이 어휘의 풍부함이라고 합니다. 《웹스터 뉴 인터내셔널 사전》에는 45만 개, 《옥스퍼드 영어사전》에는 61만 5,000개의 단어가 수록되어 있습니다. 영어 어휘의 풍부함과 다양한 동의어는 곧 비영어 사용자가 표현할 수 없는 뉘앙스(nuance)를 영어 사용자가 끌어낼 수 있다는 뜻입니다.

영어에는 다른 언어에서는 볼 수 없는 유연성이 있습니다. 그 대표적인 것이 수동과 능동을 자유롭게 취할 수 있다는 점입니다. 그리고 한 단어를 명사로도 쓰고 동사로도 써서 그 효과를 최대한 뽑아내는 역량이 있습니다. drink는 '음료'와 '마시다', sleep는 '잠'과 '잠을 자다'라는 뜻으로도 쓰입니다.

《외신으로 본 대한민국의 VOCABULARY 1》의 가장 큰 특징은 우리나라에 관한 여러 기사(BTS 등)를 통해 영어의 어휘를 익힌다는 점입니다. 이로써 가장 피부에 와닿는 공부가 된다는 점이 이 책의 장점입니다. 특히 세계 유수의 잡지인 〈Time〉에서는 2010년대 중반부터 북한의 핵에 관한 기사를 많이 다뤘습니다. 그리고 우리나라의 국제적 위상의 상승과 더불어 미국의 일간지인 〈The New York Times〉에서는 하루가 멀다고 우리나라에 관한 기사가 쏟아집니다. 이 책에서 이런 기사들을 접할 수 있습니다.

이 책의 또 다른 장점은 게재된 예문들의 강한 시사성(時事性)입니다. 세계를 불안에 떨게 한 코로나(Covid-19), Me Too, 우크라이나-러시아 전쟁 기사 등을 통해 미국 사회, 나아가 국제 정치나 국제 사회에 관한 흐름을 접할 수 있습니다. 시사성이 강하다는 의미는 현대 영어를 배운다는 맥락으로 연결됩니다.

또한 유사한 단어를 묶어 헷갈리지 않도록 하면서 풍부한 어휘를 선사합니다. 'disinformation'과 'misinformation'을 보겠습니다. disinformation은 사회문제가 되는 가짜 뉴스입니다. 의도성이 있기 때문입니다. 그러나 misinformation은 그냥 잘못된 정보일 뿐입니다. 그리고 이 책을 통해 어휘를 공부하는 과정에서 예문 속 많은 vocabulary를 만나게 됩니다. 이때 여러분은 사전을 펼치는 수고를 아끼지 말길 바랍니다. 이 세상에 수월한 일은 하나도 없습니다.

수년에 걸친 저자의 노력에 경탄하지 않을 수 없습니다. 저자의 집필 의도가 이 책 한 권에도 충분히 드러나고 있습니다. 이와 더불어 《외신으로 본 대한민국의 VOCABULARY 2》도 작업 중이라고 하니 사뭇 기대가 큽니다.

최준석
(전 조선일보 기자, 주간조선 편집장, 현 과학 칼럼니스트)

머리말

17세기 초 영어단어는 25만 개를 헤아렸다고 합니다. 1928년 옥스퍼드 영어사전에는 41만여 개의 영어단어가 등재되었고, 그 후 수십 년 동안 수만 단어가 새롭게 만들어져 현재 엄청난 수의 어휘를 형성하고 있습니다. 모든 언어가 그러하듯 생성과 사멸의 과정을 겪습니다. 그래서 연말이면 옥스퍼드 사전 등재 단어가 발표되곤 합니다. 이로 미루어보아 영어공부는 어휘공부와 별반 다르지 않다고 판단됩니다.

《외신으로 본 대한민국의 VOCABULARY 1》은 제목에서 알 수 있듯 어휘 책입니다. 대표적인 시사잡지인 미국의 〈Time〉과 일간신문 〈The New York Times〉 등에서 우리나라와 관계된 어휘(그 어휘가 쓰인 예문)를 뽑고 유사 단어끼리 묶었습니다. 2016년부터 〈Time〉은 북한의 핵 문제를 많이 다뤘습니다. 그 외에도 우리나라의 국제적 위상이 올라간 덕분인지 시간이갈수록 외신에 등장하는 횟수가 점점 잦아지고 있었습니다. 최근에는 새로운 정부 출범, 차별금지법, 저출산, 피아니스트 임윤찬 등을 보도했습니다. 자연히 이 책에도 이를 다뤘습니다. 몇 가지 예를 들어보겠습니다.

윤석열 대통령은 박빙(薄氷)으로 이재명 후보를 이겼습니다. 박빙은 본래 '얇게 살짝 언 얼음'을 말합니다. 이 뜻이 확장되어 근소한 차이를 비유적으로 이르는 말로 자주 쓰입니다. 오히려 본래의 뜻보다는 비유적 표현으로 더 많이 쓰인다고 할 수 있습니다. 그렇다면 영어에서는 이를 어떻게 표현했을까요? 'razor-thin'이라고 합니다. 면도날만큼의 차이라는 뜻이겠지요?

건강에 관심이 많은 현대인입니다. 그중에도 비만은 만병의 근원이라고도 합니다. 비만은 스트레스(stress)와 밀접한 관련이 있습니다. 스트레스를 받으면 폭식을 하는 경우가 많습니다. 영어로 'stress-eat'이라고 합니다. 간단명료함에 매력을 느낍니다. 김정은은 세계적인 trouble-maker입니다. 그의 잔혹성을 말할 때 고모부 장성택의 처형을 이야기합니다. 그때 김정은은 언론플레이를 했습니다. 장성택이 포승줄에 묶여 재판받는 광경이 전파를 탔습니다. 이럴 때 'perp-walk'라고 합니다. 'perp'는 범죄자라는 뜻의 'perperator'의 줄임말입니다.

기본적으로 이 책의 예문들은 최고로 평가받는 매체에서 쓰인 것들입니다. 이런 멋진 문장들을 암기한다면 영어 실력 향상에 도움이 될 것입니다. 더구나 헷갈리기 쉬운 단어 모음집이기에 공부하는 데도 유용할 것입니다. 그리고 보다 용이하게 공부할 수 있도록 어떤 맥락(context)에서 이런 문장이 등장하게 되었는지도 설명했습니다.

예문에서 어려운 단어를 접할 수도 있습니다. 그때는 사전을 찾아보세요. 배보다 배꼽이 커질 수도 있습니다. 진정 실력을 키울 수 있는 책으로 만들려고 노력했습니다. 이 책은 '외신으로 본 대한민국의 VOCABULARY', 즉 '외대보카' 시리즈의 첫 번째 책입니다. 계속해서 어휘 책을 발간할 예정입니다. 또한 숙어나 관용적 표현도 이 책과 마찬가지로 외신에서 만들었습니다. 당연하게도 고급 문장, 현대 영어를 만날 수 있습니다.

《도덕경》에 '궁력거중 불능위용(窮力擧重 不能爲用)'이라는 말이 있습니다. '있는 힘을 다하여 겨우 들어 올린 무거운 것으로는 쓸모있는 일을 아무것도 하지 못한다'라는 뜻입니다. 어느 철학자는 이를 '면장을 하려면 그의 능력이 능히 군수를 하고도 남을 정도여야 아주 잘 할 수 있지, 겨우 면장밖에 할 수 없는 능력이라면 힘에 부쳐서 일을 잘 해낼 수 없다'라고 해설하였습니다. 궁력거중(窮力擧重)한 자신에서 벗어날 수 있기를 바라며 책을 만들었습니다. 고맙습니다.

최홍수

* 예시의 고유명사가 가리키는 바는 다음과 같습니다

AAPI : Asian Americans and Pacific Islanders
Abe : 일본의 총리
Arden : 뉴질랜드 총리
Bang : 방시혁(Hybe 이사회 의장)
Cardin : 프랑스 패션계를 대표하는 세계적인 패션 디자이너
Castro : 쿠바의 지도자
CCP : 중국 공산당(Chinese Communist Party)
the Chancellor : 독일 총리
Choi : 최순실
Dalai Lama : 인도에 망명 중인 Tibet의 정신적 지도자
Dwight Eisenhower : 미국 34대 대통령
Elizabeth : 영국의 국왕
Fidel Castro : 쿠바의 최고 지도자
Floyd : 경찰의 목조르기로 사망한 흑인
Geguri) : 우리나라의 여자 게이머(gamer)
Goodall : 침팬지 대모 제인 구달(Jane Goodall)
Hilary : 클린턴 대통령 부인
Hollande : 프랑스의 마크롱 대통령 직전 대통령
HYBE : 방시혁(BTS 감독)의 연예기획사
IOC : 국제올림픽조직위원회(International Olympic Committee)
Kabul : 아프가니스탄의 수도
Kahlo : 멕시코 화가 칼로
Khamenei : 이란의 실질적인 최고 지도자
Kim : 김정은
Kim Jon Nam : 암살당한 김정은의 이복형
Kishida : 일본 총리(Abe 다음의 총리)
Kofi Annan : 유엔 사무총장을 역임한 아프리카 가나 출신의 외교관
Koike : 도쿄올림픽 조직위원장
Lee : 이재명

P Q R S T U V W X Y Z A B C D

Macron : 프랑스 대통령
Mao : 모택동(마오쩌둥)
Maradona : 아르헨티나의 전설적인 축구선수
Markle : 영국 해리 왕자의 부인
Merkel : 독일 여성 총리
Moon : 문재인 대통령
Norte Dame : 파리의 노틀 담 성당
Obama : 미국의 44대 대통령
Park : 박근혜 대통령
Philip : 엘리자베스 영국 여왕의 부군(consort)
Pompeo : 트럼프 시절의 국무장관
PRC : People's Republic of China
Putin : 러시아 대통령
Qaddafi : 리비아 국가원수(독재자)
Raul : Fidel의 친동생이자 공식 후계자인 라울 카스트로(Raul Castro)
Robert E. Lee : 남북전쟁 당시 남부군 군인
Rouhani : 이란 대통령
Seo : 우리나라 Me Too 운동을 촉발한 서지현 검사
Son : 손흥민
Suu Kyl : 미얀마 민주화의 싱징적 인물
Teheran : 이란 수도이지만 때로는 이란 정부를 가리키기도 함
Tiger Woods : 골프선수
Xi : 중국의 시진핑
Xinjiang : 중국의 신장지역.
Yoo : 가수 유승준
Yoon : 윤석열 대통령
Zelensky : 우크라이나 대통령

* 예시가 하나의 문장일 때는 마침표(period)를 찍었지만, 그렇지 않은 경우에는 생략하였습니다.

QRSTUVWXYZ

A

외신으로 보는
대한민국
VOCABULARY

BCDEFGHIJKLMNOP

amble, ample

- **amble** ⓥ 느긋하게 걷다(stroll)

He remembered once spotting a white dog ambling around Panmunjom.   He : 판문점 근무 미군

- **ample** ⓐ 충분한(more than enough)

Winning would give them ample opportunities to use government-funding bills to reverse or weaken the Democrats' tax-enforcement agenda.

ⓓ **amplify** ⓥ 증폭시키다   amplification ⓝ

In 2017, a parliamentarian in Jack's district stood down, and Jack saw an opportunity to amplify his call for social change by running for the seat.

amber, ember

- **amber** ⓝ (광물) 호박(琥珀)

an amber necklace

- **ember** ⓝ 잉걸불

Keep roofs and gutters repaired and clear of dead leaves and conifer needles that a flying ember could ignite.

accomplish, achieve

- **accomplish** ⓥ (마땅히 해야 할 일을) 끝내다, 달성하다   accomplishment ⓝ

but they pride themselves on being independent, accomplished 80-somethings.   노부모 기사

- **achieve** ⓥ (어려움을 이겨내고 노력해서) 달성하다   achievement ⓝ

The girls really look up to Jane and what she has achieved.

affordable, available

- **affordable** ⓐ 감당할 수 있는

In a July 2020 poll by financial-services firm TD Ameritrade, 59% of Americans said they don't plan to renew their gym memberships postpandemic, with 56% citing the appeal of more affordable ways to stay active.

ⓓ **unaffordable** ⓐ 너무 비싼

Spiraling inflation has made life unaffordable for many people.

- **available** ⓐ 구할 수 있는, 이용할 수 있는

In some states, hospitals already have more patients than beds available.

affix, annex

- **affix** ⓥ 부착하다, 붙이다   affixation ⓝ

  Pro-democracy protesters and supporters affixed messages of hope, solidarity and demands for greater political freedom to so-called Lennon Walls as protests rocked the city in 2019.   홍콩사태

- **annex** ⓥ 합병하다   annexation ⓝ

  Japan annexed the Korean Peninsular in 1910 and ruled it until the end of World War Ⅱ.

addiction, addition

- **addiction** ⓝ 중독   addict ⓥ

  He had demons : Jack struggled with addiction.

  ⓓ **addictive** ⓐ 중독성이 있는

  The difference is that opioids, unlike most other meds people take, can be highly addictive.

- **addition** ⓝ ① 덧셈 ② 첨가, 추가

  The addition of a simpler imperative to the guidelines — "move more and sit less," no matter what form that movement takes or how long it lasts — may make people more likely to meet them.   생활 속의 운동

  ⓓ **additive** ⓝ 첨가물

  The company is accused of adulterating its products with cheap additives.

assign, assuage

- **assign** ⓥ (일이나 책임 등을) 맡기다   assignment ⓝ

  She reported the incident to her managers shortly after, but was subjected to performance audits that she describes as unfair and assigned to a lower-level branch outside Seoul — a move she says did not match her strong track record at work.   She : 우리나라 Me too 운동의 물꼬를 튼 서지현 검사

- **assuage** ⓥ (안 좋은 감정을) 누그러뜨리다, 달래다   assuagement ⓝ

  Mr. Yoon's visit, which was expected to include a dinner on Thursday at the prime minister's residence and meetings between business leaders on Friday, was also a test of how well the two leaders could assuage domestic public opinion about issues that have long aroused heated passions in both countries.   대통령의 일본방문

affidavit, affiliate

- **affidavit** ⓝ 선서 진술서, 사실 확인서

A federal grand jury in Louisville charged that officers lied both before and after the raid, falsifying an affidavit to get the warrant.

- **affiliate** ⓥ 제휴하다, 연계하다　　　　　　　　　　　　　　affiliation ⓝ

They are national associations affiliated to larger organizations.

alley, ally

- **alley** ⓝ 골목 (a narrow street between or behind buildings, not usually used by cars)
- a bowling alley : 볼링장
- blind alley : ① 막다른 골목 ② 가망 없는 일 (fruitless or mistaken)

Police had been down several blind alleys in the murder investigation before the evidence being found.

- **ally** ⓝ 동맹국

Seoul is perhaps Washington's most important ally in East Asia, especially on military affairs.

- ally ⓥ 지지하다 (especially in a war or disagreement)　　　alliance ⓝ 동맹

Preemptive action, however, risks upsetting Washington's alliances in East Asia, potentially strengthening China.

미국의 북한에 대한 선제 공격

the Allies : 2차 세계대전 당시 연합국

able, capable

- **able** ⓐ 재능있는　　　　　　　　　　　　　　　　　　　ability ⓝ

a list of smart and able people

Its members refuse the minimum 18 months of military service required of all able South Korean men between the ages of 18 and 35.

여호와의 증인

- able-bodied ⓐ 신체 건강한

All able-bodied men in South Korea are mandated to start 21 months of military service before age 28.

대한민국의 군 복무

- **capable** ⓐ ~을 할 수 있는　　　　　　　　　　　　　　capability ⓝ

Pyongyang could field an intercontinental ballistic missile capable of reaching the continental US.

- incapable ⓞⓟⓟ

a weakling incapable of self-defense

allay, alloy

• allay ⓥ 가라앉히다, 누그러뜨리다(alleviate)

In June of this year, TikTok policy advisor Jack tried to allay some of the myriad security concerns.

• alloy ⓝ 합금(a metal that consists of two or more metals mixed together)

This alloy steel organizer has a rust-resistant PE coating to prevent scratches and is available in bronze, charcoal gray, and white finishes.

alternate, alternative

• alternate ⓥ 번갈아 생기다   alternate ⓐ

Periods of depression alternate with excited behavior.

• alternative ⓝ 대안, 선택 가능한 것

A strategy of maximum pressure carries heightened risks, but the alternative is almost certain defeat.   우크라이나·러시아 전쟁

audible, audit, audition

• audible ⓐ 잘 들리는

No opposition was voiced during the meeting and the resolution passed without audible dissent.

• audit ⓝ 회계 감사

Although Japan officially earmarked $12.6 billion for the Games, a government audit last year put the true figure at twice as much.   the Games : 올림픽

ⓓ audit ⓥ 청강하다

After dropping out of college, Jobs audited classes on calligraphy and dance.   Jobs : 스티브 잡스

• audition ⓝ (가수나 배우의) 오디션   audition ⓥ

The candidates audition before the five permanent members of the UN Security Council, known as the P5 : the US, China, Russia, Britain and France.   UN 사무총장 선거

aristocrat, autocrat

• aristocrat ⓝ 귀족

• autocrat ⓝ 독재자(despot)   autocracy ⓝ / autocratic ⓐ

North Korea is a cocktail of poisonous elements : autocratic, repressive, isolated and poor.

aptitude, attitude

• **aptitude** ⓝ 소질, 적성

Do Americans want leaders who are promoted based on intelligence, aptitude, skill and excellence?

• **attitude** ⓝ 태도

"In every country I've gone to, if you smile at people, they are going to be happy. This is my attitude," Son, 25, tells Time.   손흥민

affinity, affront

• **affinity** ⓝ 친밀감

And although younger South Koreans feel little affinity with the North, older generations are eager for the reunification Moon so desires.   Moon : 문재인 대통령

• **affront** ⓝ 모욕   affront ⓥ

the US Terminal High Altitude Area Defense(THAAD), antimissile defense system, which Beijing deems an affront

argue, assert

• **argue** ⓥ 언쟁하다(to disagree, in an angry way)   argument ⓝ

Harvard are still arguing over whether they should have admitted her.

• **assert** ⓥ (단호하게) 말하다(to state firmly)   assertive ⓐ
assertiveness ⓝ

But Chinese assertiveness, North Korean provocations, Japanese anxieties and South Korean political turmoil are swirling dangerously across North East Asia.

autonomous, automatic

• **automatic** ⓐ 자동의   automation ⓝ

It must also be clear that people don't automatically embark on a life of bliss the moment they touch German soil.   people : 아프리카 난민
아프리카 난민의 독일 정착

ⓓ the moment : 접속사

• **autonomous** ⓐ 자치의, 자율의(free to govern or control itself)   autonomy ⓝ
자율주행차

Hyundai Motor Group recently announced it will pilot a RoboRide, the first car-hailing service with autonomous driving vehicles, in Gangnam in Seoul, with plans to add more 300 by 2026.

ⓓ semiautonomous ⓐ 반(半)자치의

semiautonomous Hong Kong

argument, augment

- **argument** ⓝ 논쟁, 말다툼   argue ⓥ

  ⒹⒻ argumentative ⓐ 논쟁적인, 시비를 거는

  He quickly becomes argumentative after a few drinks.

- **augment** ⓥ 늘리다, 증가시키다   augmentation ⓝ

  To make the harrowing journey, they enlist the services of trans-Saharan smugglers who profit by augmenting their truckloads of weapons, drugs and other contraband goods with human cargo.

  they : 유럽에 가고자 하는 아프리카인

acid, acrid

- **acid** ⓝ 산, 산성   acidic ⓐ

  The ocean is steadily warming ; its oxygen levels are falling ; and it is becoming more acidic, making conditions for life below the waves ever harder.

- **acrid** ⓐ (냄새나 맛이) 매캐한[콕 쏘는 듯한]   acridity ⓝ

  Dust is falling in the Indian capital, and the acrid smell of burning bodies fills the air.

accredit, credit

- **accredit** ⓥ 승인하다, 인가하다

  Jack, founder and president of University of the People(UoPeople), which offers US-accredited degrees to about 100,000 students worldwide, has offered 1,000 scholarships to Afghan women, funded by the Bill Gates Foundation, Clinton Foundation, Ford Foundation and others.

- **credit**

  ① 신용, 외상

  "North Korean traders don't have cash anymore," he says, "I have to limit the amount of goods I sell to them on credit as the risk of default is so high."

  ② 영화 상영 후 관계자 자막(ending credit)

  ③ 칭찬

  It's a provocative move, especially in the context of the recent thaw in relation on the Korean Peninsular — the same thaw that President Trump was taking credit for less than a month ago.

  ④ 학점

  I don't have enough credits to graduate.

  a provocative move : 북한에서 억류되었다 풀려난 직후 죽은 미국인 대학생 아버지가 동계올림픽 개막식에 참가함. 그러나 그 자리에는 김정은의 여동생인 김여정이도 있었기에 provocative 라고 함

air, aircraft, airlift

- air ⓝ 공기, 대기

It was a cloudy day in June, but the air was thick with humid heat.

ⓓ in the air : 기운이 감도는

Optimism is in the air.

ⓓ air ⓥ (의견을) 발표하다

Residents gathered under the shade of a large tree to air their frustrations over the slow pace of development.

- aircraft ⓝ 항공기

Boeing is known for designing and manufacturing aircraft for commercial and military use.

- airlift ⓥ 항공기로 이동하다, 공수하다

airlift ⓝ

Most of them came via this expensive airlift through Nicaragua, and were released into the U.S., according to U.S. officials.

aghast, angst

- aghast ⓐ 경악한, 겁에 질린

Black Montgomery residents were aghast when two policemen dragged Colvin off the bus on March 2.

15살 소녀 콜빈이 백인 남자에게 좌석을 양보하지 않았다고 수갑이 채워져 버스에서 쫓겨난 사건

- angst ⓝ 불안

Few believe independence is feasible, but they see calling for it as a way to express their angst about the national-security law.

홍콩의 보안법

affection, affectation

- affection ⓝ 애정

But Philip and Elizabeth did exude a palpable affection when they were seen in public together.

영국의 엘리자베스 여왕 부부

ⓓ affectionate ⓐ 다정한, 애정 어린 (loving)

affectionately ⓐⓓⓥ

I have known "the boys" — as I and other fans affectionately call them — for years and had the pleasure of travelling to Korea to hang with them on multiple occasions.

- affectation ⓝ 가장, 꾸밈

Too many of their 20th-century predecessors saw opera as a bourgeois affectation, too superficial for their aesthetic philosophy.

affect, effect

• affect ⓥ

① 영향을 미치다

She is the interim deputy chief for the San Mateo County health system, responsible for public-health efforts affecting more than 700,000 Californians.

② 가장하다, 꾸미다(to pretend to have a particular feeling, way of speaking etc)

As usual, Jack affected complete boredom.

• effect ⓝ 효과, 결과

The East Coast is feeling the effects of the 1972 Marine Mammal Protection Act, which has boosted the numbers of seals to unusually high levels

cf effect ⓥ (어떤 결과를) 가져오다

Many parents lack confidence in their ability to effect change in their children's behavior.

airpower, airspace

• airpower ⓝ 공군력

In retrospect, we should have trained an Afghan fighting force that would have looked more like the Taliban — light, swift, less reliant on heavy logistics, high-tech intelligence and airpower.

• airspace ⓝ 영공

In 1996, he ordered fighter jets to shoot down two small unarmed planes piloted by Miami exiles for venturing into Cuban airspace.

append, upend

• append ⓥ (글을) 첨부하다, 덧붙이다

"Deng Xiaoping Theory" was appended only as a posthumous honor to the architect of China's economic revival. 등소평

• upend ⓥ

① (위아래를) 거꾸로 하다(뒤집다)

The Americans need their two strongest allies in the region to get along so they can focus on creating a bulwark against China, which is upending geopolitical calculations not only in Asia but across the globe. 한국과 일본

② (오리) 먹이를 찾기 위해 물속으로 뒤집어 들어가다

abstract, abstracted

- abstract ⓐ 추상적인

But so far the threat, like the debate, has been abstract.

cf concrete ⓐ ① (건축) 콘크리트로 된 ② 구체적인

The village, a small scattering of concrete huts with palm-leaf roofs, lies at the end of a severely rutted road that is all but impassable during the rainy season.

all but : almost

- abstracted ⓐ 정신이 딴 데 팔린

She seemed abstracted and unaware of her surroundings.

amass, assess

- amass ⓥ 모으다, 축적하다(accumulate)

Those traits have resonated with fans, especially on social media, where BTS has amassed millions of devoted followers.

- assess ⓥ 평가하다

assessment ⓝ

In his latest annual threat assessment, the US director of national intelligence said Kim "believes that over time he will gain international acceptance and respect as a nuclear power," as Pakistan did.

Kim : 김정은

attire, attrition

- attire ⓝ 의복, 복장

In the breezy evening some wore red attire and waved the national flag.

우리나라 축구팀 응원

- attritive ⓐ (반복적인 사용으로 인한) 소모적인

attrition ⓝ

The Russian strategy of warfare — one that is attritive and seeks to wear out their enemy — often creates risk aversion, in which commanders aren't fighting to win so much as fighting not to lose.

우크라이나-러시아 전쟁

cf a war of attrition : (전쟁) 소모전

amnesia, anemia

- amnesia ⓝ 기억상실

But the amnesia is directed inward too.

cf 일본의 잔혹한 과거사에 대해 외국은 잘 알고 있으나 일본 국내에서는 잊힌다는 의미.

- anemia ⓝ 빈혈증

anemic ⓐ

rising youth unemployment and anemic growth

cf 빈혈증적인 성장, 즉 성장이 더디다는 의미

authoritarian, authoritative

- authoritarian ⓐ 독재적인

The Chinese authoritarian-capitalist model wasn't supposed to survive in a global free market, let alone thrive.

- authoritative ⓐ 권위 있는

"Lee originated from the most backward place of 20th century Korea," says Bang Hyeon-seok, a professor at ChungAng University who authored an authoritative biography of Lee, "and is now standing on the front line of 21st century Korea."

우리나라 대통령 선거 이재명

asset, assist

- asset ⓝ 자산

One physical element is an asset : Kim resembles his grandfather Kim Il Sung, the country's founding father and a godlike figure for many north Koreans.

김정은

- assist ⓥ 돕다

America and NATO could have deployed more forces to Ukraine to train and assist Ukraine's military.

assistance ⓝ

acrimony, acronym

- acrimony ⓝ 악감정

North Korea's relationship with the US has always been rooted in bitter acrimony, with its periodic threats of annihilating America sounding almost quaint, coming, as they do, from an impoverished nation of 25 million.

acrimonious ⓐ

- acronym ⓝ 두문자어(頭文字語, 머리글자만 모아 만든 말)

ARMY, which is an acronym for Adorable Representative M.C. for Youth

ⓓ abbreviation ⓝ 축약, 축약형

'Dr' is the written abbreviation of 'Doctor'

astrology, astronomy

- astrology ⓝ 점성술
- astronomy ⓝ 천문학

ⓓ astronomical ⓐ 어마어마한

But the potential payoff for this project is astronomical.

astro~ : '별'의

anecdote, antidote

• anecdote ⓝ 일화(세상에 널리 알려지지 아니한 흥미 있는 이야기)

"There are many ways that you can learn about the world—it could be through books, it could be through anecdotes of other people," he says, "but I think actually living it yourself, experiencing it, is a different thing."

he : 이재명

• antidote ⓝ 해독제, 해결책

The real antidote to epidemics is cooperation.

assassinate, assimilate

• assassinate ⓥ 저격하다

Only the next day, Feb 14, did it emerge that what had been captured on airport cameras was a very public assassination.

assassination ⓝ
assassin ⓝ 암살범
김정남 테러 사건

• assimilate ⓥ 통합하다

At issue is how France's 7.5 million Muslims assimilate, or not, in a country whose constitution is based on an unyielding principle of secularism.

assimilation ⓝ

absolve, absorb

• absolve ⓥ 사면하다

At the outset of his insurgency in 1953, Fidel insisted, "History will absolve me."

absolution ⓝ

• absorb ⓥ 흡수하다

Scientists say the rain forest, which helps slow climate change by absorbing massive amounts of carbon dioxide, is nearing a "tipping point" after which its ecosystems cannot recover.

absorption ⓝ

adore, adorn

• adore ⓥ 좋아하다, 깊이 사랑하다(love, respect)

BTS have put their 14 best feet forward as role models to millions of adoring fans and anyone else who finds themselves drawn to BTS's undeniable allure.

adoration ⓝ
BTS member가 7명

cf adorable ⓐ 사랑스러운

They call themselves ARMY, which is both an acronym for Adorable Representative M.C. for Youth and a nod to their organized power.

• adorn ⓥ 꾸미다, 장식하다

a living room adorned with Indian devotional art

adornment ⓝ

AI

- AI : 인공지능(Artificial Intelligence)

But a 2019 study from the Brookings Institution found that workers with graduate or professional degrees will be almost four times as exposed to AI displacement in coming years as workers with a high school diploma.

- AI : 인공수정(artificial insemination)

Many urge her to take different paths to parenthood, like artificial insemination, in vitro fertilization and adoption.

in vitro fertilization : 체외수정

ⓓ 조류 인플루엔자를 AI라고 하지만 'avian influenza'로 표기하지 AI로 표기하지는 않음

adapt, adept, adopt

- adapt ⓥ 적응하다

Humans are incredibly adaptive, but when it comes to heat, there is a limit.

adaptation ⓝ
adaptive ⓐ
adaptor ⓝ 어댑터

- adept ⓐ 숙련된, 능숙한(at)

The group is also preternaturally adept at leveraging social media, both to promote their music and connect with their fans.

BTS

- adopt ⓥ ① 입양하다 ② 채택하다

Castro seemed lost as well, unable to come to grips with the need for free-enterprise reforms that even Raul, his military chief, urged him to adopt.

adoption ⓝ
adopter ⓝ
adoptee ⓝ
소련 붕괴 직후의 쿠바

aggravate, aggregate

- aggravate ⓥ (좋지 못한 상황을) 악화시키다(worsen)

Building the new road will only aggravate the situation.

aggravation ⓝ

- aggregate ⓥ 종합하다

The website aggregates content from many other sites.

aggregation ⓝ

assail, assault

- assail ⓥ 비난하다

By contrast, Macron — who has the luck of France being the EU's current rotating President — has assailed Putin and used his frequent talks with the Russian leader to cement his stature as statesman.

- assault ⓥ 공격하다

assault ⓝ

Jane's disappearance prompted an outpouring from women in Britain sharing their own experiences of harassment on social media and assault.

agitate, agony

• **agitate** ⓥ　　　　　　　　　　　　　　　　　　　　　　　agitation ⓝ

① (액체를) 휘젓다

My mother agitated the water to disperse the oil.

② (마음을) 뒤흔들다

My presence did not appear to agitate or irritate him as before, and he accepted my services quietly ….

③ (공적인 문제에 관해) 주장하다(요구하다)

She agitated for full voting rights for the rest of her life.

• **agony** ⓝ 극도의 고통 (very severe pain)　　　　　　　　agonize ⓥ

Women have suffered agony of soul which you never can comprehend, that you and your daughter might inherit political freedom.

ⓓ agonizing ⓐ 고통스러운

The process of choosing the Person of The Year — who or what most influenced the events of the past 12 months, for good or for ill — can be agonizing.

adulterate, adultery

• **adulterate** ⓥ (음식이나 음료에) 불순물을 섞다 (a foreign or inferior substance or element)

The brewer is said to adulterate his beer.

ⓓ unadulterated ⓐ 순수한

Another Olympian offered a moment of unadulterated joy.

• **adultery** ⓝ 간통

As the story goes, Jack was sentenced to death by drowning, after being falsely accused of adultery.

accrue, accurate

• **accrue** ⓥ 누적되다(누적시키다), 축적되다(축적시키다)　　　accruement ⓝ

Essentially, they are slaves : human beings who have been reduced to being possessions with a fixed value, based on assessments of the kind of income they can accrue to their owners as targets for extortion, as unpaid labor or — as is often the case with women — prostitutes.

• **accurate** ⓐ 정확한　　　　　　　　　　　　　　　　　　accuracy ⓝ

There are too many imponderables to make an accurate prediction.

ax, axis

- ax ⓝ 도끼

Captain Jack refused, and was promptly hacked to death with his own ax.

- axis ⓝ 축, 중심선

Wokeness — a term that originated in the Black community and has become a touchstone for advocates and critics alike — is now the central axis of American political controversy.

acquire, acquit

- acquire ⓥ 획득하다   —   acquisition ⓝ

Being American isn't just a state of being, whether native or acquired. It's a relationship between an individual and the nation-state.

- acquit ⓥ 무죄를 선고하다   —   acquittal ⓝ
  양심적 병역거부

In 2016, Cha was acquitted of violating conscription law.

affable, agreeable, amenable

- affable ⓐ 상냥한 (friendly and easy to talk to)   —   affability ⓝ

Unlike that of other Hong Kong politicians, his public persona is one of affability and even playfulness; every now and again he crafts riddles for a column in a local newspaper.

- agreeable ⓐ 기분 좋은 (quite enjoyable and pleasurable, pleasant)

While the Tucson is no sports car, its handling is confident, its steering is reasonably crisp, and its ride is agreeable.

- amenable ⓐ 잘 받아들이는 (open and responsive to suggestion)

Young people are more amenable than older citizens to the idea of immigration.

ambient, ambiguous

- ambient ⓐ 주위의, 주변의   —   ambience ⓝ
  지구 온난화

When the ambient air exceeds the normal body temperature of 37°, the only way to keep from overheating is by evaporative cooling — a.k.a. sweating.

- ambiguity ⓝ 애매모호   —   ambiguous ⓐ
  He : 윤석열 대통령

He also criticized Mr. Moon's stance between the United States and China, calling it too ambiguous.

acclimate, accumulate

- **acclimate** ⓥ (새로운 기후나 지역, 풍토에) 적응하다

An Iowa family, upset about what they see as "ugliness" toward refugees, volunteers to help acclimate the Syrians.

- **accumulate** ⓥ 모으다, 축적하다(amass)

The anger results from accumulated grievance.

ac*climation* ⓝ
시리아 난민의 미국 정착기

accumulation ⓝ

accident, incident

- **accident** ⓝ 사고

By definition, an accident is an unpredictable, unpreventable event.

cf **accidental** ⓐ 우연의

An autopsy showed that Jack suffered numerous broken bones and internal injuries in the fall, which was ruled an accidental death.

- **incident** ⓝ 사건(an event, especially one that is unusual, important, or violent)

Across the nine families, there were incidents of teenage parenthood, smoking pot, underage drinking, cutting school, bar fights, shoplifting and drag racing.

아홉 가정에 대한 자녀교육

accede, concede

- **accede** ⓥ 응하다(to)

Initial hopes that the Swiss-educated, third-generation dictator would be a reformer and accede to international demands to abandon his nuclear program have long died along with his victims.

- **concede** ⓥ 양보하다

Some of Trump's aides were concerned that the concession would irritate allies.

accession ⓝ

dictator : 김정은
his victims : 이복형 김정남, 고모부 장성택

concession ⓝ

accelerate, decelerate

- **accelerate** ⓥ 가속하다

Critics say the $4.5 billion of aid funneled to the regime during the "sunshine policy" of engagement actually accelerated the weapons program.

- **decelerate** ⓥ 속도를 줄이다

The Fed will want to cool down the inflationary cycle if wage growth doesn't decelerate.

acceleration ⓝ
accelerator ⓝ
한반도

Fed : (미국) 연방준비제도

abolition, abortion

- abolition ⓝ 폐지(when a law or a system is officially ended)   abolish ⓥ

It is true that Lincoln did not seek immediate abolition ; neither was he a radical racial egalitarian.

- abortion ⓝ 낙태, 인공중절   abortive ⓐ

State legislatures consider lots of bills aimed at curtailing abortion every year.

ⓓ miscarriage ⓝ 유산

anathema, anatomy

- anathema ⓝ 절대 반대, 아주 싫음

The CCP is historically anathema to Hong Kong in part because many of its people escaped Chinese communism or are descended from those who did.

- anatomy ⓝ (의학) 해부

And his drawing of *Vitruvian Man* — a work of anatomical exactitude combined with stunning beauty — became the preeminent icon of the connection of art and science.   his : 레오나르도 다빈치

appropriate, approximate

- appropriate ⓥ (자기 것이 아닌데) 자기 것으로 삼다   appropriation ⓝ

But Jack was actually a member of the centrist Indian National Congress — the BJP's biggest rival today. Critics say the BJP, which was found in 1980, is trying to appropriate Jack's legacy.

ⓓ appropriate ⓐ 적절한

clothes appropriate for a job interview

- approximate ⓐ 거의 정확한, 근사치의

From 2014 to 2017, death rates from gunshot wounds in the US. increased by approximately 20%.

abysmal, abyss

- abysmal ⓐ 최악의

For decades, the world has turned a blind eye to India's abysmal human-rights record.

- abyss ⓝ 심연

Moon helped guide the world back from the abyss.   남북관계

article, articulate

- article ⓝ (신문, 잡지의) 기사, 글

On Sept. 6, a state news outlet reported that Fan had "been brought under control" and was "about to receive legal judgment." But the article was quickly erased.

Fan : (중국) 영화배우

- articulate ⓥ (생각이나 감정을) 뚜렷이 표현하다

Arden's real gift is her ability to articulate a form of leadership that embodies strength and sanity.

articulation ⓝ
Arden : 뉴질랜드 총리

absence, abstinence

- absence ⓝ 없음, 부재

The absence of change is not, for them, an absence of information. It's an absence of will.

absent ⓐ

- abstinence ⓝ (술이나 성의) 자제, 절제

Promoting abstinence won't work because many young people who plan to abstain don't actually do so.

- abstain ⓥ 절제하다, 삼가다

Pilots must abstain from alcohol for 24 hours before flying.

acumen, acupuncture

acu- : with a needle

- acumen ⓝ 통찰력, 재능

Her integrity and analytical acumen are universally admired.

- acupuncture ⓝ 침

He has also denied accusations of an occult hand in his campaign, including links to a shaman and an anal acupuncturist.

acupuncturist ⓝ 침술사
He : 윤석열 대통령

allude, allure

- allude ⓥ 암시하다(to)

RM recorded a song with Wale that alludes to the importance of activism.

allusive ⓐ
allusion ⓝ
RM : BTS member
Wale : 미국의 rapper

- allure ⓝ 매력

The international community must also convince Bangladesh that the best means of dampening the allure of radicalization among refugees is through social integration-providing work permits and respecting fundamental rights.

미얀마의 소수민족이 탄압을 피해 방글라데시로 들어간 상황

acute, blunt

- **acute** ⓐ

① 날카로운

Japan's fears have grown more acute since North Korea conducted its sixth nuclear test on Sept. 2.

② (병) 급성

acute arthritis

SARS : severe acute respiratory syndrome

- **blunt** ⓐ

① 무딘

A robust body of research shows that these exercises lower stress, ease anxiety, improve sleep, ward off sickness, reduce depression and even blunt pain.

② 직설적인

His loud, boisterous laugh and his blunt seagoing manners....irritated the gentle King.

acuity ⓝ 명민함

blunt가 동사(verb)로 쓰임
exercise : 명상수업

his : 해군사관학교 출신인 엘리자베스의 남편
King : 엘리자베스 아버지

administer, admonish

- **administer** ⓥ

① 집행하다(manage the work of a company or organization)

It's been called a corruption-plagued bureaucratic labyrinth, an organization led by five powerful countries interested mainly in thwarting one another's plans, and administered by functionaries obsessed with protocol and lacking in common sense.

② 행하다(to give officially or as part of a ritual)

The temperature tests required to enter any shop or restaurant or even pass certain street corners are casually administered.

③ 처방하다

Paramedic crews are capable of administering drugs.

④ (타격을) 가하다

To get more, thugs might produce a mobile phone and dial a migrant's family to demand a ransom as a beating is administered.

- **admonish** ⓥ 훈계하다, 꾸짖다

According to linguistics expert, Jack, the word wasn't always used to admonish people.

administration ⓝ
administrative ⓐ

UN

코로나 사태

admonishment ⓝ

apartheid, apathy

- **apartheid** ⓝ (남아공의) 인종차별

When lives are examined in hindsight, we often forget the setting. Winnie did not live in a vacuum but in apartheid.

Winnie : 남아프리카 공화국의 인종차별철폐 (apartheid) 선봉에 섰던 만델라(Mandela) 부인

- **apathy** ⓝ 무관심

Anger has given way to apathy.

access, accession

- **access** ⓝ 접근, 접촉

Indigenous people, who were members of sovereign nations, did not have full access to citizenship until 1924.

access ⓥ

미국 시민권의 역사

ⓓ abortion access : 임신중절 가능

The high court could reshape major elements of American life in coming months with expected rulings of abortion access and gun rights.

ⓓ **accessibility** ⓝ 접근 가능성

And there are downsides to masking, like stunted communication, accessibility concerns for the deaf community, acne and even trace microplastic inhalation with long-term wear.

마스크 착용

- **accession** ⓝ (국가 지도자로) 취임

That night she rested ; the next day she signed the oath of accession before the Privy Council, and an hour later her accession was formally proclaimed.

accede ⓥ

she : 엘리자베스 여왕

ⓓ the Privy Council : 추밀원

aid, aide

- **aid** ⓝ 도움

For decades, South Korea's defense strategy relied on the assumption that the United States would come to its aid if war were to break out.

ⓓ 'come to one's aid'로 많이 씀

- **aide** ⓝ 측근, 보좌관

But in a matter of minutes, Trump had made up his mind. By quickly saying yes to a meeting, the President thought, he would test Kim's intentions and put him off-balance, explains a close aide.

북미대화 성사과정

adjacent, nascent

• adjacent ⓐ 인접한, 가까운

The schools were adjacent but there were separate doors.

• nascent ⓐ 발생기의, 초기의

Legal sports betting is a nascent industry in the U.S.

amity, enmity

• amity ⓝ 우호, 친선(friendship, especially between countries)

The presence of French troops in Scotland had produced hostility rather than amity.

• enmity ⓝ 원한, 증오(hatred)

A peace treaty was never signed, and enmity remains.

amiable, amicable, animosity

• amiable ⓐ 호감을 주는(friendly, pleasant manner, friendly and easy to like)

Everyone knew him as an amiable fellow.

• amicable ⓐ 우호적인, 원만한(friendly)

It is not an amicable divorce.   영국의 EU 탈퇴

• animosity ⓐ 반감, 적대감

Thousands of miles away, the invasion has brought back painful memories of when the Korean peninsula was occupied by the Japanese during World War II and the subsequent invasion by Soviet-backed forces in 1950, remaining today riven by Cold War animosities.   이 문장 앞에는 우크라이나 사태가 언급

alien, alienable

• alien ⓐ 생소한, 생경한   alienation ⓝ

The idea of recognizing the other party's point of view and reaching compromises is completely alien to Spanish political culture.

cf. alienate ⓥ 소원하게 하다

For the US, THAAD could protect troops in the field, but potentially at the expense of alienating the only country that may be able to alter North Korean behavior.   the only country : 중국

• alienable ⓐ 양도할 수 있는   inalienable ⓐ

inalienable human rights

values and alienable rights in our Constitution

abide, abode

• **abide** ⓥ 참다(even though you may not agree with it)

A : What kind of behavior in the workplace won't you tolerate?

B : I will not abide by someone who is nasty. This is a collaborative culture.

abide by 형식으로 사용

ⓒ **abiding** ⓐ 지속적인, 변함없는(lasting)

But we must rise to those tasks armed with courage, faith, love and an abiding commitment to justice, yet girded with a healthy sense of skepticism.

• **abode** ⓝ 거주지, 집

Once known as the "abode of the gods," Lhasa has become a warren of neon and concrete like any other Chinese city.

Lhasa : Tibet의 수도

armament, armistice

• **armament** ⓝ 무장, 군비확충

arm ⓥ
disarmament ⓝ 북한의 비핵화

He added that regime officials who are "meticulously planning" for the summit are perturbed by Secretary of State Mike Pompeo's talk of "permanent, verifiable, irreversible" disarmament, which appears to go further than the UN definition.

ⓒ **coat of arms** : (가문·도시 등의 상징인) 문장(紋章)

• **armistice** ⓝ 휴전

The Korean War armistice was signed at Panmunjom in 1953, creating the DMZ as a buffer between the two Koreas.

attach, attaché

• **attach** ⓥ 붙이다, 첨부하다

detach ⓝ
Maradona : 아르헨티나의 축구선수

Maradona is about to dribble through two English defenders in the quarterfinals of the 1986 World Cup. He spins, however, somehow keeping the ball attached to his left foot — as if it were a toy and he the child who won't let it go.

ⓒ **strings attached** : 조건이 있는 붙은 상태에서

Biden inherits a China policy with strings attached.

• **attaché** ⓝ (대사관의) 특정 분야의 담당자(in an embassy, to deal with a particular subject)

ardent, arduous

- ardent ⓐ 열정적인(passionate)   ardency ⓝ

The state's other senator, Jack, is a co-sponsor and one of the bill's most ardent supporters.

- arduous ⓐ 몹시 힘든, 고된(involving a lot of strength and effort)

The task was more arduous than he had calculated.

annals, annual

- annals ⓝ 연대기(a record of events year by year)   주로 복수형으로 씀

In the annals of human spaceflight, August 1972 is unforgettable.

- annual ⓐ 매년의

The deadly pathogen began to spread just in time for Lunar New Year(Jan. 25), when millions travel across Asia, reuniting with their families in the world's largest annual human migration.

antipathy, sympathy

- antipathy ⓝ 반감, 미움

He was also concerned by other people's growing antipathy toward masks and fears now that the virus is not going away.

- sympathy ⓝ 동감, 연민

Trump has publicly expressed sympathy for Xi and his Hong Kong predicament, and he's made clear he has no intention of siding with protesters.

sympathetic ⓐ
sympathizer ⓝ 동조자
sympathetic nervous system(교감신경)
parasympathetic nervous system(부교감신경)

apparatchik, apparatus

- apparatchik ⓝ 기관원(a member of a Communist apparat)

Before Xi rose to power, the common perception was that he was a bland apparatchik with no distinct power base.

ⓓ apparat ⓝ (특히 공산국가에서 정부가 운영하는) 기관(기구)

- apparatus ⓝ 조직(the organization or system used for doing or operating something)

Under Moon, South Korea has indicated willingness to engage more in the U.S.-led Indo-Pacific Strategy and so-called Quad Plus security apparatus, groupings of Asian-Pacific democracies united to constrain China.

B

외신으로 보는
대한민국
VOCABULARY

bump, pump

● bump ⓥ 부딪치다 bump ⓝ ① 부딪침 ② (도로 위로) 튀어나온 요철

ⓓ goose bump ⓝ 소름, 닭살

The fact that young soccer players across the region are dreaming of emulating his career gives him "goose bumps."

한국 축구
his : 손흥민

ⓓ bumpy ⓐ 울퉁불퉁한, 평탄하지 못한

The bumpy vaccination rollout and economic scar tissue of the pandemic will stoke anti-incumbent anger and public unrest in many countries.

ⓓ bumper ⓝ (자동차) 범퍼

● pump ⓥ

① (아래위로) 거세게 흔들다

The 80-year-old president, who had been questioned about his age just a few hours earlier, pumped his fists and whooped along with the crowd as Mr. Yoon performed.

윤석열 대통령이 노래를 불렀던 백악관 만찬

② 펌프질하다

Since there was no electricity, they pumped by hand.

fist bump, fist pump

● fist bump ⓝ 주먹 악수

the Blue House, where TIME's photographers found him in a jubilant mood on June 9, greeting all with smiles and fist bumps

● fist pump ⓝ (축하·지지의 표시로 가슴을 치듯) 주먹을 아래로 흔들기

Party elders were suspicious of Bo, who sidestepped the party apparatus to appeal directly to the people, reviving songs from the Cultural Revolution at fist-pumping rallies.

fist-pump ⓥ
Bo : 시진핑의 라이벌 보시라이(Bo Xilai)

base, bias

● base ⓐ 야비한, 비도덕적인 (not having good moral principles)

We hope his motives are nothing so base as money.

ⓓ base ⓝ (군사) 기지

On the last morning of September, dozens of Afghan children cheered on their older brothers as they played a lively game of soccer with US soldiers on a military base in rural Wisconsin.

ⓓ basics ⓝ 기본 원리

All Korean men know the basics of taekwondo.

ⓓ universal basic income(UBI) : 보편적 기본소득
- bias ⓝ 편견

A consistent meditation practice can help you know your biases.　　명상

boom, boon

- boom ⓝ　　　　　　　　　　　　　　　　　　　　　　　　　boom ⓥ

① 붐, 호황

The country experienced rapid economic growth from the 1960s on,　　우리나라
driven by export-led tech, automotive and ship-building booms.

② 쾅, 탕(하는 소리)

Accumulate enough, set it off and there is no other outcome but boom!　　임계질량(critical mass)

- boon ⓝ 요긴한 것

Although these policies face substantial opposition, Kim's belligerence is　　일본의 헌법개정 움직임
a boon for hawks.　　　　　　　　　　　　　　　　　　　　　　　　김정은

bigwig, wig

- bigwig ⓝ 중요인물, 거물(an important person)　　　　　　　　　　　높은 사회계층에 속할수록
a bigwig in local politics　　　　　　　　　　　　　　　　　　　　　가발도 더 풍성했던 역사에
- wig ⓝ 가발(toupee)　　　　　　　　　　　　　　　　　　　　　　서 유래

The look, which was seemingly a wig, was also a much darker shade of
hair color.

bruise, cruise

- bruise ⓥ 멍이 생기다, 타박상을 입다(입히다)

I'm making my body resistant to beating, to make sure I don't get so
bruised when I take the blows.

- cruise ⓥ 순항하다(to move at a steady speed)

A few days later, on May 10, a US guided-missile destroyer cruised past　　크루즈(cruise) 선 : 크루즈
Fiery Cross Reef, another disputed Spratly feature.　　　　　　　　　　관광을 할 수 있는 시설을 갖
　　　　　　　　　　　　　　　　　　　　　　　　　　　　　　　　춘 배

bamboo, bamboozle

- bamboo ⓝ 대나무
- bamboozle ⓥ 남을 속여 정신없게 만들다

He argues that people were initially bamboozled because they had to
communicate using a new set of rules.

budge, dodge, nudge

• budge

① 조금만 움직이다(움직이게 하다)

② 의견을 바꾸다

But Goodall refused to budge. "I did not want to leave my bed," she says. "They had to take me down with all my bedclothes." — 구달의 어린 시절

• dodge ⓥ 기피하다, 회피하다

Still, it can become a national scandal when a celebrity is thought to have dodged the draft ; after Korean-American pop star Yoo avoided military service by becoming a naturalized US citizen in 2002, he was banned from re-entering South Korea. — 유승준

• nudge ⓝ (특히 팔꿈치로 살짝) 쿡 찌르기

The move indicates the country may want South Korea to nudge the United States to relax crippling economic sanctions. — nudge ⓥ

browbeat, drumbeat

• browbeat ⓥ 협박하다, 으르다(intimidate)

He spent his childhood alongside the laborers on his father's finca, which engendered an empathy for the island's browbeaten poor.

finca : (중남미의) 대농원
browbeaten ⓐ 겁먹은, 주눅이 든

• drumbeat ⓝ 북소리, 드럼 소리

In the 1980s, during another economic crisis, Americans heard a constant drumbeat of blame as the US declared financial war on Japan, with frequent allusions to Pearl Harbour.

Pearl Harbour : (하와이) 진주만

bandage, bondage

• bandage ⓝ 붕대

The Biden Administration decided to rip the bandage off, but unfortunately it ripped off a tourniquet, and we are watching the hemorrhaging of American honor and the death of the hopes and dreams of many Afghans — particularly many girls and women.

아프간 사태
tourniquet ⓝ 지혈대

• bondage ⓝ 구속, 속박

What the ILO calls "the new slavery" takes in 25 million people in debt bondage and 15 million in forced marriage.

ILO : 국제노동기구

breastfeed, breathtaking

- breastfeed ⓥ 모유를 먹이다

She depicted taboo topics like abortion, miscarriage, and breastfeeding. 　멕시코의 화가 프리다 칼로 (Frida Kahlo)

- breathtaking ⓐ 깜짝 놀랄 만한(very impressive, exciting, or surprising)

To those in the outside world who once deified her, it was a breathtaking betrayal. 　it : 그녀의 체포

bunt, butt, buttress

- bunt ⓥ (야구) 번트 치다 　　　　　　　　　　　　　　bunt ⓝ

His bunt went foul with two strikes, resulting in a strikeout.

- butt

① 엉덩이

The hammer and sickle tattoo on their butt is exactly at my eye level.

② (담배) 꽁초

③ (총) 개머리판

cf butt ⓥ 끝을 접하다, 인접하다

Legislatures in other states butt up against deadlines, but the majority manage year after year to pass their budgets on time. 　deadline에 가까이 처리한다는 뜻

- buttress ⓝ (벽) 지지대 　　　　　　　　　　　　　　　buttress ⓥ 지지하다

The combination of low debt and sufficient cash can act as a buttress against a downturn.

bald, bold

- bald ⓐ 대머리의

The Dalai Lama engages each visitor like a big kid : slapping bald pates, grabbing onto devotee's single braid, waggling another's nose.

- bold ⓐ

① 대담한

Abe will likely wait until his third term is secure before making any bold move. 　Abe : 일본 총리

② 선명한(in a very clear way)

Besides the sirens, smart-phones beeped in unison and television stations suddenly cut to an ominous black screen with bold white script warning of a possible missile attack. 　북한의 미사일 발사에 대한 일본의 민방공 훈련

behemoth, behest

• behemoth ⓝ 거대 기업

Despite being decimated following World War II and the 1950–'53 Korean War, the nation today with its population of 50 million boasts the world's 10th largest economy, whose firms—like Samsung Electronics and Hyundai Motors—are global behemoths.

• behest ⓝ 명령

ⓓ 'at the behest of' : ~의 명령으로

In China, companies use algorithms at the behest of the government to ensure that citizens remain within the rules of order set by the political leadership.

batter, battery

• batter ⓥ 강타하다

COVID-19 has battered Italy's already sluggish economy, which sharnk by 8.8% in 2020.

ⓓ battered ⓐ 낡은, 닳은

I remember after dinner one night he picked up the battered poetry book that was always somewhere by his side and read aloud Tennyson's poem "The Charge of the Light Brigade."

• battery

① 배터리

Jack likens social-distancing motivation to a battery. When lockdowns were first announced, many people were charged with energy and desire to flatten the curve.

② 포대(several large guns used together)

anti-aircraft missile batteries

③ (야구) 투수와 포수

brigade, brigadier

• brigade ⓝ ① (군대의) 여단 ② (특정한 목적의) 사람들

Two weeks later, on April 15, came Kennedy's Bay of Pigs fiasco, a botched invasion of Cuba by a brigade of Cuban exiles.

• brigadier ⓝ (군대의) 준장(여단장)

better, bitter

- better-off ⓐ 유복한

They also drop out of school at higher rates, earn less money over time and are incarcerated far more often than their better-off peers.

- bitter ⓐ (맛) 쓴(a strong sharp taste)

And how should they navigate the increasingly bitter rivalry between the United States, South Korea's main military ally, and China, its biggest trading partner?

they : 한국민

buffer, buffet

- buffer ⓝ 완충장치, 완충제

Pyongyang's fall would rob Beijing of a buffer against a US-allied united Korea.

- buffet ⓝ 뷔페

For staying in the city of the future, the Ambassador Seoul — A Pullman Hotel reopened with six refurbished restaurants, including the King's, the first hotel buffet in Korea.

backwater, backward

- backwater ⓝ 후미진 곳, 벽지

Is London, for centuries a center of global finance, becoming a backwater?

- backward ⓐ 낙후된

And in backward and violent Oriente, Fidel also learned the power of guns.

Oriente : (쿠바 동부의) 주

- ⓓ backward ⓝ 발달이 더딘 사람, 열등생

The family maid dubbed him "der Depperte," the dopey one, and a relative referred to him "almost backwards."

him : Einstein

bemoan, moan

- bemoan ⓥ 한탄하다, 불쌍히 여기다(say that you are disappointed about something)

Advocates of debt-cancellation love to bemoan the struggles of Americans with outstanding student debt.

- moan ⓥ 신음하다, (특히 바람이) 신음하듯 불다

The wind moaned and shuddered, an eerie Halloween gale that seemed about three weeks too early.

backstab, backstop

- backstab ⓥ 중상모함하다

When Trump unilaterally withdrew the US from the 2015 deal that has significantly curtailed Iran's nuclear program, the move validated Jack's view of the US as "deceitful, untrustworthy and backstabbing."

- backstop ⓥ 뒷받침하다, 지원하다

The collapse of Silicon Valley Bank and the Biden Administration's unprecedented response, guaranteeing deposits and backstopping regional banks, has catalyzed an important and necessary national conversation over what went wrong, and what can be done to prevent future crises.

bog, bogus

- bog ⓝ 늪지, 습지

cf bog down : 교착 상태에 빠지다, 수렁에 빠지다

Yet once again Macron finds himself bogged down with domestic political resentments.

- bogus ⓐ 가짜의

But he fell afoul of local officials who accused Jack of kidnapping and extortion — charges he has always called bogus.

beam, seam

- beam ⓥ 활짝 웃다

"Football is my happiness." And with that, Son's smile comes beaming back.

Son : 손흥민

- seam ⓝ

① 솔기, 이음매

China's strongest leader since Mao Zedong was convinced that only aggressive subjugation could prevent China from following the USSR into balkanization along ethnic seams.

티베트나 신장 위구르를 말함

② (석탄 같은 광물질의) 층

An excavator used to dig through coal seams at Jharia coalfield in India's Jharkhand state.

cf seamless ⓐ 솔기 없는, (중간에 끊어짐이 없는) 아주 매끄러운

The transitions from scene to scene were seamless.

burnish, furnish

- burnish ⓥ (금속) 윤을 내다

The comments cast a shadow over a summit that Putin had hoped would burnish his diplomatic status and show he was not so internationally isolated.

- furnish ⓥ (가구를) 비치하다

The cost to move and furnish a new home are two of the most common burdens on the budget.

㏈ furniture ⓝ 가구

In 2020, the global market for eco-friendly furniture was estimated at $34.2 billion.

breeze, freeze

- breeze ⓝ 미풍   breezy ⓐ

In the breezy evening some wore red attire and waved the national flag.   우리나라 붉은 악마 응원

- freeze ⓥ   freeze ⓝ

① (얼음이) 얼다

The boy carried his few possessions in a small bag, with some donated bedding to help him sleep outdoors in near freezing temperatures.

② 동결하다

Grandparents will meet grandchildren who were born during the travel freeze.   코로나사태

balk, bulk

- balk ⓥ

① (말이 장애물 앞에서) 잠시 멈칫하다

② (야구) 보크하다

If a pitcher steps off a third time and doesn't pickoff a runner, it is considered a balk.   pickoff ⓥ (야구) 주자를 견제하여 아웃시키다

③ 망설이다

Despite the obvious benefits, many companies balk at the thought of hiring an interim executive.

- bulk ⓝ 규모, 부피

Bonus : The thin, nearly weightless sheets won't add bulk to your luggage.

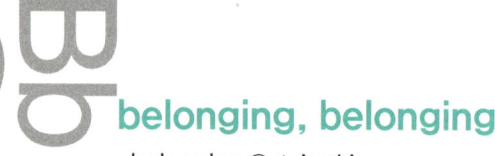

belonging, belongings

• belonging ⓝ 소속, 귀속

Cultivating a sense of belonging has become particularly important during the pandemic.

belong ⓥ

• belongings ⓝ 소지품

an insurance policy that covers your personal belongings

insurance policy : 보험증권

bereaved, bereft

• bereaved ⓐ 아주 가까운 사람이 죽은

Ahead of the first anniversary of the murders, Jane described her experience of dealing with Russian authorities over the past year, not as a journalist but as a person bereaved and looking for justice.

Jane : 미망인이자 언론인

• bereft ⓐ 상실한(deprived or robbed of the possession or use of something)

killing seven and leaving behind a father bereft of both his year-old daughter and his wife

breadbasket, breadline, breadwinner

• breadbasket ⓝ 곡창지대

• breadline ⓝ 최저 수준의 소득

Ukraine grows enough food to feed 400 million people. It went from the biggest breadbasket of the world to the longest breadlines.

우크라이나-러시아 전쟁

ⓓ on the breadline : 최저 수준의 소득에 있는

Macron's often blunt communication style has made matters worse, fueling the perception that he doesn't understand life on the breadline.

Macron : 프랑스 대통령

• breadwinner ⓝ 생계비를 버는 사람, 가장

Women are now often the breadwinners of their households.

burro, burrow

• burro ⓝ 작은 당나귀

The law created herd-management areas for wild horses and burros where they were found on public lands in the West.

• burrow ⓝ (토끼의) 굴

ⓓ burrow ⓥ 들추다

While I was writing, I was burrowing and absorbing — that's what healing required.

성폭행 피해자(I)가 폭로 글을 씀

breakout, breakthrough

• **breakout** ⓐ 갑작스런 성적, 좋은 결과(suddenly and extremely popular or successful)

The company had a breakout year last year, tripling its profits from the previous year.

• **breakthrough** ⓝ 돌파구

Moon has more reasons to hope for a breakthrough. Following Trump's short-lived bromance with Kim, the bar for a meeting is lower and politically safer, given that few Republicans could mount a serious objection.

> Moon : 문재인 대통령

bunch, bundle

• **bunch** ⓝ

① 다발, 묶음(주로 'a bunch of'로 많이 씀)

a bunch of bananas

After Phelps heard on May 31 that Naomi Osaka had pulled out of the French Open and he read her Instagram message explaining why, a bunch of thoughts rushed into his head.

> Phelps : 미국의 수영선수
> Naomi Osaka : 일본의 테니스 선수

② 많음

While Sunak claimed the support of the majority of Conservative lawmakers, they can be a mutinous bunch.

> Sunak이 영국 총리가 되기 직전의 상황

• **bundle** ⓝ

① 다발, 묶음(typically of software or hardware, sold together as a package)

a bundle of 15 desktop utilities

② 거액, 거금(a large amount of money)

The new printer cost a bundle.

③ (어떤 특징을 지닌) 사람

In 1971, my mother had me visit our neighbors to congratulate them on the arrival of their new baby, Jane. I had no idea this tiny bundle from a working-class family would become Rhode Island's first female governor and the US Secretary of Commerce.

ⓓ **bundle** ⓥ 추워서 옷을 껴입다(up)

The young kids sat before the teacher on the floor in their dimly lit classroom, all bundled up in coats.

bellicose, belligerent

- **bellicose** ⓐ 호전적인(warlike)

North Korea's bellicose leader Kim Jong Un

- **belligerent** ⓐ 적대적인

But even stronger sanctions have failed to weaken Kim's belligerence.

bellicosity ⓝ

belligerence ⓝ
대북제재

bluff, buff

- **bluff** ⓥ 허세를 부리다, 엄포를 놓다

It's like trying to bluff at poker when the other players can see your cards.

- **buff** ⓝ ~광, 애호가

a computer buff
The Civil War has always had die-hard history buffs.

barely, barley

- **bare** ⓐ 벌거벗은, 맨

People have taken comfort in their faces being concealed, and they feel some discomfort about revealing their bare faces.

마스크 착용

㎝ **barely** ⓐdv 겨우, 간신히

In Brussels, European leaders convened an emergency summit to try and fend off the contagion. Russia watched from the wings with barely concealed delight.

영국의 브렉시트(Brexit) 결정

- **barley** ⓝ 보리

The sick were typically treated with a gruel of barley meal, butter and the urine of a holy monk.

rice ⓝ 쌀
wheat ⓝ 밀
buckwheat ⓝ 메밀

bookmark, earmark

- **bookmark** ⓥ (읽던 곳을 표시하기 위해 책갈피에 끼우는) 서표(書標)로 표시하다

Moon's arrival into Seoul's presidential Blue House was bookmarked by North Korean weapons tests, including three long-range intercontinental ballistic missiles(ICBMs) and a purported hydrogen bomb, prompting then US President Trump to dispatch a US Navy carrier group and threaten "little rocket man" with "fire and fury" in riposte.

bookmark ⓝ (인터넷) 즐겨찾기

- **earmark** ⓥ (특정 목적용으로) 배정(결정/예정)하다

Although Japan officially earmarked $12.6 billion for the Games, a government audit last year put the true figure at twice as much.

earmark ⓝ
도쿄 올림픽

belie, betray

- **belie** ⓥ 착각하게 만들다

Son's natural brightness belies the responsibility he will face as South Korea's talisman at the World Cup, which will kick off in Russia on June 14.

Son : 손흥민

ⓓ talisman : (행운을 가져다 주는) 부적

- **betray** ⓥ

betrayal ⓝ

① 배신하다

Kim felt utterly betrayed by Moon for siding with the US after Hanoi, as well as by his purchase of 40 US stealth fighter jets, and sees little point in negotiating with an administration on its last legs.

② (감정 등을) 무심코 노출시키다

She does not betray even the slightest hint of envy.

benefactor, beneficiary

- **benefactor** ⓝ 후원자(someone who gives money for a good purpose)

Kim was a masterful puppeteer himself, playing his Chinese and Soviet benefactors off each other during the Cold War like two feuding parents.

Kim : 김일성(김정은의 할아버지)

- **beneficiary** ⓝ 수혜자(someone who gets advantages from an action or change)

Critics of the industry say the only beneficiaries of these so-called security measures are the people making money off them.

the industry : 미국의 총기 사고로 인한 방탄사업

breach, broach

- **breach** ⓥ

① (약속이나 계약을) 위배하다, 위반하다

Jack, however, swiftly went public to demand that Beijing clarify the situation and prove Hong Kong's constitutional autonomy had not been breached.

② (스포츠 경기에서) 수비를 뚫다

But Japan easily breached the Reds' defense and, groans rang out when opposition winger Jack completed his hat trick to end the game 3-1.

the Reds : 대한민국 축구 대표팀

- **broach** ⓥ (곤란한 이야기를) 꺼내다(embarrassing or unpleasant or cause an argument)

Is there a way to broach developing such guidelines with your manager?

bellow, billow

- bellow ⓥ 고함을 지르다, 우렁찬 소리를 내다

They use a megaphone to bellow across the gap.

- billow ⓥ (바람에) 부풀어 오르다

The loose trousers billow out from the waist, the long-sleeved tunic protects the arms, and a scarf covers the head.

blue-blooded, full-blooded

- blue-blooded ⓐ 왕족 출신의

And while George VI may have looked askance at a Greek Orthodox royal from the wrong side of the blue-blooded track, his daughter could not be argued into considering any other match.

- full-blooded ⓐ 전력을 다하는

It is a strong full-blooded fish.

blue-blood ⓝ
엘리자베스 2세의 부군 (consort) 필립에 관한 기사. Geroge VI는 엘리자베스 2세의 아버지
full-blood ⓝ

cold-blood, warm-blood

- cold-blooded ⓐ

① 냉혈 동물인

② 냉혹한(not showing or involving any emotions or pity)

They just shot those boys in cold blood.

- warm-blooded ⓐ

① 온혈 동물인

Our warm-blooded bodies are too hot for the fungus to thrive.

② 정열적인(ardent or passionate)

young and warm-blooded valor

cold-blood ⓝ

warm-blood ⓝ

befall, befit

- befall ⓥ (안 좋은 일이) 발생하다

Otto's fate deepens my Administration's determination to prevent such tragedies from befalling innocent people.

- befit ⓥ ~에 어울리다, 알맞다

They offered him a post befitting his seniority and experience.

Otto : 북한에서 죽은 미국인

bail, bill

• bail ⓝ 보석, 보석금

Ten people were arrested for offenses under the law on July 1, including several holding pro-independence flags and leaflets(most were granted bail.)

• bill ⓝ

① (법률) 법안(a written proposal for a new law)

The bill, known as the Anti-Discrimination Act, enjoys support among the general public.   우리나라의 차별금지법

② (새의) 부리

blur, slur

• blur ⓥ 흐릿하게 만들다, 흐릿해지다   blurry ⓐ

Their boundary-blurring desserts reflect their Korean background and French training.   프랑스에서 교육받은 한국인 요리사

• slur ⓝ

① 비난

Some of her supporters say the fascist label is a slur designed to weaken her appeal for Euro-skeptic Italians hungry for decisive leadership and change.

② (음악) 슬러(이음줄)

ⓓ slur ⓥ 불분명하게 발음하다

bay, bray

• bay ⓝ

① (바다) 만

Tokyo Bay

② 암갈색 말(a horse that is a reddish brown colour)

When they reached the site, they saw a blood bay mare by the side of the road.

ⓓ bay ⓥ (개가) 으르렁거리다(howl)

dogs baying at the moon

• bray ⓥ (당나귀가 시끄럽게) 울다

The donkey brayed and kicked.

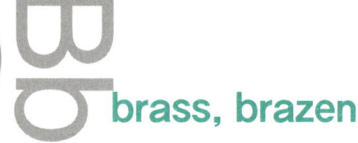

brass, brazen

- brass ⓝ 놋쇠, 금관악기
- brass band : 금관악기를 중심으로 편성된 악대
- brazen ⓐ 뻔뻔스러운

Mr. Prigozhin's blistering criticism and brazen actions called into question Russia's justifications for its war in Ukraine and the competency of its military leadership.

러시아 용병 반란

barb, barber

- barb ⓝ 미늘(낚시 끝의 안쪽에 있는, 고기가 물면 빠지지 않게 만든 작은 갈고리)
- barb ⓥ 미늘을 달다

The following year, South Korea opened the first of three "peace trails" for a limited number of visitors along the DMZ, bringing hikers past observatories and barbed-wire fences.

문재인 정부 당시 남북관계

- barber ⓝ 이발소

boo, coo, moo, woo

- boo ⓥ 야유하다(you do not like a person, performance, idea etc)

The crowd booed the opposing team.

- boo ⓝ 야유

Within seconds, loud boos and shouts of "Casse-toi"-"Go away!"- erupted from the crowd jamming the street.

- coo ⓥ ① (비둘기가) 구구구구 하다 ② (특히 사랑하는 사람에게) 달콤하게 속삭이다

Our favorite amphibians kiss and coo over their baby.

amphibian ⓝ 양서류

- moo ⓝ (소의 울음소리, 의성어) 음매
- bellow ⓥ (황소) 우렁찬 소리를 내다(to make the deep sound that a bull makes)
- woo ⓥ 지지를 호소하다, 구애하다(persuade, favor, support, the love of a woman)

In other countries, voters have been drawn to strongmen and salesmen, wooed by the promise of simple answers to complex questions.

bob, sob

- bob ⓥ (특히 물 위에서) 까닥거리다

The boat bobbed gently up and down on the water.

- sob ⓥ (흐느껴) 울다

The grandmother placed her head in her hands and began to sob.

bacon, beacon

- bacon ⓝ 베이컨
- beacon ⓝ 신호등이나 불빛(to warn or guide people, ships, vehicles, or aircraft)

All of Britain celebrated, many seeing the wedding as a beacon of hope in the post-World WarⅡ recovery period.

the wedding : 엘리자베스 2세의 결혼

bazaar, bizarre

- bazaar ⓝ 시장 거리, 상점가

Even the central bazaar was in darkness, though the vendors inside were still selling fresh fruit and cheese, pickles, and pork belly by the glow of electricity lanterns.

- bizarre ⓐ 기이한, 특이한(eccentric)

It is bizarre to me that the Biden Administration didn't use the Afghan evacuation as an opportunity to kick the refugee-resettlement program into gear.

into gear : 가동시키다

breed, brood

- breed ⓥ

① (새끼를) 낳다

② (번식시키기 위해) 사육하다

There was no factory meat industry that today breeds these animals as if they were just meat already, confining them in horrible conditions, cramped and isolated, until they die before ever having decently lived.

육식

③ 야기하다(to cause a particular feeling or condition)

Success in business does not necessarily breed success in all areas of life.

- brood ⓥ

① (알을) 품다

The male seahorses 'get pregnant' and brood the babies in their pouch.

② (걱정이나 화나는 일을) 되씹다, 곰곰이 생각하다

Jane had brooded over the subject a thousand time.

cf brood ⓝ

① (같은 때에 태어난) 새끼들

② 자녀가 많은 가족

Why would a father ask his ever-expanding brood of what became 11 children to memorize a poem about war and slaughter?

blizzard, buzzard

- blizzard ⓝ 눈보라

Let a blizzard approach or a hurricane churn toward shore, and we descend on stores, buying up more batteries, bottled water and canned foods that we could use in a lifetime.

- buzzard ⓝ (독수리과) 대머리수리

The sight of ravens, a bald eagle, or, in the warmer months, a buzzard, makes her grow tense.

her : 야생동물 보호 운동가

banquet, bouquet

- banquet ⓝ 연회

President Donald Trump and Queen Elizabeth Ⅱ arrive at a banquet at Buckingham Palace on June 3, during his first state visit to the UK.

사진설명기사

- bouquet ⓝ

① 부케(an arrangement of flowers, especially one that you give to someone)

② (포도주의) 향

An old woman picked up an empty wine-jar which had once contained a rare and costly wine, and which still retained some traces of its exquisite bouquet.

beau, beauty

- beau ⓝ 남자 친구(male friend, boyfriend)

She knows nothing about the romantic past of her current beau.

- beauty ⓝ 예쁜 여자(a beautiful woman)

Jane, a 25 year-old-ethereal beauty

bait, bite

- bait ⓝ 미끼

He found a lake and taught himself to fish by watching YouTube videos on an old wi-fi-enabled phone, using bread as bait in a cut-off plastic Coke bottle.

- bite ⓥ

① 물다

② 괴롭히다, 힘들게하다(to cause sharp pain or stinging discomfort to)

If you are my friend, why do you bite me?

barrel, barren

• barrel ⓝ ① 배럴(한 통의 양) ② 총신

Oil prices on both sides of the Atlantic briefly jumped above $100 per barrel to their highest levels since 2014.

ⓓ lock, stock and barrel : 몽땅, 모조리   stock ⓝ 개머리판

"The chance of North Korea believing in U.S.-offered security assurance in return for nuclear disarmament — lock, stock and barrel — is now close to zero," Jack says.

ⓓ over a barrel : 아주 어려운 입장인

The North Korean regime is fully aware that it has the Chinese leadership over a barrel.   it : 한국 주도의 통일

• barren ⓐ 불모의, 척박한

The artists in my generation experimented in a very barren environment, because the art we were taught was based on the education Koreans received during the Japanese colonial period.

burst, bust

• burst ⓥ (갑자기) 어떤 행동을 하다(suddenly begin doing or producing something)

V, Jimin and J-Hope spontaneously burst into song as they discuss Jin's upcoming birthday.   BTS

• bust ⓝ ① 흉상, 반신상 ② (수사 당국의) 급습   bust ⓥ 급습하다

Although Yoon has no governing experience, he's seen as a populist whose following is owed to a graft-busting image.

ⓓ busted-up ⓐ 망가진

Polls suggest 3 out of 4 Brazilians, including large numbers who voted for the former President in the October election that he lost to Lula, were horrified to see the ransacked offices, busted-up equipment and furniture, broken windows and violence between rioters and police.

브라질 대선 불복 폭동
bust up : 못 쓰게 만들다
(to damage or break something)

blacklist, whitelist

• blacklist ⓥ 블랙리스트에 올리다

Any of the P5 can blacklist any candidate for any reason.   유엔사무총장 선거
P5 : 상임이사국

• white list ⓝ 바람직한 것의 리스트

Both nations removed each other from their so-called white list of preferential trade partners.

Both nations : 한국과 일본
white list : 띄어쓰기도 함

bit, bitt

- bit ⓝ 조금

Almost seven decades later, she oversees an island nation reduced to a bit player on the world stage.   영국의 엘리자베스 여왕

- bitt ⓝ (배를 매어 두기 위하여 부두 따위에 세워 놓은) 기둥, 계주

I'm being towed by a fish and I'm the towing bitt.

blind, blink

- blind ⓐ 앞을 못 보는

Without the rules of transparency written into the nuclear treaties between the US and Russia, he says, both sides would become blind to each other's nuclear arsenals.   be blind to: 모르다

- blink ⓥ (눈을) 껌벅거리다

The man blinked in incomprehension, then rushed to the terminal help desk, trying to explain to the orange-jacked staff what had just taken place.   김정은의 이복형 김정남

breadth, breath

- breadth ⓝ 폭, 너비

I had long admired him for his success and dedication, and the breadth of his work across Europe, West Africa and the US allowed me to imagine possibilities for my own career.

- breath ⓝ (한번 들이쉬는) 숨

ⓓ in the same breath : 같은 반열에 있는 (you think they are alike or are related)

After her release in 2010, she became an even greater icon of human rights, mentioned in the same breath as Gandhi or Mandela.   her : 미얀마의 민주화 상징인 아웅산 수치 여사

baggy, buggy

- baggy ⓐ 헐렁한

The baggy suit is hanging a bit more loosely.

- buggy ⓝ (말 한 필이 끄는) 마차

Ulysses Grant was the first President to be arrested for speeding on a horse and buggy in 1872.   미국 18대 대통령

ⓓ bug ⓥ 괴롭히다

I began to be bugged by the teaching of American history, because it seemed that history had been taught without cognizance of my presence.   I : 흑인

brim, brink

- **brim** ⓝ (컵이나 그릇의) 끝부분
- **brim** ⓥ (넘칠 듯) 그득하다(with)

Volunteers hand out steaming bowls of miso soup brimming with pork belly and root vegetables

- **brink** ⓝ ① (벼랑·강가 등의) 끝 ② (위험하거나 흥미로운 상황이 발생하기) 직전

During the 1980s, rhinos were on the brink of extinction as poachers killed creatures for their horns.

- **brinkmanship** ⓝ 벼랑 끝 전술

In 2011, ending weeks of political brinkmanship, Congress advanced legislation to avoid a partial government shutdown.

buddy, bully

- **buddy** ⓝ 친구
- **buddy up to** : 친구로 지내다

His political opponents are aghast that a former human-rights lawyer, imprisoned as a student activist for opposing South Korea's own military dictatorship, could buddy up to a man like Kim.

a former human-rights lawyer : 문재인 대통령
Kim : 김정은

- **bully** ⓝ 괴롭히는 사람

Hell hath no fury like a rejected bully.

영화제작자 와인스타인 (Weinstein) 성추행

- **Hell hath no fury like a woman scorned**(여자가 한을 품으면 오뉴월에도 서리가 내린다)
- **Cyber Bullying** : (사이버) 특정인을 집단적으로 따돌리거나 집요하게 괴롭히는 행위

burden, burdensome, overburdened

- **burden** ⓝ 부담, 짐

For Olympians, the burden of expectation can be debilitating.

- **burdensome** ⓐ 부담스러운, 힘든

An increasingly burdensome "zero COVID" policy and President Xi Jinping's reform plans will unsettle markets and companies in 2022.

- **overburdened** ⓐ 부담이 과한

The Biden Administration inherited a very broken, underresourced, overburdened, and overcomplicated program, and humanitarian parole was the easy way out.

미국의 이민정책

C

외신으로 보는
대한민국
VOCABULARY

charisma, chasm

- charismatic ⓐ 카리스마의

Jack is revered among the Taliban as a founding member of the movement in 1994, a charismatic military leader and a deeply pious figure.

charisma ⓝ

- chasm ⓝ (사람·집단 사이의) 큰 차이(갈등)(schism)

It could inject significant light into America's chasm of toxicity.

it : meditation

consecrate, desecrate

- consecrate ⓥ 성스럽게하다

consecration ⓝ

In the years since Mao founded the People's Republic in 1949, no leader since the Great Helmsman himself has been consecrated by name in the constitution while alive.

Mao, Great Helmsman : 중국의 마오쩌둥
helm : (배) 키

- desecrate ⓥ (신성한 것을) 훼손하다

desecration ⓝ

Vandals desecrated gravestones in Jewish cemeteries in Philadelphia and Missouri.

calligraphy, chemotherapy, choreography

- calligraphy ⓝ 서예(artistic, stylized, or elegant handwriting or lettering)

Its original Christian art was then covered up and Islamic calligraphy was displayed instead.

- chemotherapy ⓝ (암에 대한) 화학요법

For months, we've gotten nothing but terrible news — the cancer is everywhere; it's not responding well to chemotherapy.

- choreography ⓝ 안무

BTS hits the expected high notes of traditional K-pop : sharp outfits, crisp choreography and dazzling videos.

clot, clout, cot

- clot ⓝ 혈전(blood clot)

He developed a blood clot on his brain and died.

- clout ⓝ ① (손이나 물건으로 강력하게) 때리기 ② 영향력

But prosecutors accuse her of actually boosting their clout through her longtime confidante, Choi Soon-sil.

her : 박근혜 대통령
their : 재벌들

- cot ⓝ 간이침대

Water, meals, cots and blankets were pre-positioned in San Juan.

태풍 대비

crude, cruel

- crude ⓐ

① 대충한

The gnarled scar that covers most of the left side of his face appears to show a crude number 3. His jailer carved it into his cheek with a fire-heated knife, cutting and cauterizing at the same time.

② 원래 그대로의, 미가공의

There is room for Beijing to do more : suspending the 500,000 tons of crude oil it sends to North Korea annually, for example, was what brought Kim Jong Il to the six-party talks in 2003.

crude oil : 원유

- cruel ⓐ 잔인한

Pandemics are cruel thing. Their gradual end can be deeply sweet.

cf cruelty ⓝ

The stress of the times, combined with the cruelty of the act and Floyd's desperate plea, broke me.

Flyod : 백인 경찰의 목 눌림으로 죽은 흑인
desperate plea : 죽어가면서 하는 호소

cannon, canon

- cannon ⓝ (무기) 대포

Those crowds today on the streets of Hong Kong braving riot police, water cannons, and tear gas understand that the Chinese judicial systems is a tool of state.

cf cannon fodder : 총알받이

The pain of our most vulnerable citizens has been turned into political cannon fodder.

- canon ⓝ ① 규범, 일반적 규칙 ② (작가의) 작품 목록

Although he produced an astonishing canon chronicling life in 20th century America,

he : 작가(writer)

crucial, crucible

- crucial ⓐ (앞으로의 상황에 영향을 미친다는 점에서) 대단히 중요한(critical)

Missile defense is an element that will be crucial to defend both South Korea and Japan.

- crucible ⓝ ① (쇳물을 녹이거나 하는) 도가니 ② (창조하는 과정에서) 호된 시련의 장

The crucible of the pandemic became a pretense of stifling dissent.

clean, clear

- clean ⓐ

① 깨끗한

the WHO helps provide access to medicine and clean drinking water.

② (마약 같은) 불법적인 약물을 하지 않는

I was 17 when I started shooting heroin. Since then, I've gotten clean, gotten high again, gotten clean, gotten high.

high ⓐ 마약에 취한

ⓓ cleanse ⓥ (바람직하지 않은 것을) 제거하다, 청소하다

a campaign of ethnic cleansing

인종청소

- clear ⓐ

① (날씨가) 맑은

Stillness is drenched in humidity and scorched by a sun blasting down from the clear skies that will eventually follow a hurricane.

② 분명한

it must also be clear that people don't automatically embark on a life of bliss the moment they touch German soil.

유럽에 도착하는 아프리카 난민

ⓓ crystal clear : 너무나 분명한

The Iranian government wants to kill the messengers in order to conceal the truth — but for the Iranian people, the truth is crystal clear.

ⓓ the coast is clear : 붙잡힐 위험은 없다

It wasn't until the middle of 1920 that the pandemic was finally over in many places, though there was no official declaration that the coast was clear.

ⓓ clear ⓥ 치우다

clearance ⓝ

She also oversaw a remorseless slum-clearance drive in Delhi and forcible-sterilization campaigns across India.

clean-cut, clear-cut

- clean-cut ⓐ 말쑥한, 용모 단정한(neat, clean, have a good moral character)

Macron's youth and clean-cut looks set him in contrast to France's political grandees.

Macron : 프랑스 대통령
grandee : 고위층

- clear-cut ⓐ 분명한, 명백한(easy to understand or be certain about, sharply defined)

This year's choice was the most clear-cut in memory.

unclean, unclear

- unclean ⓐ 더러운, 부정한

The whole world has grown more apprehensive about taking children into highly trafficked unclean areas, especially since the pandemic began.

- unclear ⓐ 불확실한

It's unclear whether she has been charged with a crime.

She : 중국에서 행방불명된 여배우

cadet, cadre

- cadet ⓝ 사관생도

Years before, Elizabeth had visited a naval college at Dartmouth where she had been greeted by a towering 18-year-old cadet.

영국 여왕의 젊은 시절

ⓓ midshipman : (해군) 장교 후보생

As a midshipman at the US Naval Academy in the 1970s, I had my first close-up look at Jack.

- cadre ⓝ 핵심그룹

Since its genesis in the '90s, Korean pop—or K-pop—has become synonymous with what studios call "idols" : a cadre of young, polished, perfect-seeming pop stars whose images are often rigorously controlled.

clarify, classify

- clarify ⓥ 분명하게 하다, 명백하게 하다

clarification ⓝ

I should clarify something before going further.

ⓓ clarity ⓝ 명확성, 명료함

Her uncompromising clarity may be what I most admire about Jane.

- classify ⓥ 분류하다

classification ⓝ

Under the rules of Russian criminal procedure, they had classified him as a victim in the case.

ⓓ declassify ⓥ (국가 기밀에 관한 정보에서) 제외시키다

The United States military investigated the case just days after the killings occurred, according to declassified American documents.

criticize, critique

• criticize ⓥ 비난하다

Others have criticized the Pope for caving in to the demands of an authoritarian state with a record of religious intolerance and human-rights abuses.

🅒 critical

① 비판적인(criticize)

There's really an opportunity for everyone to critically reflect on a racist and racialized past.

② (앞으로의 상황에 영향을 미친다는 점에서) 대단히 중요한(crucial)

Peace-keeping will be even more critical in the years ahead.

③ 위태로운

Officers under attack shot and critically injured two teenagers in early October.

• critique ⓥ 비평하다   critique ⓝ

In BTS's debut 2013 single, "No More Dream," they critiqued Korean social pressures, like the high expectations placed on schoolkids.

critical mass, critical point

• critical mass ⓝ 임계질량

Critical mass has its roots in physics : it's the amount of material needed to sustain a nuclear explosion.

What happens when women reach a critical mass of influence.   미투(Me Too) 기사 제목

• critical point ⓝ 임계점

In 2011, when famine was declared in Somalia, things escalated to a critical point, but only briefly.

chore, core

• chore ⓝ (정기적으로 해야 하는) 귀찮은 일

But they didn't have chores in the same way their friends did. In the Jack household, less was required—but more was expected.   가정교육
they : Jack의 아이들

• core ⓝ 핵심

The core was, We've had a sick kid, we've had a kid who's died, so let's get real about what's important here. You've got to find a path in life that yor're really happy with.   가정교육

circle, cycle

- circle ⓝ 원   circular ⓐ

Obama warned against assuming history turns in circles. "We're not bound by our genetic code to repeat the mistakes of the past, we can tell our children a different story."

cf circle ⓥ (공중에서) 빙빙 돌다

Conversations circle around the incomprehensible fact that the United Kingdom voted on June 23 to leave the European Union.

cf encircle ⓥ 둘러싸다

a courthouse encircled by concrete boundaries, chain-link fencing and citizen-soldiers dressed for war

- cycle ⓝ ① 사이클 ② 순환   남북문제

Certainly there are few original ideas on how to break this cycle : engagement, negotiation, provocation, estrangement, rapprochement.

circuitous, circulate,

- circuitous ⓐ 길이 빙빙 돌아가는 (longer than the most direct way)

At the time, all the salt produced had to be transferred to a market 40 miles away via circuitous 217mile-route, as there was no road through the desert to the nearest train depot.

- circulate ⓥ 순환하다, 유포하다

Dangerous variants of the virus are circulating.

captive, captor

- captive ⓝ 억류된 자, 포로

North Korea's history of captive-taking reaches back decades and contributed to Trump's decision to order all US citizens out of the country by September 2017.

cf captive ⓐ 사로잡힌 (held under control, but having the appearance of independence)

He governed a nation in which a violent and vociferous element was captive to its onw visions and controlled by its own interests.   He : 링컨 대통령

- captor ⓝ 억류자, 포획자

For the next five hours, his gun-toting captors mocked and hit him.

commute, telecommute

• commute ⓥ 통근하다   commute ⓝ
                                              생활 속의 운동
Ditch the car! If you have a short commute, leave traffic behind and sneak in exercise with person-powered transport. Think bikes, scooters and your own two feet.

• telecommute ⓥ 재택 근무하다

Many workers would like to continue to telecommute post-pandemic.

castrate, castigate

• castigate ⓥ 비난하다

An editorial in the Sankei Shimbun, a right-leaning newspaper in Tokyo, castigated Japan's welcoming response to Mr. Yoon's plan last week as "extremely regrettable" and "pandering" to South Korea for "distorting and denouncing historical facts."   대통령의 일본방문

• castrate ⓥ 거세하다(to remove the testicles of a male animal or a man)

The videos showed a group of men, one whom was seen wearing pro-Russian symbols, castrate and execute a prisoner dressed in military fatigues with Ukrainian military insignia.

civic, civil

• civic ⓐ 시민의

For many, wearing one has become a symbol of civic duty during an uncertain time.   코로나 관련 마스크 착용

• civil ⓐ   civility ⓝ
                  civilian ⓝ 민간인
① 민간의(종교나 군대와 상대되는 의미)(civilian)

a civil-society organization that tracks hate crimes against intolerance in Germany

civil engineer : 토목기사

② 정중한, 예의 바른 (courteous and polite)

They defend the police. They condemn the violence. Civility matters more to them than justice.   흑인 목조르기 사망사고

ⓓ incivility ⓝ 무례함

It's not a coincidence, psychologists say, that much of the incivility occurs toward people in customer-service industries.

carcass, corpse

- **carcass** ⓝ (동물) 사체

Blood trickles into gutters as the buffalo become carcasses. — 도축장

- **corpse** ⓝ (사람) 시체

Their family waited for weeks, months, then years as the military worked to find their corpse.

couch, crouch

- **couch** ⓝ 긴 의자

It's late October, and Suga is sitting on a couch strumming a guitar. — Suga : BTS member

cf **couch** ⓥ (특정한 방식으로) 표현을 하다

The measures of American success in Afghanistan have been couched in kilometers of roads built, money spent, insurgents killed.

- **crouch** ⓥ 쭈그리고 앉다(squat)

The government says you have a much higher survival rate if you crouch rather than stand up. — 지진 대비 훈련

copper, corpulent

- **copper** ⓝ (화학원소) 구리, 동

Pipelines and dams in Myanmar, ports in West Africa and hydroelectricity plants and copper mines in Afghanistan could all be held ransom to strife. — hold somebody to ransom

- **corpulent** ⓐ 살찐(fat, obese)

There are men who prefer very small breasts, men who prefer corpulent women, and so forth.

commodity, commonality

- **commodity** ⓝ 상품

Its chief export, milk in some form, is not the kind of commodity nations fight over. — It : New Zealand

- **commonality** ⓝ 공통점, 공통성

But none of the parents in this story set out to raise successful children. Instead, the six commonalities of our nine families combined to create drive, grit and social consciousness that propelled all the siblings on their own chosen paths. — 미국 이민 간 아홉 가정의 자식 교육

crackle, crinkle

• **crackle** ⓥ 딱딱 소리를 내다 (장작이 탈 때) 탁탁 소리를 내다

The banshee wail of the emergency siren reverberates across the school field, conjuring a primal fear even before the words "Missile launched!, Missile launched!" crackle over the loudspeaker.

민방공 훈련

• **crinkle** ⓥ (많은) 잔주름이 생기다(wrinkle)

Children ran forward and tore open the packages, only to crinkle their noses.

chart, charter

• **chart** ⓝ
① 해도(바다의 상태를 자세히 적어 넣은 항해용 지도.)
② 도표, 차트
③ (음반 판매고에 따른 대중음악 주간) 인기 순위표

BTS isn't just the biggest K-pop act on the charts.

ⓓ **chart** ⓥ (특정한 결과를 내기 위한 절차를 담은) 계획을 세우다

That speech was the first by a South Korean leader in North Korea and the high point of a long, often agonizing process of engagement that Moon had charted since his election in May 2017.

that speech : 문재인 대통령의 평양 연설

ⓓ **uncharted** : 해도에 없는

This corner of Spain is now in uncharted territory.

• **charter** ⓥ (항공기나 배를) 전세내다

The boat is jointly chartered by international medical humanitarian organization, Medicins Sans Frontieres(MSF), or Doctors Without Borders, and the search-and-rescue organization SOS Mediterrane.

collide, collude

• **collide** ⓥ 충돌하다, 부딪히다

There is no longer any doubt that Hong Kong is on a collision course with the Chinese government, which has ruled the former British colony since 1997.

collision ⓝ

• **collude** ⓥ 공모하다, 한 통이 되다

The legislation's full text—which targets secession, subversion, terrorism and collusion with foreign forces—was not made public until after it became law.

collusion ⓝ

classic, classical, classified

• classic ⓐ 전형적인

The first lady, Jill Biden, arranged for a classic American menu with a Korean flair. — 윤석열 대통령 미국방문

• classical ⓐ 고전적인

He has become a symbol of pride in South Korea, where he has been described as classical music's answer to K-pop. — He : 피아니스트 임윤찬

• classified ⓐ 기밀의

Besides Choi, two former Park aides have been hit by various charges related to abuse of power, fraud and coercion, as well as leaking classified documents. — Choi : 최순실(최서원)

culinary, cutlery

• culinary ⓐ 요리의

He acknowledged that many people still use onggi as a piece of culinary equipment, but he said that it is also transitioning from a purely functional object into an art piece with cultural and symbolic significance. — 김치와 장독

• cutlery ⓝ (식탁용) 날붙이류(나이프·포크·숟가락 등)

Activists are attempting to rid the island of Anglesey of single-use plastic bottles, cutlery and straws to make the entire district plastic-free. — 1회용품 근절

accord, cord

• accord ⓝ (국가 사이의) 공식적인 합의

Kim even gifted Moon a pair of snow white Pungsan hunting dogs — Gomi and Songgang — to symbolize their flourishing accord.

• cord ⓝ 줄, 선

She wore the key on a cord around her neck.

cucumber, sea cucumber

• cucumber ⓝ 오이

She walked in as cool as a cucumber, as if nothing had happened.

• sea cucumber ⓝ (바다의) 해삼

as cool as a cucumber : (햇볕에 탔을 때 오이 마사지를 상기하면서 곤란한 상황에서도) 대단히 침착한

sea squirt : 멍게

corridor, corrode

• corridor ⓝ 복도, 회랑

The corridor from Arica's most populous country to its northern Mediterranean shores has proved especially lucrative.

• corrode ⓥ 부식시키다

He limits his use of social media, he says, because he believes it is corrosive to creativity and because he wants to live as much as possible as his favorite composers did.

corrosion ⓝ
He : 피아니스트 임윤찬

cardinal, cordial

• cardinal ⓐ 중요한

This was the ancients' guide for placing the four cardinal signs in the zodiac.

• cordial ⓐ 화기애애한

Talks with European leaders have been cordial but not particularly productive.

cardinal ⓝ (천주교) 추기경

considerable, considerate

• considerable ⓐ 상당한, 많은

The economic damage to Hong Kong is already considerable.

• considerate ⓐ (남에 대한) 배려심이 깊은

Jane described her mother as generous and considerate.

carriage, coach

• carriage ⓝ 마차(pulled by a horse, used in the past)(buggy)

Sharpshooters were stationed on rooftops along the avenue, "with orders," an officer recalled, "to watch the windows on the opposite side, and to fire upon them in case any attempt should be made to fire from those windows on the presidential carriage.

링컨 취임식 당일

• coach ⓝ

① 마차(pulled by horses and used in the past for carrying passengers)
② 코치

At Oklahoma State, star running back Jack called out his coach, Tom, for wearing a shirt supporting a news outlet that called Black Lives Matter a "farce."

cement, cemetery

- cement ⓥ 강화하다

But no legislation has cemented full protections for sexual minorities into law.   우리나라 차별금지법

- cemetery ⓝ 묘지

Jack was buried in a cemetery in suburban Chicago, said Tom, Jack's longtime friend.

component, composure

- component ⓝ 요소, 부품

The 5,000 gold, silver and bronze medals are cast from metal components harvested from defunct gadgets, including 6.21 million cell phones.   2021 도쿄 올림픽

- composure ⓝ 평정, 평정심

She had the unimaginable composure to understand the historical and public importance of her reaction to her husband's assassination, even amid her personal grief and trauma.

correlate, corrugate

- correlate ⓥ 연관성을 보여주다

Colleagues noted a correlation between increased nighttime temperatures and suicide rates in the US and Mexico.   correlation ⓝ
지구 온난화

- corrugate ⓥ 물결 모양으로 주름 잡다   corrugation

Also, some of the seawalls are made of vertical corrugated steel, which is inadequate, officials said.

cf seawall : 방파제

coda, coma

- coda ⓝ (음악) 종결부 혹은 연설이나 문학작품의 마지막 부분

In London, he has enjoyed a coda as businessman, restaurateur, and thorn in the side of Russian President Putin, supporting democratic causes in Russia and its periphery by funding opposition parties and issuing scathing critiques.   he : 영국에 망명한 러시아인

- coma ⓝ 혼수상태   comatose ⓐ

Jack was found unresponsive, in a coma.

convey, convoy

- convey ⓥ 전달하다, 실어 나르다

He also conveyed his views and the views of the bureaucracy.

cf conveyer belt : 컨베이어 벨트

- convoy ⓝ (군인이나 다른 차량의) 호송대

A : Do you have documents on you?
B : Good, then we'll know how to mark your grave if you fall behind the convoy.

전쟁터에서 검문소 통과 joke

canvas, canvass

- canvas ⓝ 캔버스, 화폭

Almost all of these paintings are on paper, not canvas.

- canvass ⓥ (선거에서) 유세하다

Jane had canvassed with an abortion-rights group for months, urging Kansas residents to vote no on a ballot measure that would have amended the state constitution to say there was no right to an abortion in the state.

capitulate, catapult

- capitulate ⓥ 굴복하다, 항복하다

Putin, however, seems to be stubbornly sticking to the same strategy, banking on his conviction that Western support for Ukraine will crumple, forcing Ukraine to capitulate in time.

- catapult ⓝ (옛날의) 투석기

cf catapult ⓥ (갑자기) 내던지다

In 1960, at 26, she sat for months in the forests of Tanzania, biding her time until Chimpanzees accepted her presence and she could observe them up close. When she finally did, she made the seismic discovery that they use tools, transforming our understanding of the relationship between humans and animals and catapulting her to global fame.

제인 구달

carton, cartoon

- carton ⓝ (특히 음식이나 음료를 담는) 갑(통), 한 갑(의 양)

America has fallen out of love with drinking milk, as lower-calorie options have proliferated and people are substituting water bottles for milk cartons.

- cartoon ⓝ 만화

crowdfund, crowdsource

• crowdfund ⓥ 크라우드펀드하다, 인터넷 모금하다

The gargantuan sculpture, which was partly crowfunded but mostly paid for by the state, took 33 months to build and cost $400 million.

• crowdsource ⓥ 크라우드 소스하다(인터넷을 통해 여러 사람의 정보나 도움을 받다)

How Ukraine is crowdsourcing digital evidence of war crimes 〔기사 제목〕

collective, collectible

• collective ⓐ 집단의

As another Black man lost to senseless violence activates our collective moral outrage, that burden remains as we strive to reach the full promise of America.

• collectible ⓐ 모을 수 있는, 수집할 수 있는

Similarly Jack has observed that we often opt for "collectible experiences" that give us a story to tell and help build our "experiential CV," as we like to feel we're accomplishing something.

ⓓ CV : 이력서(curriculum vitae)

collaborate, corroborate

• collaborate ⓥ 공동으로 작업하다, 협력하다   〔collaboration ⓝ〕

In the past few months, tensions between the US and China have dramatically worsened. A relationship that has swung between outbreaks of hostility and grudging collaboration is now settling into long-term estrangement.

• corroborate ⓥ (증거나 정보를) 제공하다, 입증하다   〔corroboration〕

This chatbot, created by Ukraine's Digital Ministry and dubbed "e-Enemy," is one of a half dozen digital tools the government in Kyiv has set up to crowdsource and corroborate evidence of possible war crimes.

communicable, communicative

• communicable ⓐ 전염성이 있는

communicable diseases that are usually transmitted sexually

• communicative ⓐ 대화를 잘 하는, 속내를 드러내는

Jack spent the afternoon horseback riding with Jane and was especially communicative about his feelings.

clatter, clutter

- clatter ⓥ 덜커덕거리며 가다(rumble)

Subway trains clattered along their tracks, their doors squealing open to disgorge crowds of passengers.

- clutter ⓝ 잡동사니, 어수선함

The cavernous terminal 2 departure hall at Kuala Lumpur International Airport was filled with its usual morning clutter of giddy vacationers and harried businesspeople.

communicate, communique

- communicate ⓥ 의사소통하다

communication ⓝ

Experts stress governments must have a sound strategy to communicate to the public.

- communique ⓝ 공동 선언문

The Nicaraguan government signed an official communique to reestablish diplomatic ties with China in Tianjin on Friday, according to Chinese state broadcaster CCTV.

console, consolidate

- console ⓥ 위로하다

consolation ⓝ
BTS와 코로나

The idea was to release new music to console people and heal their minds through our music during these hard times, when it's difficult to physically meet and interact.

- consolidate ⓥ 굳히다, 강화하다

consolidation ⓝ

There is also some evidence that Kim Jong Un is in the final stage of consolidating power and moved on his half brother to eliminate any remaining rivalry.

clomp, clump

- clomp ⓥ 쿵쿵거리며 걷다

But in the village, burros still clomp up narrow streets, and 1 in 5 homes lacks running water.

burro ⓝ 작은 당나귀

- clump ⓝ 덩어리, 군집(a small mass of something)

Hindu devotees bathe among clumps of toxic foam in the river in New Delhi on Nov. 10, as part of rituals during the four-day festival.

constable, constant

- constable ⓝ 경찰관(police officer)
- constant ⓐ 항상(happening regularly or all the time)   constantly ⓐⓓⓥ

New buildings spring up constantly in Pyongyang, where flatscreen TVs and karaoke machines are common, and locals now talk of a "rush hour."

ⓒⓕ constant ⓝ 상수   variant ⓝ 변수

contend, content

- contend ⓥ (언쟁 중에) 주장하다, 다투다   contention ⓝ

What would it take to bring Asian nations into contention with the European and South American stalwarts at the top of the FIFA rankings?

ⓒⓕ contender ⓝ 도전자, 경쟁자

It has been six years since baseball's superstars faced off in the sport's version of a World Cup. The U.S., Japan, the Dominican Republic and others are top contenders.

- content ⓐ 만족하는

They seem content to blame their own inaction on the police in central Africa.   수사가 미진함에 대한 내용

ⓒⓕ contents ⓝ (속에 든) 내용물

Much has been written about the trash problem created by the billions of disposable plastic drinking-water bottles sold each year in the US. Far less is understood about the contents of those bottles.

bone of contention, point of contention

- bone of contention ⓝ 미해결된 이슈(something that causes arguments between people)

If Biden reverses the policy, China hawks in Washington will accuse him of appeasing Beijing. If he doesn't, he inherits a tough bone of contention with China.

ⓒⓕ 개들이 뼈를 두고 서로 다투는 것을 비유

- point of contention ⓝ 논쟁 지점 (argument and disagreement between people)

When the 1979 Islamic Revolution overthrew Reza Shah's son, the last monarch of the Pahlavi dynasty, the hijab became mandatory (and a major point of contention between the people and the new regime).   이란

clash, crash, crush

- clash ⓥ 충돌하다, 차이를 보이다

South Korea's position has been that it will cooperate with the United States while not clashing with Russia.

clash ⓝ a short fight
우크라이나·러시아 전쟁

- crash ⓝ

① (자동차 충돌, 항공기 추락) 사고

Twelve of the migrant laborers, who had spent a grueling day working the harvest, died in the crash.

② 요란한 소리, 굉음

Then he fell into the water with a crash that sent spray over the old man and over all of the skiff.

skiff ⓝ 아주 작은 배

③ (경제) (가격, 가치의) 붕괴

Soon after the 2008-9 financial crash tanked the economy, Americans' unflagging faith in higher education started to falter.

㏇ crash ⓥ

① 자동차 충돌하다, 비행기가 추락하다

A Ukraine International Airlines passenger jet bound for Kyiv crashed shortly after taking off from Tehran, killing all 176 on board.

② 붕괴하다

Who could imagine a virus that crashes the entire global operating system, or an attack that narrowly fails to decapitate the US government?

㏇ crash ⓐ 단기에 집중적인

crash diet

- crush ⓝ

① 강렬한 사랑, 홀딱 반함(infatuation)

It's an intimate moment, the kind you'd spend with a new crush in a college dorm room while they confess rock-star ambitions.

BTS member인 Suga의 기타 치는 모습

② (좁은 곳에) 잔뜩 몰려든 군중

Soon a new crush of refugees was pouring into neighbouring Bangladesh.

㏇ crush ⓥ 으스러(쭈그러)뜨리다

One day, Lee got his wrist crushed in a pressing machine.

Lee : 이재명

crashing, crushing

• **crashing** ⓐ 완전한, 철저한(utter, absolute)

Apple's once-unstoppable growth had come to a crashing halt : The number of iPhones sold was down 13 percent, and the company posted its first revenue decline in 13 years.

• **crushing** ⓐ 참담한(causing overwhelming disappointment or embarrassment)

In April, Moon's Democratic Party suffered crushing defeats in the mayoral elections in South Korea's two largest cites.

2021년 4월 서울시장과 부산시장 재보궐 선거

ⓓ **soul-crushing** ⓐ 엄청 힘드는

Young Koreans have well-documented reasons not to start a family, including the staggering costs of raising children, unaffordable homes, lousy job prospects and soul-crushing work hours.

cereal, cerebral

• **cereal** ⓝ 시리얼

a bowl of breakfast cereal

• **cerebral** ⓐ

① 뇌(brain)의

cerebral palsy : 뇌성마비(spastic)

cerebral cortex : 대뇌피질

② 이지적인(complicated ideas rather than strong emotions)

The band does take a cerebral approach to music and has a lot of sonic ambition.

sonic ⓐ 소리의

contagious, contiguous

• **contagious** ⓐ

contagion ⓝ

① 전염성이 강한(be passed from person to person by touch)

Another study this summer found that students had higher levels of the stress hormone cortisol if their teachers reported being burned out. But if stress is contagious, so is its opposite.

② (태도나 감정 등이) 전염성이 강한

Jane talks in a direct manner, with a sort of contagious defiance.

• **contiguous** ⓐ 인접한(next to something, or next to each other)

America's 48 contiguous states

contain, contaminate

- contain ⓥ

① ~이 들어 있다, 함유되어 있다   container : 그릇, 용기

Also, nobody got an allowance. Instead, a drawer in the living room table, contained petty cash for anyone to use.   자녀교육

② (좋지 않은 일을) 방지하다, 억제하다   containment ⓝ

South Korea's political stability is critical in the multilateral effort to contain North Korea, a rogue state that aspires to become a member of the nuclear-power club.

- contaminate ⓥ 오염하다, 오염시키다   contamination ⓝ

And much of our time is "contaminated time" — when we're doing one thing but thinking about something else.   "Do you have enough time?" 제목에 대한 기사

conscience, prescience

- conscience ⓝ 양심

The savagery of Jack's killing pained anyone with a conscience.

- prescience ⓝ 예지, 혜안, 통찰

But whether by sheer luck or keen prescience, Bong Joon-ho's parasite is the movie for right now.   (영화) 기생충

conscientious, conscious

- conscientious ⓐ

① 양심적인

As a conscientious objector in South Korea, Hye-min fought conscription for years.

ⓓ conscientious objector : 양심적 병역거부자

② 착실한, 충실한

She has always been a very conscientious worker.

- conscious ⓐ 의식하는   consciousness ⓝ

You talk to the subconscious. You don't talk to the conscious   자식 교육을 위해 잠자는 자식 옆에서 주문을 외움

click, clock

- click ⓥ 찰칵하는 소리를 내다

The door to the Oval Office clicked shut.

- clock ⓥ (경기에서 속도가 얼마의 시간을) 기록하다

the fastest 800-m time ever clocked on American soil

cloak, cluck, croak

- cloak ⓝ ① 망토 ② 은폐   cloak ⓥ 가리다, 숨기다

If anything, the upcoming election is a test of limits of populism when stacked against the entrenched powers of dictatorship, cloaked in a facade of democracy.

- cluck ⓥ ① (닭) 구구 소리 내다 ② 혀를 차다

Tongues clucked when word got out that a Missouri man whose daughter had tested positive for COVID-19 broke quarantine in early March to attend a father-daughter school dance with her sister.

- croak ⓝ 개구리, 까마귀 울음소리

carry, miscarry

- carry ⓥ

① (무거운 물건을) 받치고 있다

He is morbidly obese, carrying upwards of 300lb. on a 5-ft. 8-in frame.

② 임신하다

But armed with birth control and evolving scientific information about this virus, I have some ability to predict whether I'll carry and deliver my next child during this pandemic.   코로나

- miscarry ⓥ 유산하다   miscarriage ⓝ

She miscarried several times ; her relationship with her husband was vexed by infidelity.   abortion ⓝ 인공중절

ceiling, cellar

- ceiling ⓝ (건물) 천장

ⓓ glass ceiling ⓝ 유리천장

It had not occurred to me, frankly, that I would ever be in a position to break a glass ceiling.   me : (미국) 여성 국무장관

- cellar ⓝ (wine 등의) 지하의 저장창고

As soon as the artillery barrages began, the informal village leader, a man named Jack, made a bomb shelter out of his cellar.

complex, compound

- **complex** ⓝ 복합 건물(premises), (건물) 단지(for a particular purpose)

a leisure complex

- **complex** ⓐ 복잡한

While being a former head of state might look more impressive, deep experience with a complex bureaucracy is crucial for any bid to make the UN run more effectively and efficiently.   *UN 사무총장 선거*

- **compound** ⓝ 구내(an area, by a fence or wall)

All students live on a closed compound outside the city.

- **compound** ⓥ

① 더욱 악화시키다

Prisoners' lack of contact with the outside world compounds their problems.

② 구성하다, 이루어지다

Everything he has learned in school about the American right has taught Jack the power of endurance as a compounding political power.

③ (이자) 복리 계산하다

the yield at which the interest is compounded

connection, connectivity

- **connection** ⓝ (두 가지의) 관련성   *connect ⓥ*

Some people kept up the tradition, but its religious connection faded, even among Catholics.   *Halloween*

- **connectivity** ⓝ (컴퓨터의) 연결성

By boosting connectivity, China can spur growth, gain access to valuable natural resources and create new markets for its goods.

claim, clamor

- **claim** ⓥ 목숨을 앗아 가다

As of mid-December, the pandemic has claimed more than 1.6 million lives worldwide.

- **clamor** ⓥ 시끄럽게 요구하다

Her 2020 run for office against Jack — Europe's longest-serving leader — galvanized support throughout Belarus, as citizens clamored for a fresh face in government.

cornerstone, millstone, milestone, touchstone

• **cornerstone** ⓝ 초석, 주춧돌

Biden has a chance to make national service the cornerstone of his legacy.

• **milestone** ⓝ
① 이정표(mile을 돌에 표시하여 앞으로의 거리를 말함)
② 중요한 사건 (a very important event in the development of something)

She doesn't feel like she's missing adolescent milestones as she travels the world for tennis.   테니스 스타

• **millstone** ⓝ
① 맷돌(방앗간에서 곡식을 빻을 때 사용하던 돌)
② 골치거리

To do so, he must clip the wings of China's mammoth state-owned enterprises, which helped propel its export-led growth for close to four decades but risk becoming a millstone.   To do so : 경제발전

• **touchstone** ⓝ 시금석(something used as a test or standard)

At a time when indigenous art wasn't taken seriously, she incorporated Mexican folkloric touchstones into both her paintings and her unique fashion sensibility.   she : 멕시코 화가 프리다 칼로(Frida Kahlo)

comparable, comparative, compatible

• **comparable** ⓐ 비교할 만한

On Sept. 9, North Korea conducted its fifth nuclear test — the largest to date, with a yield of some 10 to 20 kilotons, comparable to the Hiroshima bomb.

• **comparative** ⓐ 상대적, 비교적

Even by the comparatively lax standards of the 1970s, the Jack girls had more freedom than most.   가정교육

• **compatible** ⓐ
① 호환이 되는

By combining two seemingly incompatible ideas like unstable atoms in a molecule,

② 양립되는

ⓓ **incompatible** ⓐ 양립이 불가능한

It would end the Supreme Court's right to strike down pieces of legislation that the court finds incompatible with Israel's Basic Law, which serve as the country's constitution.   it : 이스라엘 정부의 개혁안

clamp, cramp

• clamp ⓥ 꽉 물다(잡다)(in a position so that it cannot move)

Jane had to clamp a hand over her mouth to stop herself from laughing.

• cramp ⓝ (근육에 생기는) 경련, 쥐

Center back Jack played the final half-hour with Tom suffering what appeared to be a cramp.

ⓓ cramps ⓝ 생리로 인한 복통

cram, cramped

• cram ⓥ

① (좁은 공간 속으로 억지로) 밀어(쑤셔) 넣다

The wooden boat carried 416, several of them crammed belowdecks, in the storage area.

② (시험을 앞두고 벼락치기) 공부하다

Lectures were called off so students could cram for the semester finals.

ⓓ crammer ⓝ 시험준비학교(a special school that prepares people quickly for examinations)

Many send them to private crammers, known as hagwon, after school.

Many : 부모님
them : 자녀들

• cramped ⓐ 비좁은

The only way to stretch your legs in those cramped conditions was to stand up.

cause, clause

• cause ⓝ (조직의) 대의명분, 이상

She rejected traditional gender roles, instead committing herself to the cause of the Chinese Communist Party.

• clause ⓝ (법률의) 조항

Abe had wanted to add a clause on the existence of Japan's military, the Self-Defense Forces, to clarify its status.

calamity, catastrophe

• calamity ⓝ 재앙, 재난

Nuclear calamity

• catastrophe ⓝ 참사, 재앙

We are on track for a catastrophe that dwarfs the COVID-19 crisis.

cataclysm ⓝ
세 단어 모두 같은 뉘앙스

catastrophic ⓐ
지구 온난화

celebrate, celestial

• **celebrate** ⓥ 기념하다, 축하하다   celebration ⓝ

We need not to celebrate our sugar high but to diet.   경제 기사

• **celestial** ⓐ 하늘의, 천상의

The precious toddler seemed to recognize objects belonging to the 13th   달라이라마
Dalai Lama, prompting the lamas to proclaim him the celestial heir.

chalk, choke

• **chalk** ⓝ 분필

It was also seen written in chalk on a sidewalk at the University of Alabama on Jan. 26, 2023.

ⓓ chalkboard ⓝ 칠판

• **choke** ⓝ 숨이 막힘, 질식

ⓓ choke-hold ⓝ 목 졸림

As public outcry grew, France announced a ban on choke-hold arrest tactics on June 8.

ⓓ choke point ⓝ 요충지

The Strait of Malacca, the choke point that links the Indian and Pacific oceans at the southern end of the South China Sea, handles four times as much oil as the better-known Suez Canal.

crass, cross

• **crass** ⓐ 무신경한(not understand or care about other people's feelings)

the crass assumptions that men make about women

• **cross** ⓥ   cross ⓝ 십자가

① 가로질러 건너다

In this image by photojournalist Jack, a trail of civilians crosses the Myanmar border seeking sanctuary on the muddy banks of Bangladesh.

② (사람의 계획 등을) 반대하다

The purging of senior officials and generals during Xi's first term as he pursued an antigraft campaign demonstrated that he was not a leader to be crossed.

ⓓ cross-legged : 책상다리하고

Sit comfortably. You don't have to be cross-legged—a chair will do.   명상

confab, confide

- confab ⓝ 대화, 담소

One report suggests that Xi was injured by a chair hurled during a fractious confab of CCP princelings.

confabulation ⓝ

- confide ⓥ (속마음을) 털어놓다

President John F. Kennedy, Lyndon Johnson and Richard Nixon privately confided that the conflict could not be won, yet publicly pretended otherwise.

베트남전쟁

- confidential ⓐ 비밀의

Doctors are required to keep patients' records completely confidential.

chafe, chaff

- chafe ⓥ

① (피부를) 쓸리게 하다, 쓸려서 아프다 (sore because of something rubbing against it)

Soft leather straps don't chafe the tops of your feet and the thong won't cause painful blistering between the toes.

② (어떤 제한 또는 불편함 때문에) 짜증내다, 신경 쓰이다

This crisis is driven not just by a desire for independence by a region with its own language, identity and history of chafing at Spanish dominance that dates back centuries.

- chaff ⓝ (곡식의) 겉껍질, 왕겨

Crises always help separate the wheat from the chaff, including in government.

separate the wheat from the chaff : 알갱이와 쭉정이를 구별하다, 가치 있는 것과 가치 없는 것을 가른다

clench, clinch

- clench ⓥ

① (주먹 등을) 꽉 쥐다

Protesters raise clenched fists in solidarity.

② (근육이) 수축하다

a military-grade chemical weapon that makes muscles clench uncontrollably

- clinch ⓥ 성사시키다, 이루어내다

This makes South Korean officials nervous that Trump may give away too much to clinch a deal.

Trump의 노벨평화상에 대한 욕심으로 북한에 너무 많은 양보를 하지 않을까 하는 내용

- clinch ⓝ (권투 시합 중에) 끌어안음, 클린칭

capital, capitol

- capital ⓝ

① 자본

Indeed, capital flight is a growing threat to the economy ; China's foreign-exchange reserves dropped $36.6 billion from January to April.

② 수도, 서울

parts of San Juan, the capital of this US territory

- capital ⓐ 사형의

Aside from capital punishment, the only way to legally kill someone in the US is in self-defense, but what that means can vary state by state.   정당방위

cf capitalist ⓝ 자본가, 자본주의자

Still, his ostentation and defense of China's strict "996" work culture — 9 a.m to 9 p.m, sixdays a week — also led some to decry him as a "capitalist bloodsucker."

- capitol ⓝ 국회 의사당(Capitol)

Like our pandemic response, the US Capitol riot is the latest cataclysm to be blamed on a failure of imagination.

crotch, crutch

- crotch ⓝ 사타구니

Researchers examining the mummy at the British Museum thought the remains were male after x-ray images from the 1960s revealed dense packing in its crotch area.

cf groin ⓝ 사타구니

I was 13 weeks pregnant with my first child when I felt a sharp, tearing pain in my groin.

- crutch ⓝ 목발

I went from exercising daily to needing a crutch to walk.

condolence, condone

- condolence ⓝ 애도, 조의   condotent ⓐ

I signed 2,026 letters of condolence to the families of those killed under my NATO mission.

- condone ⓥ 용납하다

I can't condone the use of violence under any circumstances.

credence, credential

• **credence** ⓝ 믿음, 신임

Begin with the reality that while NATO support increases pressure on Moscow, it also places a weapon in Putin's hand by lending credence to his claims that the West is at war with Russia.

우크라이나-러시아 전쟁

• **credential** ⓝ (대사에게 주는) 신임장, 자격 증명서

Kubuqi's transformation burnishes China's credentials as an environmental leader at a time when the US is retreating from its international commitments.

Kubuqi : 몽고 사막

credible, credulous

• **credible** ⓐ 믿을 수 있는

Even something as simple as checking a credible news source you don't usually follow, or catching up on headlines from another part of the country, could help your brain reset.

미디어 다이어트(media diet)

ⓓ **incredible** ⓐ 믿을 수 없는

It's very dangerous, They are making incredible progress.

북한

• **credulous** ⓐ 잘 믿는

Medieval people weren't more superstitious or credulous than modern ones.

credulity ⓝ
incredulous ⓐ

costume, custom

• **costume** ⓝ 의상, 옷

dancers in national costume

• **custom** ⓝ 관습

By the 1840s, when a wave of Irish and Scottish immigrants brought the custom to the US, it was basically secular pastime.

Halloween 축제

ⓓ **customs** ⓝ 세관

The first time we travelled back to the US from a visit to Colombia, I was questioned heavily at customs.

competition, competitiveness

compete ⓥ

• **competition** ⓝ 경쟁

Prices are lower when there is competition among the stores.

• **competitiveness** ⓝ 경쟁력

Her competitiveness was honed in fierce board games with her parents and two older sisters.

center, centralize

- center ⓥ 중심에 두다

Despite origins in pagan and Christian tradition, the modern American Halloween is often a purely secular celebration centered on candy and costumes.

- centralize ⓥ 중앙집권화하다

centralization ⓝ

The Pahlavi monarchy, which ruled Iran from 1925 to 1979, tried to centralize control by assimilating Kurds, sometimes by force, and reducing the power of tribal leaders.

crawl, creep

- crawl ⓥ 기다, 기어서 가다

A female employee says Jane, the supervisor, forced her to crawl along the factory floor as punishment for being late.

- creep ⓥ 살금살금 움직이다

Diagnoses for attention-deficit-hyperactivity-disorder(ADHD) in kids show no signs of slowing, creeping up from 7% in 2003 to 11% 2011.

'천천히 움직이다'는 뜻보다는 눈치채지 못하게 움직인다는 뉘앙스

creeping, creepy

- creeping ⓐ 서서히 진행하는

whether in the face of a creeping pandemic or a megastorm warning, supermarkets are quickly emptied of staple foods, batteries, and ever and always toilet paper, far more than the circumstances call for in most cases.

- creepy ⓐ 오싹하게 하는(an unpleasant feeling of fear or unease)

There's no fixed line between friendship and creepy.

성추행

cant, canter

- cant ⓥ 기울다, 기울어지다

To the astonishment of Merkel's liberal supporters, she canted to the right in December and called for a ban on full-face veils.

- canter ⓥ (말이) 보통 구보로 달리다

말의 빠르기 정도 : walk, trot, canter, gallop

The horses cantered across the grass.

crumble, crumple

- **crumble** ⓥ 바스러지다, 허물어지다

The vision contrasts starkly with US President Trump, who can't pass his $1 trillion plan to rebuild the nation's crumbling roads, bridges and electricity grid, despite the fact that the vast majority of Americans recognize the need.

ⓒ crumb ⓝ (빵이나 케이크의) 부스러기

- **crumple** ⓥ 구기다, 구겨지다

One bad slip on a too-polished floor could break not only a hip but a majority, crumple a President's agenda or upset the balance of power.

고령의 바이든

confess, profess

- **confess** ⓥ (잘못을) 자백하다, 고백하다

Booksellers who published salacious tomes about the party leadership vanished in 2015, reappearing on state-run television issuing confessions.

confession ⓝ

홍콩사태

- **profess** ⓥ 자신의 감정을 말하다 (a personal feeling or belief openly)

Both Rouhani and Trump professed an appetite for sitting down and talking over the ever more treacherous rift between their nations.

profession ⓝ

미국과 이란

commission, commitment

- **commission** ⓥ (그림 등의) 주문(의뢰)하다

Portraiture is based on this idea of people having the money to commission an artwork, or having done such great things that an artwork is commissioned in their honor.

commission ⓝ

portraiture ⓝ (그림이나 조각) 초상화 기법

ⓒ decommission ⓥ (핵무기 등을) 해체하다

Although Trump triumphantly tweeted, "There is no longer a Nuclear Threat from North Korean," in June 2018, he left office without a single warhead decommissioned.

ⓒ NCO : (군대) 하사관(non-commissioned officer)

- **commit** ⓥ

① (그릇된 일이나 범죄를) 저지르다

One does not commit suicide for fear of suicide.

② 의무를 지우다

That deal took nearly a decade to negotiate, and it committed the Islamic Republic in 2015 to halt its nuclear-weapons program.

③ (어떤 문제에 대하여) 입장을 분명히 하다, 약속하다

South Korean companies committed to invest nearly $40 billion in innovative technologies in the US — such as semiconductors, AI, electric-vehicle batteries, 5G and 6G — that are vital for Biden's ambitious plans to extricate sensitive supply chains from Beijing while building infrastructure to "win the future."

④ 회부하다, 위탁하다

On trade, Abe can be firm with Trump. In particular, he can resist pressure to commit to bilateral trade talks because he now has more confidence that he'll be around long enough to persuade a future US President to return to the Trans-Pacific Partnership, a multicountry deal that Trump has rejected and Abe still wants.

cf commitment ⓝ

① 약속(a promise to do something or to behave in a particular way)

Instead, American officials say, Mr. Biden's most vivid commitment to Mr. Yoon will focus on what arms control experts call "extended deterrence," renewing a vow that America's nuclear arsenal will be used, if necessary, to dissuade or respond to a North Korean nuclear attack on the South.

한미관계

② 헌신(the hard work and loyalty that someone gives to an organization, activity etc)

"With this year marking the 70th anniversary of the alliance between our two countries, it is an especially important time to reflect on the achievements of our partnership and to reaffirm our shared commitment to democracy, economic prosperity, and global peace."

construct, deconstruct

• construct ⓥ 건설하다

He was forced to work off his debt on a construction site.

construction ⓝ

cf construct ⓝ 생각(combining several pieces of information or knowledge)

Many of the stereotypical traits that our culture associates with boyhood — things like achievement, adventure and risk — are not inherently harmful cultural constructs that should be engineered out.

• deconstruct ⓥ 해체하다

deconstruction ⓝ

Through her deconstruction of long-held beliefs about artistry — and her ability to express both tortuous pain and unfettered joy in her art — she remains one of the most enduring artists of the 20th century.

화가 프리다 칼로(Frida Kahlo)

confidant, confident

- confidant ⓝ (사적인 것도 털어놓을 수 있는) 친구

On Jan. 18, Samsung's de facto chief, Lee Jae-yong, appeared in Courts after being accused of bribing impeached Park and one of her confidantes.

- confidence ⓝ 신뢰, 자신, 확신

ⓓ confidence-building ⓝ 신뢰구축

Several years of engagement and confidence-building would likely be needed just to bring Pyongyang's nuclear program to the table, as well as significant concessions by Seoul, such as suspending the annual joint naval exercises with the US.

confidante ⓝ (여성) 친구
one of her confidantes
: 최순실

confident ⓐ

clang, clank

- clang ⓥ 쨍그랑 소리를 내다(특히 금속끼리 부딪힐 때)

The horrors of the auction block, the brutality of the lynching tree, the backbreaking work of the cotton field and the slaughterhouses, the sounds of clanging chains on the chain gang, and the daily disregard fuel the rage.

- clank ⓥ 철커덕 소리를 내다

tanks clanking through the streets

미국의 인종차별, chain gang : (강제 노역을 하느라) 사슬로 함께 묶인 죄수들

clink, clunk

- clink ⓥ 쨍그랑 소리를 내다

The two delegations mixed easily, clinking porcelain cups of soju, the Korean spirit.

- clunk ⓝ '쾅'(나는 소리)

the clunk of the car door being shut

ⓓ clunky ⓐ 투박한(solid, heavy and old-fashioned)

Clunky and awkward as it sounds, the phrase *people with disabilities* became the standard.

clink ⓝ 감옥(prison)

장애인

coalesce, coarse

- coalesce ⓥ (더 큰 덩어리로) 합치다

Jack believes the divide between the sides is too wide to coalesce.

- coarse ⓐ (옷감이나 천을) 성기게 짠

The fabric varies in texture from coarse to fine.

coalescence ⓝ

comprise, compromise

- **comprise** ⓥ 구성하다

Somewhere in that zone, when women comprise 20% to 30% of an institution, things begin to change.

that zone : 미투가 일어난 지역

- **compromise** ⓝ 타협

The age of compromise with Iran is over for Saudi Arabia.

- **compromise** ⓥ 위태롭게 하다

If I go to see her, carrying germs — no matter how careful I try to be, how many times I wash my hands — I might be the one to compromise her fragile, hard-won stability.

her : 요양원의 엄마

- **uncompromising** ⓐ 타협하지 않는, 단호한

Jack is honest and brave, uncompromising, and hilarious.

compassion, compensate

- **compassion** ⓝ 연민, 동정심

There's something powerful about hope, compassion, caring for others, altruism.

- **compassionate** ⓐ 연민 어린

Befitting his reputation, Moon, then the opposition party leader, was compassionate and engaged.

- **impassion** ⓝ 열정

In an impassioned speech outside city hall on Oct. 23

impassioned ⓐ

- **compensate** ⓥ 보상하다

The government said it had created a foundation that would pool funds from South Korean businesses and use the money to compensate Koreans who were forced into labor by companies in Japan, which then ruled Korea as a colony, during World War II.

compensation ⓝ
일본과의 과거사 문제

commensurate, commiserate

- **commensurate** ⓐ 상응하는

Salary will be commensurate with age and experience.

commensuration ⓝ (수학) 약분

- **commiserate** ⓥ 위로를 표하다, 동정하다

You see people commiserating with victims of hurricanes across the Caribbean or Texas.

commiseration ⓝ

T U V W X Y Z A B C

D 외신으로 보는
대한민국
VOCABULARY

E F G H I J K L M N O P Q R S

don, doff

- don ⓥ (옷 등을) 입다

Lots of world leaders try the trick of celebrating a nation's first peoples by donning the local dress.

first people ⓝ 토착민

- doff ⓥ (옷 등을) 벗다

At the beginning of the pandemic, nurses or techs would be stationed outside the COVID rooms to watch us don and doff the P.P.E.

PPE : Personal Protective Equipment (개인 보호 장구)

distract, distraught

- distract ⓥ 주의를 산만하게 하다

I turn up the volume on the television so that the sounds of shelling outside don't distract me.

ⓓ distraction ⓝ

Some experts think mindfulness is the antidote to distraction, misbehaving — even poor math scores.

명상

- distraught ⓐ (흥분해서) 완전히 제정신이 아닌

Relatives are tonight comforting the distraught parents.

detract, retract

- detract ⓥ (중요성, 영향력 등을) 감소시키다

The brave men, living and dead, who struggled here have consecrated it, far above our poor power to add or detract.

detraction ⓝ

링컨의 Gettysburg 연설
it : 미국

- retract ⓥ (했던 말을) 철회하다, 취소하다(withdraw)

Jack retracted his statements and apologized to the country's LGBT community, many of whom now back him.

retraction ⓝ

LGBT : lesbian, gay, bisexual, transgender

de facto, de jure

- de facto ⓐ (법률과는 관계없이) 사실적으로는

This summer, Iran will turn into a de facto "threshold nuclear" state — one with enough highly enriched uranium for one nuclear device and the technology to make it a weapon.

- de jure ⓐ 법률에는, 법률에 따르면

Once Russia has completed the de jure annexation of its conquered lands, re-taking them will become a risky endeavor.

discus, discuss

- discus ⓝ (육상 경기) 원반

She and her husband, former US discus and shotput thrower Jack   shotput ⓝ (육상) 투포환

- discuss ⓥ 논의하다   discussion ⓝ

V, Jimin and J-Hope spontaneously burst into song as they discuss Jin's upcoming birthday.   BTS 기사

déjà vu, de rigueur

- déjà vu ⓝ 기시감

There is a sense of déjà vu in the US medical community right now, a year and a half after COVID-19 first slammed into the health care system and knocked it down like a feather.

- de rigueur ⓐ (사회 관습상) 필요한

Dark sunglasses are de rigueur these days.

de-mine, demise

- de-mine ⓥ 지뢰를 제거하다   mine ⓝ 지뢰

The Ukrainian Agricultural Ministry surprised many by saying that it expects 70% of spring crops to be planted, and up to 80% if "de-mining" is completed in northern areas previously occupied by Russia.

- demise ⓝ 종말, 죽음

Then, with the Soviet Union's demise, Cuba was cut adrift economically.

dandle, dangle

- dandle ⓥ (갓난아이를 두 손으로) 흔들다 (in affectionate play)

The day after the election, Jack, a fellow third-year, posted a picture on Buckingham's Facebook page of Donald Trump as an infant being dandled by Vladimir Putin.

- dangle ⓥ

① 대롱대롱 매달리다

It was satisfying to have tied off loose ends, but I still had one dangling string.   tie off ⓥ 매듭을 짓다

② ~을 (남의 눈앞에) 어른거리게 하여 주목을 끌려고 하다

And Kim's stated refocus on improving the lives of his 25 million compatriots provides room for the US to dangle economic carrots.   Kim : 김정은

dawdle, doodle, dwindle

- **dawdle** ⓥ 꾸물거리다

The opposition has been dawdling, largely to better prepare for presidential election slated for next fall.   *박근혜 탄핵 관련 야당 이야기*

- **doodle** ⓥ (특히 지루해하거나 딴생각을 하면서) 뭔가를 끼적거리다

Jack, who is illiterate, wasn't sure if they were numbers or letters or merely the twisted doodles of deranged men who saw their black captives as little more than livestock to be bought and sold.

- **dwindle** ⓥ 점점 줄어들다, 축소하다

The Queen was also the constitutional head of state for 14 other nations, which have been paying their own tributes — even as the debate reignites about the legacy of the British Empire, which was already dwindling at the time of her coronation in 1953.   *엘리자베스 여왕의 죽음*

drawl, drool

- **drawl** ⓥ (모음을 길게 빼며) 느릿느릿 말하다

Only a few hours later, on the television, Johnson withdrew, solemnly drawling, "I shall not seek, and I will not accept, the nomination of my party for another term as your President."   *Johnson : 미국의 36대 대통령*

- **drool** ⓥ 침을 흘리다 (to let saliva come out of your mouth)

detonate, donate

- **detonate** ⓥ 폭발하다   *detonation ⓝ*

But hope collapsed anew on Oct.14, when two truck bombs detonated downtown, killing over 300 people in the worst terrorist attack the country has seen.

- **donate** ⓥ 기부하다   *donation ⓝ*

Many rushed to answer his call and donate blood.

dairy, diary

- **dairy** ⓝ 낙농업(낙농 : 젖소나 염소를 기르는 농업)

a dairy farmer

- **diary** ⓝ 일기

The nearly 6,000 photographs form an intimate visual diary of a disease that is often invisible, cloaked in shame, fear and stigma.   *정신병 환자*

detain, deter

- **detain** ⓥ (경찰서 등에) 구금하다

Pyongyang returned remains of U.S. servicemen and released three detained Americans.

detention ⓝ

- **deter** ⓥ 단념시키다, 그만두게 하다

South Korea has kept Japan at arm's length, even though Washington urged its two key allies to work closely together to deter China and North Korea.

deterrence ⓝ

detergent, deterrent

- **detergent** ⓝ 세제

Bottles of laundry detergent — and beer — have subbed in as weights.

- **deterrent** ⓝ 제지하는 것, 못하게 하는 것

Abe will also try to persuade the US President during his visit to sell Japan cruise missiles as a deterrent against North Korea.

deter ⓥ
Abe : 일본 총리

detriment, detritus

- **detriment** ⓝ 손해, 해(damage or injury to something or someone)

He maintained this position to his political detrimen throughout the 1850s — he won no major office between a single term in the US House and his election to the presidency in 1860.

He : 링컨
this position : 처음부터 과격한 노예해방론자가 아니었던 입장

- **detritus** ⓝ 쓰레기, 폐기물

Patches of the street are covered in soapy water and last night's party detritus — cups, cigarettes, and ripped wristbands dot the sidewalks.

dip, drip

- **dip** ⓥ ① (액체에) 살짝 담그다 ② (아래로) 내려가다

As a result, the number of successful crossings has dipped slightly from last year.

🔸 **dip** ⓝ (일시적인) 하락, 감소

Since his dip in the polls, Mr Yoon has repeated his victory promise to "follow the people's will"

- **drip** ⓥ (물방울이) 뚝뚝 떨어지다

The faucet won't stop dripping.

dim, dime

- dim ⓥ 어둑해지다　　　　　　　　　　　　　　　　dim ⓐ 흐릿한

But then that hope starts to dim as you get older and you confront a lot of barriers.

- dime ⓝ 다임(미국·캐나다의 10센트짜리 동전)
- ⓓ dime store ⓝ 싸구려 가게

Local mothers raised their eyebrows when the girls rode their bikes alone to the dime store a mile away.

- ⓓ a dime a dozen ⓐ 매우 흔한(그래서 별로 가치가 없는)

Being a genius is different than merely being supersmart. Smart people are a dime a dozen, and many of them don't amount to much.

dire, dour

- dire ⓐ 매우 심각한

Dire Warning. Australia's historic drought and a world transformed by climate change.　　　　　　　　　　　　　　　　　　　　잡지 표지

- dour ⓐ 진지한, 심각한(stern, harsh)

She had a dour expression on her face.

- ⓓ dour는 사람의 태도나 매너(manner)를 표현함

destiny, destination

- destiny ⓝ 운명

She learned that people should be politically and socially engaged in shaping their own destiny.

- destination ⓝ 목적지, 도착지

The push to get rid of no-kids zones gained momentum last week when the health and welfare safety committee on Jeju Island — a popular tourist destination off the southern tip of the Korean Peninsula — deliberated an ordinance that would abolish no-kids zones island wide.

den, din

- den ⓝ (야생동물이 사는) 동굴(lair)

A lion was lying asleep at the mouth of his den.

- din ⓝ (오래 계속되는 크고 불쾌한) 소음

She said over the din.

defang, default

- **defang** ⓥ 엄니를 빼다(to make something ineffectual)

For one thing, the pretext for the Iraq invasion was the need to defang a monster who threatened regional peace with weapons of mass destruction.

fang ⓝ (뱀이나 개의) 송곳니

- **default** ⓝ 채무불이행

"North Korean traders don't have cash anymore," he says, "I have to limit the amount of goods I sell to them on credit as the risk of default is so high."

he : 북한과 무역하는 조선족

cf **default** ⓥ 채무불이행하다

Loans are more regularly defaulted than paid.

device, devise

- **device** ⓝ (특정 작업을 위한) 장치, 기구

On the surface, addressing the issue appears simple : countries need to expand access to air-conditioning and provide public cooling locations for people who can't afford their own devices. This is under way.

the issue : 지구 온난화

- **devise** ⓥ 창안하다, 고안하다

Pyongyang's isolationism means it has devised darker ways to bring in foreign capital.

dramatic, drastic

- **dramatic** ⓐ

① 드라마와 관련된

② (변화나 사건 등이) 극적인(sudden, striking)

Following his election to the presidency in 2017, Moon has made dramatic moves with regard to North Korea.

문재인 대통령

cf **drama** ⓝ

Yet to focus on a cultish hand in the presidential drama is to overlook some very real-world grievances.

박근혜 대통령

- **drastic** ⓐ 과감한(extreme, basic), 커다란(great)

If you think other countries will then come to your aid, you will be more likely to adopt this drastic measure sooner.

코로나

dynamic, dynamo

- **dynamic** ⓐ 정력적인, 역동적인, 활발한 (energy, new ideas, positive in attitude)

cf **dynamic** ⓝ 역학

With a few notable exceptions, most described a sibling dynamic that was wildly competitive at best and physically violent at worst. — 자식교육

cf **dynamics** ⓝ 동학, 역학관계

Of course, genetics plays a role for every family, but we focused on upbringing and sibling dynamics instead.

cf **static** ⓐ 고정적인, 정적인.

The static installation of the statue in that niche means that no one will ever see its back, which is also of interest.

- **dynamo** ⓝ ① 발전기 ② 정력이 넘치는 사람

After a series of particularly devastating famines in East and West Africa in the early 1980s — the ones that sparked the Live Aid concert and set Bono on his path from rock star to humanitarian dynamo — the US set up an early-warning system for when a region's food supply was going to fail. — Bono : 가수(singer)

deadline, deadlock

- **deadline** ⓝ 기한, 마감 시간

Advocates are using victims to come forward before the chance expires: a court will set a deadline, likely one to two years from now, for individuals to file claims. — come forward ⓥ 도움을 주기 위한 정보 제공 / 성추행 사건 / deadlock ⓥ

- **deadlock** ⓝ 교착상태

Both sides are deadlocked and neither gives the public impression that it genuinely wishes to reach a settlement.

domestic, domesticated

- **domestic** ⓐ 국내의

A stronger domestic league "is a must," he says. — domus(라틴어) : 집 / He : 한국 축구 비평가

- **domesticate** ⓥ 길들이다 (tame)

She jokes that dogs are easier to domesticate than men.

cf **domestication** ⓝ 국산화

I won't say it was an easy change, but my domestication was a much needed one.

delude, deluge

- delude ⓥ 착각하게 하다, 속이다

Just as Ukraine demonstrated in the war's early weeks that Russian victory plans were pure delusion, its latest gains again make clear that Putin's war refuses to go to plan.

delusion ⓝ
delusional ⓐ

- deluge ⓝ 폭주, 쇄도

Since the January 2019 revelation that 12,245 children had reported experiencing sexual abuse in the Boy Scouts from 1944 to 2016, the organization has faced a deluge of lawsuits.

drab, drag

- drab ⓐ 생기 없는

The consensus among these enthusiasts : plants are an accessible, interesting way to make an otherwise drab space more inviting, and there's a unique thrill to watch them grow.

집에서 'houseplant' 키우기

- drag

① 방해물

Any slowdown in the economy is going to be a drag on the president's re-election campaign.

② (담배 연기 등을) 빨아들이기

He took a long drag on his cigarette.

cf drag ⓥ (힘들여) 끌고가다

Others bled to death on prayer mats as people tried to drag them to safety.

cf the main drag ⓝ 중심가 (the biggest or longest street that goes through a town)

Our hotel is right on the main drag.

cf drag queen ⓝ 여장 남자 (a man who performs as an entertainer in usually female drag)

dinghy, dingy

- dinghy ⓝ 소형 보트

At a nearby beach, at the same hour, another group of smugglers inflated a white rubber dinghy.

- dingy ⓐ 우중충한, 거무칙칙한 (dark, dirty, and in bad condition)

Bleary-eyed gamblers hammer away at betting machines in dingy casinos.

demean, demeanor

- **demean** ⓥ 비하하다(degrade)

Today, there are millions of Iranians — especially women — who have suffered from the many corrupt, discriminatory, and demeaning policies of the regime.

- **demeanor** ⓝ 품행, 태도, 성격(deportment)

His sunny demeanor made him a hit with his North London teammates, whom he treated to a Korean barbecue buffet shortly after his arrival to the UK.

손흥민

dismal, dismay

- **dismal** ⓐ 음울한, 울적한(unhappy and hopeless)

The average US life expectancy has hit its worst decline in 100 years, and America's standing is dismal among peer nations.

cf **dismally** ⓐⓓ

Attempts to coax better behaviour with aid have failed dismally.

북한 설득 실패

- **dismay** ⓝ 실망, 경악(the worry, disappointment, or unhappiness)

The Western world reacted with dismay, and the US and Europe imposed steep sanctions on Russia.

deferment, deference

- **deferment** ⓝ 연기(postponement)

One of the 700,000 immigrants with DACA status plans her future in the Trump era.

defer ⓥ

cf DACA : Deferred Action for Childhood Arrivals(불법체류 청년 추방유예 제도)

- **deference** ⓝ 존중, 존경

deferential ⓐ

In deference to these local interests, the federal government had resisted engaging in draconian deportation measures.

dab, dub

- **dab** ⓥ (가볍게) 토닥거리다, 만지다(touch something lightly several times)

She dabbed her eyes with a handkerchief.

- **dub** ⓥ 별명을 붙이다

His regime was dubbed "Europe's last dictatorship" by President Bush in 2005.

dud, dude

- **dud** ⓐ 제대로 작동 못 하는

Several of the fireworks were duds.

- **dude** ⓝ 놈, 녀석 (a city dweller unfamiliar with life on the range)

A : What was your first corporate job?
B : I was in the oil industry for 10 years, worked for Mobil oil on the tanker, the marketing and refining side. I worked the night shift ; it was me and the dudes.

dearth, death

- **dearth** ⓝ 부족, 결핍

Trump's ad lib diplomacy may be partly in response to that dearth of good information. *폐쇄적인 북한에 대한 정보의 한계*

cf **ad lib** ⓐ 즉흥적인

- **death** ⓝ 죽음

One does not commit suicide for fear of death. *예문이 좋음*

depart, deport

- **depart** ⓥ   *departure* ⓝ

① 죽다

So little is clear that Castro's departure took on the quality of a test case for the incoming leader of the new world. *트럼프 대통령(the incoming leader of the new world)*

② 출발하다

Within hours of Pelosi's departure, China began several days of live-fire drills and missile tests that encircled Taiwan. *Pelosi(미국 하원 의장)의 대만 방문*

- **deport** ⓥ 추방하다   *deportation* ⓝ
  deportee ⓝ 추방당한 사람

1954 : The US begins mass deportation of Mexican immigrants.

cf **deportment** ⓝ 몸가짐, 행실 (demeanor)

The new students were instructed in proper dress and deportment.

depot, despot

- **depot** ⓝ 정거장, 정류장 (A railway or bus station)

There was no road through the desert to the nearest train depot.

- **despot** ⓝ 독재자, 폭군 (autocrat)   *despotic* ⓐ

Castro was hardly as bloodstained as other 20th century despots like Stalin.

dressage, dressing

- dressage ⓝ 마장마술

an equestrian school at which her daughter, a dressage champion, trains   최순실의 딸

- dressing ⓝ ① (요리용) 드레싱(소스) ② 상처 치료

㏇ dress ⓥ

① 옷차림하다

I spend most of my time in the house with young children, so I dress casually.

② 상처를 치료하다, 소독약을 바르다

He accordingly removed it and dressed the wound as well as he could.   it : a large thorn

dessert, desert

- desert ⓝ 사막

The journey of more than 2,500 miles would take him across the trackless desert plains of Niger and through the lawless tribal lands of southern Libya.   him : 아프리카 난민

㏇ desert ⓥ (어떤 장소를) 떠나다, 저버리다

What was once a city of 200,000 is now all but deserted.

- dessert ⓝ 디저트, 후식 (sweet food served after the main part of a meal)

At the Park Hyatt hotel in Paris, Narae Kim combines the Nashi pear she grew up eating in Dangjin, South Korea, and the Williams pear often used in eau de vie into an eye-catching dessert.   eau de vie ⓝ (음료) 오드비

despoil, spoil

동의어

- despoil ⓥ 훼손하다

despoliation ⓝ =
despoilment ⓝ

environmental despoliation

For decades, he was mocked for his jeremiads about climate change and the despoilment of the English country-side.   he : (영국 국왕) 찰스

- spoil ⓥ

spoilage ⓝ

① 훼손하다

For their part, many on the mainland regard dissenters in Hong Kong as unpatriotic and the city as spoiled and insufficient grateful for the opportunity to ride the economic juggernaut that the motherland has become.   juggernaut ⓝ 통제할 수 없는 거대한 힘(조직)

② (아이를) 응석받이로 키우다

Spare the rod and spoil the child.   영국 속담

defuse, diffuse

- **defuse** ⓥ 진정시키다, 뇌관을 제거하다

The Winter Olympics in PyongChang in February shone a spotlight on the role that international sports competitions can play in defusing tensions between nations.

- **diffuse** ⓐ 분산된

And much like the groundswell among Britons that led to their vote to leave the EU in June, many French blame a diffuse set of elites — politicians in Paris, bureaucrats in Brussels — for seemingly leaving them behind, with even the Socialist government of President Hollande seeking to undercut labor protections.

- **cf fuse** ⓥ 연결시키다, 결합시키다

There were glimpses of these qualities when Khan rose to become Prime Minister : running on an antigraft ticket, he fused a disparate band of students and workers, Islamic hard-liners, and the nation's powerful military to derail the Sharif political juggernaut.

fuse ⓝ ① 퓨즈 ② (폭약의) 도화선

them : 노동자

앞 문장에서 cricket에서 성공을 거둔 기사가 있음
Khan과 Sharif은 정적관계

delinquency, relinquish

- **delinquent** ⓝ 비행자

juvenile delinquency ⓝ 미성년 범죄

If we award delinquents and validate their violence as a way to advance in negotiations with the government, we will only be sowing more violence.

- **relinquish** ⓥ (마지못해 소유권 등을) 포기하다

Raising optimistic kids is hard, in part, because it demands that parents relinquish the cynical perspective that's the easiest response to an era of pessimism.

delinquency ⓝ 비행(非行)

반란세력과의 협상

relinquishment ⓝ

demagogue, demography

- **demagoguery** ⓝ 선동정치

National service can provide economic opportunity while preserving the planet, creating a more informed public that rejects misinformation and demagoguery, and strengthening the cohesion of the American citizenry.

- **demography** ⓝ 인구동태, 인구변동

Automation has already upended labor demographics in the developed world.

demagogue ⓝ 선동정치가

demo~ : 사람들의
demographics ⓝ 인구통계

dimple, pimple, wimple

- **dimple** ⓝ 보조개, (표면에 작게) 옴폭 들어간 곳

If left this way before painting, a small dimple will be visible.

- **pimple** ⓝ 여드름, 뾰루지

The anti-inflammatory effect applies to the elevation of your pimple too.

- **wimple** ⓝ 수녀(nun)가 쓰는 머리 가리개

At the end of her life, she lived in Buckingham Palace, walking the halls in her wimple. *(앞 문장에서 수녀가 되었다고 함)*

disinformation, misinformation

- **disinformation** ⓝ 허위 정보(deliberately false information)

Disinformation will further undermine public faith in democracy, particularly in the US.

- **misinformation** ⓝ 잘못된 정보(incorrect or misleading)

Yet misinformation is rife and official protection lax. *(몸에 좋다고 남획되는 야생동물)*

drawback, drawdown

- **drawback** ⓝ 결점, 문제점

Despite these challenges, the benefits of digital ads in political campaigns far outweigh the drawbacks.

- **drawdown** ⓝ 축소, 감축

Russia's Defense Ministry said the drawdown would be complete by May 1, part of a routine training exercise ; Ukrainian, European and US officials were waiting to exhale.

despair, desperate

- **despair** ⓝ 절망

The world loves to crown heroes from despair. Jane, 72, comes from one of her country's most storied families.

- **desperate** ⓐ 필사적인

That desperate sense has definitely been a driving force for me in pursuing my political career. *(이재명 이야기)*

- ⓓ **desperation** ⓝ 필사적임

The scammer had ravaged his savings, damaged his self-confidence, and set him on a path of desperation.

downmarket, upmarket

- downmarket ⓐ 저가의, 대중적인

The company wanted to break away from its traditional, downmarket image.

- upmarket ⓐ 부자들을 상대로 하는

a short drive from her country's modernist embassy in upmarket Knightbridge to an Icelandic ice cream shop on the west side of town

아이슬란드 여성 총리에 관한 내용

disparage, disparate

- disparage ⓥ 폄하하다, 깎아내리다

He has an edge and has to restrain himself from being nasty, sarcastic and disparaging about people.

- disparate ⓐ 이질적인, 서로 다른

It is a discussion that is long overdue and wrapped up in highly disparate viewpoints of policing in the country.

경찰의 과잉진압

dividend, divine

- dividend ⓝ 배당금

The show of unity at the Olympics sparked a backlash among South Korean conservatives, who clashed with riot police and burned North Korean flags. But sports diplomacy paid real dividends, prompting a series of meetings between North and South that led to a historic summit on April 27, where Kim became the first North Korean leader to step across the border line and visit the South.

평창 올림픽

- divine ⓐ 신의, 신성한

His uncle Kim Pyong Il returned to North Korea last year after decades overseas, but is not considered to be from the same divine bloodline as the late leader Kim Jong Il because he had a different mother.

김평일 : 김정일(김정은 아버지)과의 이복형제

downtime, uptime

- downtime ⓝ (컴퓨터가) 작동하지 않는 시간, 한가한 시간

It's a rare moment of downtime for the boys.

BTS 기사

- uptime ⓝ (컴퓨터나 기계의) 가동시간

Look for a solution that has an uptime above 99.5%.

downtick, uptick

- **downtick** ⓝ 약간의 감소 (a small decrease or slight downward trend)

Pennsylvania saw a slight increase in traffic-related fatalities last year despite a national downtick, according to the National Highway Traffic Safety Administration.

- **uptick** ⓝ 약간의 증가 (a small increase or slight upward trend)

For the professional middle class in particular, an uptick in innovation and a return to faster economic growth would solve many problems, and likely reignite income growth.

downsize, upsize

- **downsize** ⓥ 축소하다, 줄이다

As part of those efforts, he has built up his credentials among South Korean conservatives by reinstating the joint U.S.-South Korean military exercises which were canceled or downsized under Mr. Moon and Mr. Trump.

- **upsize** ⓥ 늘리다, 확대하다

They are considering upsizing their information systems.

he : 윤석열 대통령
those efforts : 한미관계를 바로잡는 노력

downside, upside

- **downside** ⓝ 단점

One of the biggest downsides is that these sandals lack arch support, which could lead to discomfort.

- **upside** ⓝ 장점

The upside : Your relationship will have plenty of alone time for each of you to do your own things.

downbeat, upbeat

- **downbeat** ⓐ 침울한

But the mood in the room was downbeat and his friends' questions were full of reproach.

- **upbeat** ⓐ 긍정적인, 낙관적인

As of Sept. 14, Ukraine has regained more territory than Russia has captured in months, and the mood of its political and military leaders has turned dramatically upbeat.

dialect dialectic

- dialect ⓝ 방언, 사투리

But behind those three letters are seven astounding young men who believe that music is stronger than the barriers of language. It's a universal dialect.   three letters : BTS

- dialectic ⓝ 변증법

This tension is often observed in the dialectic between a founder's organization and a successor's organization.

discreet, discrete

- discreet ⓐ 신중한(careful, not offend, upset)   indiscreet ⓐ

Men everywhere should be able to address this issue in a discreet way without shame.

cf. discretion ⓝ 재량

But the revised Wildlife Law allows the government the discretion whether to grant that protection or not.

- discrete ⓐ 별개의

Eliminating stress entirely is not an option. If there are discrete sources of stress in your life — a relationship, a job, a health problem — you can and should take action to try to mitigate them.

discriminate, incriminate

- discriminate ⓥ 차별하다   discrimination ⓝ 박근혜 대통령

Violence and discrimination against women have actually increased during Park's term, and women find the glass ceiling lower and tougher to crack.

- incriminate ⓥ 유죄로 보이다, 잘못한 것처럼 보이게 하다   incriminate는 crime, criminal에서 파생됨 홍콩 보안법

Many have started scouring their social-media accounts, deleting posts they fear could be incriminating once the law comes into force.

deduce, deduct

- deduce ⓥ 추론하다, 연역하다   deduction ⓝ 추론, 연역

From her son's age, I deduced that her husband must be at least 60.

- deduct ⓥ 공제하다   deduction ⓝ 공제

What he didn't mention was that the cost of transportation to the fields would be deducted from his wages, along with his water and his food.

diverse, divert

• **diverse** ⓐ 다양한   diversity ⓝ

It's one thing to say we have a diverse management team or diverse population. It's another thing to say they feel inclusion, that they feel connected, that they feel listened to.

cf **diversify** ⓥ 다양화하다

Mohammed tried to shift the kingdom from 20th century petrostate to divesified 21st century economy.

• **divert** ⓥ 다른 곳으로 돌리다

But internally, top aides to President Yoon Suk Yeol were worried that their American ally would divert them to Ukraine.

them : (미국에 판매한) artillery shells

cf **diversion** ⓝ 우회로

Bad weather forced the diversion of several flights.

cf **diversionary** ⓐ 주위를 딴 데로 돌리는

This is nothing more than a diversionary tactic to distract attention from the issues.

deliberate, deliberative, debilitate

• **deliberate** ⓐ 의도적인(intended or planned)

Open modeling can also identify oversights or deliberate omissions.

• **deliberate** ⓥ 깊이 생각하다(to think about something very carefully)

The jury deliberated about five hours over two days before reaching a verdict.

cf **deliberative** ⓐ 깊이 생각하는, 심의하는

the world's greatest deliberative body

• **debilitate** ⓥ 몸을 약화시키다   debility ⓝ

At 18, she was the victim of a horrific bus accident that left her in debilitating pain.

deprave, deprive

- **deprave** ⓥ (도덕적으로) 타락하다, 부패하게 하다   depravity ⓝ

But in the State of the Union, he returned to form: "We need only look at the depraved character of the North Korean regime to understand the nature of the nuclear threat it could pose to America and to our allies."

the State of the Union: 연두교서
he: Trump

- **deprive** ⓥ 빼앗다, 박탈하다   deprivation ⓝ

Public money diverted to private use deprived South Africa of the funding for infrastructure needed to create jobs and spark growth and for social safety net protections.

doubt, suspect

- **doubt** ⓥ ~을 하지 않을 것이라 생각한다

In a survey by the Seoul-based Chey Institute for Advanced Studies late last year, nearly 49 percent of respondents said they doubted that Washington would fight for South Korea at the risk of a North Korean nuclear attack on mainland United States.

㎝ **doubtful** ⓐ ~일 것 같지 않은

When he dies, it's doubtful the revolution will last long without a Castro at the helm.

helm ⓝ (배) 키
at the helm: 책임지고 있는

㎝ **no doubt**: 분명히, 틀림없는

Jack, Kono's district chief, says he has no doubt the government will deliver.

- **suspect** ⓥ

① ~의 혐의를 두다

Analysts had suspected that North Korea was developing a solid-fuel ICBM, and Mr. Kim had vowed to add it to its growing nuclear arsenal.

② 알아채다

After working as a teacher and playground supervisor in the 1960s, she began to suspect that early childhood education was more crucial than anyone then thought.

㎝ **suspect** ⓝ 용의자, 혐의자

㎝ **suspicion** ⓝ 의심, 혐의

In the track world, where the use of performance-enhancing drugs is prevalent, Jane's records will forever be viewed by some with suspicion.

육상선수

dibs, digs

• dibs ⓝ 권리, 우선권

One result of that is that the well-connected often get first dibs, Jack wrote.

• digs ⓝ 숙소

A few blocks away, a disused underpass serves as a temporary digs to about 30 Afghan men ; a few sat huddled over a small fire at 2 a.m.

ⓓ dig ⓝ 빈정거림, 비꼬기(a joke or remark, to annoy or criticize someone)

Apart from a dig at Trump, the clear implication that Kim is illegitimate is a problematic starting point for diplomacy.   Biden의 대북 정책

defunct, defund

• defunct ⓐ 지금은 사용하지 않는

The 5,000 gold, silver and bronze medals are cast from metal components harvested from defunct gadgets, including 6.21 million cell phones.   2021년 도쿄 올림픽

• defund ⓥ 재원을 고갈시키다

Amid all the long-needed national debate following the murder of George Floyd, one element is emerging as particularly polarizing : the discussion over "defunding the police."

digit, digital

• digit ⓝ (0에서 9까지의 아라비아) 숫자

His biggest political problem at the moment is economic : unemployment stands near 14%, inflation remains in double digits, and the pandemic grinds on.

• digital ⓐ

① 디지털의

And he speaks in a 21st century, digitally savvy language : mordant, ironic and thoroughly unimpressed by an authority. More important, he gets results.

PDA ⓝ 개인정보단말기(Personal Digital Assistants)

② 손가락의, 발가락의(relating to the fingers or toes)

ⓓ digitize ⓥ (데이터를) 디지털화하다

Singapore, Hong Kong and Taiwan have also digitized data to improve transparency.   코로나 사태

daze, doze

- daze ⓥ 멍하게 하다(unable to think or react properly)   daze ⓝ

Videos showed people being beaten on the floor and left bloodied and dazed.

- cf in a daze ⓐ 멍한 상태로(confused, unable to think or react properly)

London is in a daze. At the posh bars in SOHO, at the kebab shops on Edgware Road and in the halls of Westminster, conversations circle around the incomprehensible fact that the United Kingdom voted on June 23 to leave the European Union.   영국의 EU 탈퇴

- cf half-dazed ⓐ 반쯤 멍해서

They were sluggish and never climbed and may have seemed half-dazed in daylight.

- doze ⓥ 깜빡 졸다(lightly for a short time)

Each villa also comes with a retractable roof, so kids can doze off beneath the stars.

dissect, disseminate

- dissect ⓥ 해부하다   dissection ⓝ

Jane had long been a tabloid fixture, and her death prompted calls for newspapers to stop publishing invasive stories dissecting celebrities's private lives.

- cf tabloid fixture ⓝ 타블로이드(선정적인 기사를 주로 취급) 신문에 고정 등장
- disseminate ⓥ 퍼뜨리다(propagate)   dissemination ⓝ

When the Shah exiled Khomeini in 1963, Khamenei remained in Iran disseminating his mentor's unorthodox teachings about Islamic government.

dole, sole

- dole ⓥ 조금씩 나눠주다(out)

Although dissidents is still ruthlessly quashed, he has permitted a free market to take root, and the much maligned state distribution bureaus — once responsible for doling out all provisions — are shuttered.   북한

- sole ⓐ 단 하나의

The story was published with the sole purpose of selling newspapers.

degenerate, denigrate

- **degenerate** ⓥ 악화하다

History has shown how systematic victimization of so-called degenerates(communists, counterrevolutionaries, homosexuals and now criminal elements, like alleged drug pushers) can easily swing to anyone else being targeted for voicing unpopular opinions.

degenerate ⓝ 타락한 사람

- **denigrate** ⓥ 폄하하다, 깎아내리다(belittle)

Yet both the left and the right denigrate direct cash aid as a waste and an inducement to laziness and abuse.

사회적 약자에 대한 현금 지원

decisive, decided, divisive

- **decided** ⓐ 확실한

But Mr. Yoon now returns home to South Korea to a decidedly colder audience.

대통령의 미국방문

- **decisive** ⓐ 결정적인

But in Ukraine, as winter sets in and the war enters its second year, time will prove decisive.

- **divisive** ⓐ 분열을 일으키는

Such laws are deliberately anti-union and divisive.

diagonal, diagnose

- **diagonal** ⓝ 대각선, 사선

Grabbing noodles with my wife means sitting diagonally across a four-person table to comply with social distancing rules.

diagonal ⓐ

코로나 사태

- **diagnosis** ⓝ (병) 진단

Months after my dad's death in 2018, my mom was diagnosed with cancer.

diagnose ⓥ
prognosis ⓝ (병의) 진행, 예후

devolve, dissolve

- **devolve** ⓥ 어떤 다른 상태로 변하다

In the absence of a government, the country has devolved into a brutal marketplace of human lives.

- **dissolve** ⓥ

① 용해되다(to mix with a liquid and becomes part of it)

They learn how to savor the taste of a mint until it dissolves on their tongue.

명상

② (의회 등 공식기구) 해산하다(close down)
Gaddafi was toppled and the country dissolved into a vicious civil war.
cf dissolution ⓝ 해산
the dissolution of the Soviet Union
cf dissolve ⓝ (영상의) 디졸브(화면이 사라지면서 다음 장면이 겹쳐 나타나는 장면 전환법)
Transitions are not slow dissolves into tinkling piano but abrupt metallic rips, the sound of a sword pulled from a scabbard.

devoted, devotional, devout

• devoted ⓐ 헌신적인(a lot of love and attention)

Queen Elizabeth II was also devoted to upholding the "special relationship" between the UK and the US, engaging with every President from Truman to Biden over a period of more than 70 years.

• devotional ⓐ 종교적인

If such a thing as a devotional folkloric genre painting could exist, this might be its textbook example.

• devout ⓐ 열렬한, 진심으로부터의(earnest)

Still a college sophomore, Lim has inspired a devout following in the United States, Europe and Asia.   피아니스트 임윤찬

delete, delve

• delete ⓥ 삭제하다   deletion ⓝ

Christian's sister later uploaded the clip to Twitter, where it has been viewed more than 40 million times prior to being deleted.

cf delible ⓐ 지울 수 있는   indelible ⓐ

The precious stones paid for the rebel's weapons, inspiring the 2006 DiCaprio blockbuster *Blood Diamond*, which indelibly linked sparkling engagement rings with their high human cost for a generation of consumers.

• delve ⓥ (무엇을 찾으려고) 뒤지다, 탐구하다

research that delves deeply into this issue

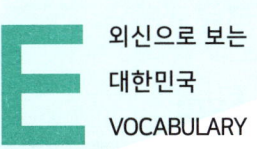

E

외신으로 보는
대한민국
VOCABULARY

elegy, eulogy

- elegy ⓝ 비가, 애가(a sad poem or song, about someone who has died)

The history at hand is too recent for elegy.

- eulogy ⓝ 고인에 대한 추도연설

She delivered the eulogy at his funeral.

enclave, exclave

- enclave ⓝ (한 국가나 도시 내의) 소수 민족 거주지

At the time a capitalist enclave in a communist empire, the regional finance hub once served as the conduit for almost all commerce between East and West. — 홍콩

- exclave ⓝ 고립 영토, 비지(飛地)(본국에서 떨어져서 다른 나라의 영토에 둘러싸인)

Poland and Lithuania border the Russian exclave of Kaliningrad, the most militarized territory in all of Europe.

endonym, exonym

- endonym ⓝ 토착지명(그 지역에서 그 지역 사람들에 의해 사용되는 명칭)

Nippon, the endonym for Japan, means 'land of the rising sun.'

- exonym ⓝ 외국어 지명(특정한 지역에 대해 각국에서 부르는 다른 이름)

Manchuria is an exonym for several large overlapping regions in north-east Asia. — Manchuria ⓝ (중국) 만주

excoriate excruciating

- excoriate ⓥ 혹평하다, 맹비난하다 — excoriation ⓝ

Millions of students are regularly skipping school to protest, bearing slogans that excoriate adult politicians.

- excruciating ⓐ 몹시 고통스러운 — crucify가 어원

The deadly toxin in the handkerchief was VX, a military-grade chemical weapon that makes muscles clench uncontrollably and causes death through excruciating asphyxiation in just 15 to minutes. — 김정남 암살

egalitarian, egregious

- egalitarian ⓝ 평등주의자

It is true that Lincoln did not seek immediate abolition ; neither was he a radical racial egalitarian.

- **egregious** ⓐ (부정적 의미로서) 엄청난, 터무니없는

Among the more egregious incidents was the June 22 killing of Jack, a 16-year-old Muslim.

ennoble, noble

- **ennoble** ⓥ 품위있게 하다, 고상하게 하다

You will find yourself ennobled by Johnson's example and may wield this book like a sunlit talisman against your post-holiday depression.

- **noble** ⓐ 고결한   nobility ⓝ

History teaches us that if we sit idly by, even the most noble laws can be distorted by bigotry — and bigoted laws, left unchecked, can lead to immense suffering.

excommunicate, incommunicado

- **excommunicate** ⓥ (종교) 파문하다   excommunication ⓝ

As part of the deal, Pope Francis has recognized the legitimacy of seven previously excommunicated, Beijing-appointed bishops.

- **incommunicado** ⓐ 말을 걸 수 없는

He is reportedly being held incommunicado at a military prison.

endemic, epidemic, pandemic

- **endemic** ⓐ 고유의, 고질적인(주기적으로 발생하거나 풍토병으로 굳어진 감염병)

Drought is endemic on the world's driest inhabited continent.

ⓓ 대규모 감염을 일으키지 않고 사회의 각 기능이 작동하는데 차질을 일으키지 않을 정도로 파괴력이 낮아진 상태

- **epidemic** ⓝ 유행병 (a large number of cases of a disease that happen at the same time)

During the start of the HIV epidemic, there was debate about whether health care professionals could refuse to care for people who were suspected of having HIV.

ⓓ **epidemiology** ⓝ 전염병 역학

a professor of pediatrics and epidemiology at the University of California

- **pandemic** ⓝ 세계적인 유행병   pan~: 전체를 아우르는

South Korea's response to the COVID-19 pandemic has become a global example.

en masse, en route

- en masse ⓐⓓⓥ 집단으로

Yet I do not worry that young Japanese will suddenly militarize en masse.

- en route ⓐⓓⓥ 도중에

He was strapped onto a stretcher and sent to a hospital in an ambulance — but died en route.

enlist, enroll

- enlist ⓥ 입대하다, 징집하다

In 1942 and 1943, the US Armed Forces finally allowed women to enlist.

- enroll ⓥ 이름을 올리다, 입학하다

In 2009, 70% of recent high school graduates enrolled in collage.

enlistment ⓝ
enlistee ⓝ 지원병
enlister ⓝ 징병관, 모집관
enrollment ⓝ

engine, engineer

- engine ⓝ 기관차

Economic integration will not only benefit the North, but also will give the South a new growth engine, which will revive the South Korean economy.

- engineer ⓥ 수작 부리다

Jack, an unremarkable 60-year-old cleric, was anointed Iran's President in an engineerd June 2021 election.

engineering ⓝ 공학

enfold, unfold

- enfold ⓥ 안다, 감싸다 (to cover or surround someone or something completely)

He reached out to enfold her in his arms.

- unfold ⓥ 전개되다

People in poverty in America in 2018 are not a world apart — they are all around us, and their lives unfold next to, but are cut out from, any prosperity that this nation experiences.

exhale, inhale

- exhale ⓥ 숨을 내뱉다

The pores also allow the pottery to exhale some of the carbon dioxide produced by fermentation, creating an ideal environment for lactic acid bacteria to flourish.

exhalation ⓝ
김치와 장독

- inhale ⓥ 숨을 들이마시다

But many experts in Asia say that wearing a mask can keep a person from inhaling the respiratory droplets of someone else — the main way COVID 19 spreads.

explicit, implicit

- explicit ⓐ 분명한

On the South China Sea, the Trump Administration announced that it had officially aligned with a 2016 ruling from the Hague that explicitly denies Chinese claims there.

explicitly ⓐᵈᵛ

- implicit ⓐ (직접적으로 표현되지 않지만) 내포된

This is happening with the implicit acceptance of the US., which under President Trump has rejected its role as a champion of universal values like human rights.

implicitly ⓐᵈᵛ
This : 국제적인 인권유린

exuberant, exude

- exuberant ⓐ 활기 넘치는, 생동감 있는

When Time sat down with Koike in late 2019, Tokyo's governor was exuberant in anticipation of the approaching Olympic and Paralympic Games.

2021 도쿄 올림픽 기사
Koike : 도쿄 도지사

- exude ⓥ 물씬 풍기다, 흘리다

The leather cover has intricate designs that exude old world charm.

exit, exodus

- exit ⓝ 출구, 떠남

Some in the city are eyeing the exits.

홍콩사태

ⓓ exit poll : (선거) 출구조사

ⓓ exit clause : (계약대로 이행하지 않아도 되는) 조항

His agent cuts off any more questions about the subject. An exit clause for Son exists in the form of the Asian Games, which will be held in Indonesia in August.

the subject : 손흥민 군대 이야기

- exodus ⓝ (많은 사람이 동시에 하는) 대량 탈출

It is very little known that the great majority of Muslims in the state have not joined the exodus.

emergence, emergency

- **emergence** ⓝ 출현

But he is now the leading voice of an emerging political force.

emerge ⓥ

- **emergency** ⓝ 비상

On paper, the emergency measures expired in June, but the government's grip on power has not loosened.

emergency exit ⓝ 비상구

endanger, engender

- **endanger** ⓥ 위험에 빠지게 하다

If Trump misplays his hand, it could endanger millions of lives.

endangerment ⓝ
북한의 핵무기

- **engender** ⓥ (어떤 상황을) 낳다

Over time, this conversation can engender a change.

engenderment ⓝ

evoke, invoke, revoke

- **evoke** ⓥ 떠올리다, 환기시키다

Asked how she'd like to be remembered, she evoked Abraham Lincoln: "I have planted a rose where only thistles grew."

evocation ⓝ

thistle ⓝ (식물) 엉겅퀴

- **invoke** ⓥ

invocation ⓝ

① (법·규칙 등을) 들먹이다(적용하다)

He is now set to invoke a never-before-used constitutional provision, Article 155, to reinstate home rule over the region.

스페인에서 분리 독립(the region)하려는 지역

ⓓ never-before-used : 과거에는 사용한 적이 없는

② 환기시키다(evoke)

Flag waving is still taboo in mainstream German politics, as are most gestures that invoke the still-sensitive specter of nationalism.

- **revoke** ⓥ 취소하다, 무효화하다

revocation ⓝ

The university revoked his teaching qualifications, issuing a public statement saying it found Jack had sexually harassed students.

erratic, erroneous

- **erratic** ⓐ 불규칙한, 변덕스러운(not regular)

North Korea has both an erratic leader and nuclear weapons.

- **erroneous** ⓐ 잘못된(incorrect)

His economic predictions are based on some erroneous assumptions.

high-end, low-end

• **high-end** ⓐ 고가의, 고급의

Zelensky and his government would like to see more support, especially high-end weapons.

• **low-end** ⓐ 저가의(inexpensive), 저질의

In general, low-end buyers are the most willing to embrace products without pedigrees.

ⓓ pedigree ⓝ (동물) 족보

eradicate, erase

• **eradicate** ⓥ 근절하다, 뿌리 뽑다   eradication ⓝ

Some cities, like Berkley, Calif., have eradicated single-family zoning.

• **erase** ⓥ 지우다   eraser ⓝ 지우개

By saying we put our own interests first, with no regard to others, we erase what a nation holds dearest... its moral values.

embody, embolden

• **embody** ⓥ 실현하다, 구현하다

The spirit of Ukraine was embodied by countless individuals inside and outside the country.

ⓓ embodiment ⓝ 구현

The artist Suh Seung-Won may be the embodiment of the tumultuous history of South Korea and the youthfulness that seems to dominate this country and its ever-present K-pop stars.

• **embolden** ⓥ 대담하게 하다

The more impoverished the country from whence you come, the more emboldened one's work ethic is.   whence : from where

expert, expertise

• **expert** ⓝ 전문가

Medical experts believe he is obese.   he : 김정은

• **expertise** ⓝ 전문 지식, 전문 기술

As a former vice president of the influential Agricultural Bank of China, she is also emblematic of the CCP's new efforts to promote cadres with financial expertise.

eject, evict

- **eject** ⓥ

① 추방하다

If Ukrainian forces do manage to rout Russian forces and eject them from Ukraine, Putin might lose credibility inside the Kremlin.

② (조종사가) 탈출하다

The pilots in the crash managed to eject and survived.

- **evict** ⓥ 쫓아내다

On Nov.4, police dismantled a tent camp that sprung up along the freeway in northern Paris, evicting about 3,000 people.

ejection ⓝ

eviction ⓝ

equivalent, equivocal

- **equivalent** ⓐ 동등한 것

It's the equivalent of having Bill Gates, Warren Buffet and Colin Powell arrested.

- **equivocal** ⓐ 애매한(ambiguous)

His answer was equivocal.

equivalence ⓝ

사우디 왕자의 체포를 두고 한 말

evacuate, evaporate

- **evacuate** ⓥ (위험한 지역에서) 대피시키다

When 21 Jewish community centers across the US received bomb threats on Feb. 27, the JCC staff knew what to do : notify the authorities and confirm the evacuation routes.

- **evaporate** ⓥ (액체가) 증발하다, 증발시키다

Higher temperatures cause water to evaporate faster, making plants less water efficient.

evacuation ⓝ
evacuee ⓝ 피난민

JCC : Jewish Community Center

evaporation ⓝ

ensue, ensure

- **ensue** ⓥ 뒤따르다(follow)

At least 300 people died and 40,000 fled Juba in the ensuing four days, casting fresh doubt on the viability of the world's youngest nation.

- **ensure** ⓥ 반드시 ~하게 하다, 보장하다

Unfortunately, there are no easy and painless ways of ensuring that the economy enjoys a soft landing.

ⓒf **insure** ⓥ 'ensure'의 미국 영어

Juba : 남수단 공화국

ensurance : 사용하지 않음

insurance ⓝ 보험

erode, erupt

- **erode** ⓥ 부식시키다, 약화시키다   erosion ⓝ

The national-security law is just the latest "milestone" in a long erosion of freedoms.

- **erupt** ⓥ 분출하다, 터뜨리다   eruption ⓝ

They erupted in jubilation.

express, expressive

- **express** ⓐ 급행의, 신속한   expressly ⓐⅾv

But those of us who stayed stuck around expressly to preserve the New York we knew. This city is haughty and knows its self-worth.   pandemic의 뉴욕

- **express** ⓥ 표출하다, 나타내다

Nearly 40 years after Chin's murder, I am dismayed that so many have expressed surprise, even shock, at the existence of anti-Asian racism.   Chin : 중국계 미국인

- Ⓓⓕ **expressive** ⓐ 나타내는, 표정이 있는

Vehicle interiors are becoming more expressive, too.

exquisite, inquisitive

- **exquisite** ⓐ 매우 아름다운 (extremely beautiful and very delicately made)

Jack says the experience of writing a biography is an "exquisite pain" — a phrase his mother used to describe childbirth.   Jack : 전기 작가

- **inquisitive** ⓐ 호기심이 많은

What I found very different about him than other Chinese leaders I met with was that he's much more outgoing and inquisitive.   him : 시진핑

explode, implode

- **explode** ⓥ   explosion ⓝ
    explosive ⓝ 폭약, 폭발물

① 폭발하다

But once the opening ceremony's fireworks explode across the night's sky, sporting prowess take over and all people can recall are grinning medalists and cheering crowds.   올림픽 개막식

② (화의 강도가 아주 셀 때) 화를 내다, (갑자기 강한 감정을) 터뜨리다

He exploded.

- **implode** ⓥ (안으로) 폭발하다   implosion ⓝ

The windows on both sides of the room had imploded.

entranced, entreat

- entranced ⓐ 넋을 잃은

I was entranced by the sweetness of her voice.

- entreaty ⓝ 간청

Even as bombs fell on Buckingham Palace, the royal couple refused entreaties to abandon London and evacuate Princess Elizabeth and Princess Margret to Canada.

entreat ⓥ
2차 대전 당시의 영국

electric, electronic

- electricity ⓝ 전기

Einstein proved, by flying a kite, that lightning is electricity, and he invented a rod to tame it.

electric ⓐ

ⓓ electrify ⓥ 전기를 통하게 하다, 흥분시키다

A 19-Year-Old Pianist Electrifies Audiences.

피아니스트 임윤찬

- electronic ⓐ 전자의

Tibetan society is divided into a "grid system" of five to 10 households, each with a nominated representative responsible for political activities forced to keep track of individuals via an integrated electronic system.

ⓓ electromagnetic ⓐ 전자기의

Experts say North Korea could potentially strike the American mainland with a nuclear electromagnetic pulse that would wreak havoc on power grids, utilities, infrastructure and any industry dependent on them.

electromagnetism ⓝ 전자기

elevate, escalate

- elevate ⓥ 승진시키다, 고양시키다(to a more important level or rank)

She is a rare female rising star of the ruling Chinese Communist Party(CCP), whose elevation to No. 2 in Fujian — where President Xi Jipping cut his leadership teeth and retains a power base — signals the possibility of further growth.

elevation ⓝ

- escalate ⓥ 악화하다(to become much worse)

With politics deadlocked, many fear violence will continue to escalate.

escalation ⓝ

ⓓ escalatory ⓐ (특히 전쟁이) 확대되는

If they do such a test, from our perspective, that would clearly constitute a grave escalatory action.

북한의 핵실험

ethic, ethnic, ethos

- **ethic** ⓝ 윤리, 도덕   ethical ⓐ

  ⓓ unethical ⓐ 비도덕적인

  She began meditating and doing yoga, and soon switched to the a vegan diet after deciding it was unethical to eat meat.

- **ethnic** ⓐ 민족의   ethnicity ⓝ

  Each of these families is different in thousands of ways, from their ethnicities to their incomes to their sleepover policies.

  아이들을 훌륭하게 키운 아홉 가정 이야기

- **ethos** ⓝ (특정 집단의) 기풍, 정신

  Jack, who wrote about his post-Olympic depression in his book *Bravey*, released earlier this year, sees Jane as someone who can help us move away from the win-at-all-costs ethos in sports.

  운동선수들의 스트레스

extinct, extinguish

- **extinct** ⓐ 멸종된, 사라진   extinction ⓝ

  You're probably aware of overfishing and the harmful practices of fisheries driving a third of the planet's fish stocks toward extinction.

  ⓓ extinct volcano(사화산), active volcano(활화산), dormant volcano(휴화산)

- **extinguish** ⓥ 불을 끄다(put out)

  Brave domestic reporters are the lone reason its light still flickers. The arrests of Jack and Jane — and of nearly 100 other journalists since the protests started — show how far the regime will go to extinguish it.

  언론탄압

establishment, antiestablishment

- **establishment** ⓝ 기관, 시설   establish ⓥ

  Surveillance images released by the department show the men sitting in an unknown establishment.

  ⓓ the Establishment ⓝ (사회의) 기득권층, 지배층

  Voters in the US and Europe, meanwhile, have been in revolt against the Establishment.

- **antiestablishment** ⓐ 반체제의

  But unlike their peers, BTS had an antiestablishment streak, both in the activism and in the way they contributed to their songwriting and production — which was then rare in K — pop, although that's started to change.

elide, elude

- **elide** ⓥ (한 단어에서 일부의 발음을) 생략하다   elision ⓝ

The desire to belong to the people we love is powerful. It can be tempting to elide differences and emphasize similarities : I am Black like my father, Latinx like my husband.

cf Latinx ⓝ 라틴계 사람

- **elude** ⓥ 교묘히 빠져나가다(trick, cunning way, skillful)   elusive ⓐ / elusion ⓝ

Justice is elusive when policing goes wrong.

earthy, earthen, earthly

- **earthy** ⓐ 흙의   earth ⓝ

It was a chilly Friday afternoon in early February, and a group of young activists huddled around a table inside a modern, earthy cafe.

cf **earthen** ⓐ 흙으로 만든

The best kimchi is made in earthenware pots.

- **earthly** ⓐ 세속적인, 지상의(terrestrial)

But Jack was murdered. I will never see or have the chance to meet with him again in the earthly realm.

emigrate, immigrate

- **emigrate** ⓥ 이민을 가다(to leave your own country in order to live in another country)   emigration ⓝ

In a survey of 21,000 South Koreans last year, 88% of respondents said they were considering emigrating to another country because of a sluggish economy, distrust in the government and a lack of social mobility.

- **immigrate** ⓥ 이민을 오다(to live permanently in a foreign country)   immigration ⓝ

Incheon International Airport is set to become one of the world's smartest and greenest, equipped with state-of-the-art self-driving shuttle buses, automated immigration processing, and disinfecting robots.

envisage, envision

뉘앙스는 같음

- **envisage** ⓥ (미래의 일을) 예상하다

"I don't envisage a return to the past. Even if the people's demands are not met, the reality will have shifted permanently."

- **envision** ⓥ 마음속에 그리다(to picture to oneself)

I don't envision a nuclear conflict in the foreseeable future.

expand, expanse

- expand ⓥ 확장하다

In an interview with The New York Times on Wednesday, the South Korean president said it had become necessary — even inevitable — for Seoul to expand its security cooperation with Washington and Tokyo as North Korea intensified its nuclear threat.

- expanse ⓝ 넓게 트인 지역(a very large area of water, sky, land etc)

The 500-ft.-long expanse gives visitors plenty of space to take in the scenic views.

expansion ⓝ
expansive ⓐ
the South Korean president : 윤석열 대통령

expend, expense

- expend ⓥ (많은 돈·시간·에너지를) 들이다, 사용하다

More than 3,000 US and allied dead, tens of thousands with significant wounds and a few trillion dollars expended — to say nothing of hundreds of thousands of Afghans killed and wounded as well.

ⓓ to say nothing of ~ : ~은 말할 것도 없고

- expense ⓝ 비용

In a sense, the growth for New Zealand has been at the expense of its most marginalized children for the last 30 years.

ⓓ at the expense of ~ : ~을 희생하면서

expenditure ⓝ

expendable, expensive

- expendable ⓐ 소모용의

It's a sad moment when a man loses his job and discovers that he is expendable.

- expensive ⓐ 비싼(exorbitant)

Demonstrators there unfurled a banner reading, "Rather on strike than in a suit," a reference to an earlier encounter with Macron, when a protester mocked his expensive suits.

inexpensive ⓐ

exploit, explore

- **exploit** ⓥ (부당하게) 이용하다, 착취하다

Activists accuse many employers worldwide, including tea plantations in India, of exploiting their workers.

ⓓ **exploit** ⓝ 위업, 공적(a bold or daring feat)

About midnight the gang returned, with various articles of plunder, and talked over their exploits.

ⓓ **exploitation** ⓝ   exploitative ⓐ 착취하는

① 착취

South Korea's history of sexual exploitation is not always openly discussed.   기지촌 여성

② 개발(development)

the controlled exploitation of resources

- **explore** ⓥ 탐사하다, 탐험하다   exploration ⓝ

He was one of the first French designers to tap then unexplored markets in Asia and Russia, where he found immense popularity.

expatriate, expatiate, repatriate

- **expatriate** ⓝ (고국이 아닌) 국외 거주자   expatriate ⓐ

Qatar is renewing efforts to make real estate more attractive to expatriate residents, foreign investors and real estate funds.

- **expatiate**(on) ⓥ 상세하게 설명하다(on)   expatiation ⓝ

The naturalist is known for her willingness to expatiate on any number of issues relating to wildlife and the environment.

- **repatriate** ⓥ 본국으로 송환하다   repatriation ⓝ

Meanwhile, donor governments and humanitarian agencies should withhold both political and financial support to the hastily planned repatriation process for refugees in Bangladesh — unless Myanmar can ensure that returns are safe, voluntary, dignified and sustainable.   Myanmar 정부의 소수민족 탄압으로 방글라데시로 피난감

extend, extent

- **extent** ⓝ (크기·중요성·심각성 등의) 정도, 규모

I bought them clothes and installed a thingummy to extent the reach of their wi-fi.   them : 부모님

ⓓ **thingummy** ⓝ (이름을 정확히 모를 때) 거시기(hard to classify, whose name is unknown or forgotten)

- **extend** ⓥ 확대하다, 연장하다   extension ⓝ

Xi joins Mao on Mount Olympus at a time when China boasts the world's second biggest economy and is extending its global influence.

- **extensive** ⓐ 광범위한

We need to replace the ruined stones. We need to replace the joints with traditional materials. This is going to be extensive   노틀담 대성당 화재

existent, existential

- **exist** ⓥ 있다, 존재하다   existence ⓝ / 미국의 인종 차별

It's central to understanding that black oppression still exists today.

- **coexist** ⓥ 공존하다

The US cannot coexist with a nuclear-capable North Korea.

- **nonexistent** ⓐ 존재하지 않는

We still live in townships, we still have pit latrines, the electricity is nonexistent, and most of my friends are unemployed.

- **existential** ⓐ 실존주의적인 (relating to the existence of humans or to existentialism)

Following a historic summit with Kim in Singapore in 2018, the first between the leaders of these existential foes, Trump declared: "We fell in love."   김정은

entitle, entity

- **entitle** ⓥ 자격을 주다, 권리를 주다   entitlement ⓝ

People feel almost entitled to be rude to people who are not in a position of power.

- **entity** ⓝ 독립체 (something that exists as a single and complete unit)

She became the go-to person for sympathetic international entities.   남아프리카 민주투사 만델라 (Mandela)가 감옥 간 뒤 그의 부인 이야기

- **go-to** ⓝ (도움을) 찾는 사람

emphasis, empathy

- **emphatic** ⓐ ~을 강조하는   emphasis ⓝ

The governor issued an emphatic denial of all charges.

- **empathy** ⓝ 감정이입, 공감   empathic(empathetic) ⓐ / I : 코로나 치료 의사

I have plenty of empathy for people who did get vaccinated but got sick in spite of it.

exalt, extol

- **exalt** ⓥ 승격시키다(into a high rank or position)   exaltation ⓝ

Jack has always been wary of programs that exalt donors as saviors.

- **extol** ⓥ 극찬하다(to praise something very much)   extolment ⓝ

Hong Kong — a city that the economist Jack extolled as a temple of "capitalism in action,"

exhort, extort

- **exhort** ⓥ 촉구하다, 열심히 권하다   exhortation ⓝ

For the past year, and especially since the devastating Atlanta-area murders on March 16, many of my Asian American friends have been sharing deeply personal, painful stories of talking with their parents and elders, pleading with them to take care, being exhorted to be careful in turn.

동양계에 대한 묻지마 폭행

- **extort** ⓥ 강요하다, 갈취하다   extortion ⓝ

In Honduras, extortion is often backed up by murder.

extricate, intricate

- **extricate** ⓥ 구출하다, 해방시키다

Every day I typed alone in the quiet, my sole job being to extricate the story.

ⓓ **inextricable** ⓐ 불가분한, 떼려고 뗄 수 없는

His words and music are inextricable.

- **intricate** ⓐ 복잡한   intricacy ⓝ

With positive messages of self-confidence, intricacies of philosophy hidden in their sparkly songs, true synergy and brotherhood in every step of their elaborate choreography, and countless charitable and anthropological endeavors,

BTS

equestrian, pedestrian

- **equestrian** ⓝ 승마자(A rider or performer on horseback)

an equestrian school

- **pedestrian** ⓝ 보행자(walking rather than travelling in a vehicle)   ped : 발을 뜻하는 접두사

The downtown pedestrian mall is filled with these restaurants, as well as coffee shops, bars, outdoor cafes, music halls, bookstores, galleries.

enjoin, enjoy

• enjoin

① ~을 하도록 하다

The organization has been enjoined to end all restrictions.

② 금지하다

He was enjoined by his conscience from telling a lie.

• enjoy ⓥ 즐기다

Since becoming Prime Minister in 2017, Arden has enjoyed stardom outside of New Zealand. But her reception back home had been more ambivalent.

eclipse, elapse

• eclipse ⓥ 빛을 잃게 만들다(oveshadow)

The pressure may be even greater at this World Cup as South Korean soccer's big outing on the world stage is at risk of being eclipsed by theater of a political kind.

트럼프, 김정은 정상회담과 손흥민

• elapse ⓥ (시간이) 흐르다(go by)

If an intercontinental ballistic missile (ICBM) were fired at a US target, roughly 25 minutes would elapse between detection and impact.

embargo, embark

• embargo ⓝ 금수 조치, 통상금지령

At the time of the 1973-74 Arab oil embargo, the energy crisis was seen as a symptom of the West decline, akin to the end of the gold standard, Watergate, the failure of the Vietnam War and more.

gold standard : 금본위제

• embark ⓥ (배에) 승선하다

ⓓ embark on : ~에 착수하다

Since taking China's top job in 2013, he has launched an unprecedented anticorruption drive within the Communist Party and riled Asian neighbors by embarking on military expansions.

disembark ⓥ 하선하다
embarkation ⓝ
embarkment ⓝ
he : 시진핑

F

외신으로 보는
대한민국
VOCABULARY

formative, formidable

- **formative** ⓐ (성격 등의) 형성에 중요한

The pain of those formative years opened the young Lee's eyes to social injustice that still plagues Korean society. 　　이재명

- **formidable** ⓐ 어마어마한(very powerful or strong)

The obstacles that Ukrainian farmers face at the present time are certainly formidable.

flax, flex

- **flaxen** ⓐ ① 엷은 황갈색의 ② (목소리) 다듬어지지 않은(raw) 　　flax ⓝ 아마, 아마 섬유

Her silky, flaxen voice-in pillowy ballads like "Have You Never Been Mellow" and subtly foxy seductions like "A Little More Love"-always brought with it a rush of joy and warmth. 　　(가수) 올리비아 뉴턴 존

- **flex** ⓥ (관절을) 구부리다

He hoisted a stuffed Olympic mascot, mugged for selfies and crouched low and flexed in his trademark lightning-bolt pose 　　He : 우사인 볼트(Bolt) 육상선수

- **inflexible** ⓐ 유연하지 않은

And if a firm does take back a working mother, she will face a stark choice: drop off the fast track or work long and inflexible hours. 　　대한민국 경단녀

fluke, flux

- **fluke** ⓝ 요행(something good that happens because of luck)

But her breakout effort is far from a fluke.

- **flux** ⓝ 끊임없는 변화

In the two months since Afghanistan's government collapsed on Aug. 15, thousands of Afghan girls and women like Farah have been shut out of their high schools and universities, their studies over and futures in flux.

fester, foster

- **fester** ⓥ (상처가) 곪다(infected), 나쁜 감정·생각이 곪아 터지다

In March, the two countries began taking steps to address a long-festering dispute over wartime forced labor. 　　한일관계

- **foster** ⓥ 조성하다, 발전시키다(foment)

That shows how badly the EU has failed in trying to foster a sense of belonging among its older citizens. 　　That : 은퇴한 국민들이 EU에 남지 말고 떠나라는 정서

disfigure, prefigure

- disfigure ⓥ 외양을 흉하게 만들다

Then in 1831 came Victor Hugo's book *The Hunchback of Notre Dame*, whose hero was the disfigured bell ringer Quasimodo.

- prefigure ⓥ 예시하다

At home, she was seen as power-hungry but, through her New Life Movement, helped foster an upright Chinese identity in opposition to supposed Western decadence, prefiguring some of the ideological zealotry of the Cultural Revolution.

> she : (중국) 송미령

fraught, freight, fright

- fraught ⓐ 불안한, 불편한

The long-fraught relationship between South Korea and Japan appears to be entering a phase of détente.

> 윤석열 정부

- freight ⓝ 화물

We'll send your personal belongings by air freight and your furniture by sea freight.

- fright ⓝ 두려움, 무서움

Any predator clever enough to see through its arboreal disguise and mount an attack will be in for a fright.

> arboreal ⓐ 나무의

- frighten ⓥ 무섭게 하다

A suddenly unshackled press was free to report on the frightening hyperinflation, unemployment and official corruption that left many Russians eager for a restoration of order.

fatigue, fatigues

- fatigue ⓝ 피로

We're all suffering from coronavirus caution fatigue.

- fatigues ⓝ 군인들의 작업복

As the Soviet Union was collapsing in 1991, Fidel Castro met with a group of journalists on a visit to Mexico. We pressed him repeatedly about the fall of communism until, chafing in his olive fatigues and the Yucatan humidity, he stopped stroking his beard and instead pounded his fist.

fisherman, fishmonger
- fisherman ⓝ 어부
- fishmonger ⓝ 생선 장수

~monger : 상인

fruiter, fruiterer
- fruiter ⓝ 과일이 열리는 나무
- fruiterer ⓝ 과일 장수

ferment, foment
- ferment ⓥ 발효하다

fermentation ⓝ

The juice already fermenting in tanks and barrels should be fine.
- foment ⓥ (문제·폭력을) 조성(조장)하다(foster)

fomentation ⓝ

So Kim knows China would never squeeze enough to foment its collapse.

Kim : (북한) 김정은

forge, forgo
- forge ⓥ

① 구축하다

Despite no formal secondary education, Lee was accepted to law school on his first attempt, later forging a career in politics.

이재명

② 위조하다

His forged Dominican passport bore the name Pang Xiong, or "Fat Bear" in Mandarin.

김정은의 형인 김정남

- forgo ⓥ ~없이 때우다(forego)

Moms are being discharged from hospitals more and more quickly to reduce the possibility of exposure to the virus, forced to forgo around-the-clock postnatal care.

팬데믹(pandemic) 상황에서의 산부인과 모습
around-the-clock : 24시간 내내

ⓓ foregone conclusion : 처음부터 알고 있는 결론

And it should be a foregone conclusion that primary and secondary education prepares all students for going to college.

fauna, flora
- fauna ⓝ 특정 지역, 특정 시대의 동물(in a particular area or period in history)
- flora ⓝ 특정 지역, 특정 나라의 식물(in a particular place or country)

Tourism is damaging the flora and fauna of the island.

fault line, front line

- **fault line** ⓝ ① (지질) 단층선, 분명한 구분 ② 분쟁의 씨앗

It can be argued that the 1992 Los Angeles riots helped create a new racial fault line in the United States.

- **front line** ⓝ 최전선, 최전방(the place where fighting happens in a war)

War is again a possibility on the Korean Peninsula — and Moon may soon be once again at the front line.

flag, flog

- **flag** ⓥ

① (중요한 정보에) 표시하다

Although Harvard's reviewers looked on Jone's application favorably, two professors flagged it for review, and the university decided against admitting her.

살인죄로 수감 중 공부하여 하버드에 입학

② 시들해지다

Your strength flags ; your world narrows ; much of what once gave you pleasure and satisfaction is now gone.

- **flog** ⓥ 매로 때리다

Video from the protests shows police aggressively flogging protesters with nightsticks.

forceful, forcible

- **forceful** ⓐ 강력한, 단호한

The one new wrinkle appears to be that the Administration will seek to forcefully hold China responsible for North Korean provocations.

- **forcible** ⓐ 강제할 수 있는

Unfortunately, this isn't the first instance of a child receiving a forcible haircut at school.

fairway, faraway

- **fairway** ⓝ (골프) 페어웨이(the part of a golf course that you hit the ball along toward the hole)

- **faraway** ⓐ 멀리 떨어진

Graphic scenes from other faraway conflicts make it easy to forget the ongoing war in Ukraine.

fort, fortress

- fort ⓝ 요새
- fortress ⓝ 요새

Four centuries after the Dutch West India Company built Manhattan's first fort near here, New York has erected another kind of fortress, part high-tech, part slapdash.

force, forced

- force ⓝ 세력, 힘

The grandson has adopted the look and mannerisms of the first Great Leader, and voices the same desire to control a reunified Korea, by force if necessary.

the grandson : 북한의 김정은

cf force ⓥ ① 강간하다(force oneself on)

Her professor Jack drove her to his sister's home and tried to force himself on her.

② 강요하다

It's forcing the United States and its allies to spend billions of dollars to upgrade their defenses.

it : 북한 미사일 개발

cf forces ⓝ 군대

Memories of his youth are now colored by the atrocities that Russian forces committed this year in service of Moscow's imperial ambitions

우크라이나 대통령 젤렌스키 (Zelensky)

- forced ⓐ 강요된, 강제적인

For women, the forced transaction is often sexual assault ; many female migrants take contraceptives to at least avoid pregnancy by their rapists.

cf unforced ⓐ 본인 잘못에 의한

She learned she had made just six unforced errors in her straight-sets win.

she : 테니스(tennis) 선수

fickle, flicker

- fickle ⓐ 변덕이 심한

The real issue is that America is now considered a very fickle ally.

- flicker ⓝ 빛의 반짝거림(an unsteady light that goes on and off quickly)

flicker ⓥ

In the summer of 2015, a curious piece of world news brought a flicker of hope to the wretched Syrian city of Palmyra.

fungible, fungus

- fungible ⓐ 대체할 수 있는

Putting Tubman on legal tender, when slaves in the US were treated fungible commodities, is a supreme form of disrespect.

ⓓ tender ⓝ 입찰

- fungus ⓝ 곰팡이류, 균류

This will help to kill any bacteria or fungus on the skin that may be causing the itchiness.

Tubman : (흑인) 흑인해방 운동가

afflict, inflict

- afflict ⓥ 괴롭히다, 피해 입히다

Throughout history, health care personnel have been vulnerable to the infectious agents that afflict their patients.

- inflict ⓥ (괴로움 등을) 가하다

No effort was made to inflict harm on Russia preinvasion.

의미는 같으나 쓰임은 다름

affliction ⓝ

infliction ⓝ

fragile, frail

- fragile ⓐ 허약한, 부서지기 쉬운

But can the fragile truce between the two countries last?

- frail ⓐ (병이나 나이로) 노쇠한

Testing 700 residents, many of whom are immobile, frail and elderly, also takes time.

fragilily ⓝ

한일관계

florid, fluid

- florid ⓐ 얼굴이 발그레한 (a red or flushed complexion)

I had expected that Jack would be a florid and corpulent person in his middle years.

- fluid ⓐ 유동적인 (likely to change)

Their centralized command structure has made it difficult for them to respond to a more fluid, decentralized Ukrainian military command.

ⓓ fluid ⓝ 유동체

a lab, where they took samples of their blood and knee-joint fluid before and after a 30-minute run on a treadmill

우크라이나-러시아 전쟁
them : Russian troops

ferry, fury

- **ferry** ⓥ (보통 짧은 거리를 작은 보트나 다른 차량으로) 옮기다

No charges were ever brought, but she spent the next 15 months being ferried between five different prison camps with barbed wire and watchtowers, during which she was interrogated 19 times and tortured with electric batons.

cf ferry ⓝ (사람·차량 등을 운반하는) 연락선(카페리)

- **fury** ⓝ 분노

Within a year of Moon-led diplomacy, Trump went from fire and fury to outright affection.   남북관계

familial, familiar

- **familial** ⓐ 가족의   family ⓝ

For the Jacks, having a parent who was an educator created an unspoken expectation of academic achievement that was almost as powerful as familial love.

- **familiar** ⓐ 친숙한   familiarity ⓝ

The assassination kept North Korea squarely on the world stage and in the familiar role of villain.   김정남 암살

fervent, feverish

- **fervent** ⓐ 열렬한 (ardent)

With no political experience or knowledge of the outside world, he was thrust into negotiations with an invading army while trying to calm his fervent but poorly armed subjects.   he: 달라이라마

- **feverish** ⓐ 열이 나는   fever ⓝ

You bring your feverish baby to the hospital in the middle of the night.

foothill, foothold

- **foothill** ⓝ 작은 언덕

Morning has broken on the cedar-strewn foothills of the Himalayas.

- **foothold** ⓝ ① (등산 때) 발 디딜 곳 ② (사업·직업 등에서 성공의) 발판(기반)

A deal would help Kakao establish a foothold in the K-pop business and offer a chance to expand abroad.

flash, flesh, flush

- flash ⓐ 순식간의

Flash floods tore through valleys, and hillsides collapsed, pulling down houses already shorn of their roofs.

ⓓ flash ⓥ (잠깐) 비치다

In one snapshot, she even flashed a grin — between the metal bars.

she : 철창 안에 있는 죄수

ⓓ flash-bang ⓝ 섬광탄

The National Guard, state and local law enforcement — equipped with guns, batons, tear gas, rubber bullets and flash-bangs — have since been dispatched to restore what's known as order.

ⓓ flashlight ⓝ 섬광

Soldiers peered out of pillboxes hidden among the trees, and flashlight beams flickered in the windows of Zelensky's office on the fourth floor.

- flesh ⓝ (사람의) 살, 피부

He peeled flesh off the faces of cadavers, delineated the muscles that move the lips and then painted the world's most memorable smile.

He : 레오나르도 다빈치
cadaver ⓝ 사체
delineate ⓥ 기술하다

ⓓ

- flush ⓝ 물을 왈칵 쏟음

What the British tabloids especially love to hate about the EU is the red tape churned out by Brussels in an attempt to regulate every aspect of the European market, from the maximum wattage of vacuum cleaners to the amount of water used in a toilet flush.

영국의 EU 탈퇴

fandom, fathom

- fandom ⓝ 팬층 (all the fans)

BTS is not the first Korean act to establish a secure foothold in the West, yet their outsize success today is indicative of a sea change in the inner workings of fandom and how music is consumed.

fan ⓝ

- fathom ⓥ

① 헤아리다

I still can't fathom out what she meant.

② (물의) 깊이를 가늠하다

The pilot had to continually fathom the river, which drought conditions had lowered to unprecedented levels.

ⓓ pilot ⓝ 수로 안내인, 도선사

flash ⓝ

fallow, fellow

- **fallow** ⓐ

① (농토) 놀리는, 농사를 안 짓는

The bridge plunges abruptly into fallow cornfields. 　　중국과 북한을 잇는 다리

② (이용가치가 있는데도) 사용하지 않는 　　lie fallow

At this very moment there are probably important inventions lying fallow.

- **fellow** ⓝ 동료

That promise is so fundamental to what it means to be an American that 　　기회와 자유의 땅이라는 약속
millions of my fellow veterans have fought and died to defend it.

ⓓ **fellowship** ⓝ 유대감, 동료애

traditions that bind us together in fellowship

florescent, fluorescent

- **florescent** ⓐ 꽃이 활짝 핀 　　florescence ⓝ 개화

the potent florescence of youth

- **fluorescent** ⓐ ① 형광의 ② 화사한, 밝은, 야광의 　　fluorescence ⓝ 형광

fluorescent shopping arcades

fodder, folder

- **fodder** ⓝ

① (가축의) 사료

② ~에만 쓸모가 있는 사람(것)(that is useful only for a particular purpose)

young people ending up as factory fodder

ⓓ cannon fodder : 총알받이

- **folder** ⓝ 서류철

ⓓ **fold** ⓝ

① (같은 사상이나 신념을 가진) 집단(단체)

In a blow to the Tibetan exile community, China has set about bringing the
leadership of Tibetan Buddhism into the party fold

② 배(~fold)

GDP per capita rose 40-fold from 1978 to 2012. 　　중국

ⓓ fold ⓥ 중단하다, 사업을 접다

More than 200 businesses in the city folded between March and September 2020.

flank, flunk

- flank ⓝ 옆구리   flank ⓥ 옆에 서 있다

President Xi of China, center, flanked by new members of the Politburo's Standing Committee, on Oct. 25   사진 설명

- flunk ⓥ 시험에 떨어지다

But given that applications already vastly outnumber available jobs, why the imperative to consider candidates who flunk the exam?

filch, filter

- filch ⓥ 좀 도둑질하다

Since the Philippine navy sends fresh water, fuel and other provisions only once every two months, the soldiers must survive on their spear-fishing catch and filched seagull eggs.

- filter ⓥ ① 여과하다 ② 서서히 들어 오다   filtering ⓝ

But hundreds, and at times thousands, of migrants have filtered back to the capital since then, many huddling at night under freeways, or in doorways.

facade, facet

- facade

① (건물의) 정면

The story quickly circulated across Korean news and social media, giving rise to an outpouring of homophobia. The club's facade was vandalized.   동성애 이야기

② 허울 (a way of behaving that hides your real feelings)

Her flawless public facade masked private despair.

- facet ⓝ ① (보석의) 깎인 면 ② 측면 (aspect)

Much uncertainty remains about the rights of women and girls to access to education — or participate in many facets of public life — in the country following the recent Taliban takeover.

fortuitous, fortunate

- fortuitous ⓐ 우연의

The similarity between the paintings may not be simply fortuitous.

- fortunate ⓐ 운 좋은   fortune ⓝ 운, 해운

We should try to help others who are less fortunate than ourselves.

a few, few

- a few ⓐ 몇 개의

The space to help Myanmar correct course is narrow and shrinking, although a few imperfect options exist.

- few ⓐ (숫자가 적음을 강조할 때) 불과 얼마 안 되는

Jane was cooking dinner when the smugglers told her they had a boat. Even though the 20-year-old African hadn't eaten all day, she abandoned her pasta in the rush to gather her few belongings.

유럽으로 가려는 아프리카 난민

foresight, hindsight

- foresight ⓝ 예지력, 선견지명

It was an example of the authorities' lack of foresight.

ⓓ foreseeable ⓐ 예측할 수 있는

But for the foreseeable future, China is likely to remain strong and stable.

- hindsight ⓝ 뒤늦게 깨달음

When lives are examined in hindsight, we often forget the setting. Winnie did not live in a vacuum but in apartheid South Africa.

Winnie : 만델라 부인

fillet, filly

- fillet ⓝ (육류생선의 뼈를 발라내고 저민) 살코기

This fish is a Mediterranean staple. Roast a fillet of mackerel (or the whole fish if you're up for it) with a generous helping of herbs, oliver oil and lemon.

고등어(mackerel) 이야기

- filly ⓝ 새끼 암말(a young female horse)

Not far away, behind a stand of junipers, the mare's filly stood alone, lost.

fraction, fractious

- fraction(n) ① 분수 ② 부분, 일부

My situation happened in less than a fraction of a second, and it changed my life forever.

- fractious ⓐ 쉽게 화를 내는(tending to be troublesome)

It will be interesting to see how long this fractious mood lasts.

fertile, futile

- fertile ⓐ ① 비옥한 ② 생식력 있는
- fertile crescent ⓝ (역사) 비옥한 초승달지대
- fertilizer ⓝ 비료

fertility ⓝ
infertile ⓐ

Other parts of the country so far spared fighting still face shortages of fuel, labor, and other crop inputs, especially fertilizer.

the country : 우크라이나

- fertility rate ⓝ 출생률

For three years in a row, the country has recorded the lowest fertility rate in the world, with women of reproductive age having fewer than one child on average.

우리나라 저출산

- futile ⓐ 헛된, 소용없는(pointless)

In 1845 explorer Jack led an expedition through these parts on a futile search for an inland sea.

funeral, furnace

- funeral ⓝ 장례식

Seo, a top-level prosecutor in South Korea, alleges that a senior male colleague repeatedly groped her at a funeral in 2010, while the country's Justice Minister sat nearby.

서지현 검사(미투 촉발 장본인)

- furnace ⓝ
① 용광로
② (건물의) 난방장치, 보일러 시설

Jack, 27, died after snow covered a furnace and sent carbon monoxide into his home.

③ 아주 더운 장소(a very hot place)

Her car was a furnace.

flaunt, flout

- flaunt ⓥ 과시하다

They waved their rebel battle flags, oblivious to the fact that Robert E. Lee told his men to put them away. They flaunted their swastikas.

남북전쟁

- flout ⓥ 비웃다

Cardin embraced designing for the masses, flouting couture traditions and championing ready-to-wear (or mass market) clothes far ahead of many contemporaries.

couture ⓝ 고급 여성복

flatline, flatten, headline

- **flatline** ⓥ 나아지지 않다

But with his approval ratings flatlining at 23%, he doubts Macron will be re-elected in 2022.

- **flatten** ⓥ 평평하게 하다

The window for flattening the curve in the US is rapidly closing, but it's still open.

curve : 코로나가 급증하는 곡선

- **headline** ⓝ (신문기사나 뉴스 등의) 헤드라인

North Korea's missile tests are so frequent that they prompt more shrugs than big headlines in Seoul.

- **headline** ⓐ 주목할 만한

A shared desire in Washington and Beijing for stability in US-China relations will ease headline tensions.

farther, further

- **farther** ⓐⓓⓥ (시공간 상으로) 더 멀리

They had enough fuel to make the 12-nautical-mile distance to international waters but no farther.

- **further** ⓐⓓⓥ (정도의) 더 멀리

On Thursday afternoon, Japan gave a further indication that it was reciprocating South Korea's move when the trade ministry in Tokyo announced that it was moving to drop restrictions on technology exports to South Korea that had been imposed since 2019.

flagrant, fragrant

- **flagrant** ⓐ 노골적인, 명백한

This kind of flagrant assault on the US Constitution may not be limited to Texas and Mississippi for long.

- **fragrant** ⓐ 냄새 좋은(a pleasant smell)

Bake until crust is fragrant and beginning to brown, 16 to 18 minutes.

- **fragrance** ⓝ 향수

Even more revolutionary was his vision for a diversified namesake brand; Cardin licensed his name on everything from fragrances and furniture to pickle jars and car interiors.

faction, fiction, friction

- **faction** ⓝ 파벌, 파당   factious ⓐ

Indonesia is on the verge of outlawing all sexual intercourse outside marriage, as conservative political factions in the majority-Muslim nation compete for votes ahead of provincial elections.

- **fiction** ⓝ 허구, 픽션   fictional ⓐ

All the figures I make are fictional, because I'm trying to critique the whole concept of portraiture.

I : 조각가

- **friction** ⓝ 마찰

China's fraying international relations and economic doldrums are creating frictions domestically.

faint, feint

- **faint** ⓥ 실신하다, 기절하다(pass out)   faint ⓝ
- cf **faint** ⓐ

① (소리, 빛, 냄새 등이) 희미한(barely perceptible)

② 어지러운

The old man felt faint and sick and he could not see well.

③ (가능성 등이) 아주 적은

I had faint hopes of my own when Kim came to power in 2011, knowing that he had encountered democracy and capitalism studying in Switzerland.

김정은

- **feint** ⓝ 페인트(특히 스포츠에서 상대방을 속이는 동작)

Early on Oct. 30, the deposed Catalan president Jack posted a photo on Instagram from inside the seat of his government. In fact, Jack was nowhere near the Generalitat. He had fled to Belgium. The photo was apparently a feint.

Catalonia : 분리 독립운동이 활발한 지역

Generalitat : 자치정부

ferocious, fierce

- **ferocious** ⓐ 흉포한   ferocity ⓝ

The 120-kiloton explosion was about eight times the ferocity of the bombs that devastated the cities of Hiroshima and Nagasaki at the end of World War Ⅱ.

북한의 여섯 번째 핵실험

- **fierce** ⓐ 맹렬한(a lot of energy and strong feelings)   fierceness ⓝ

Jane, in her signature white sari paired rubber flip-flops, has become the face of fierceness in Indian politics.

feast, feat

- feast ⓝ 잔치

"People jumped into the pit with the bodies," says one six months later, recalling the ordeal, at a feast for those who emerged alive. Many had not.

전쟁 피난민
the pit : hell

- feat ⓝ 업적, 공

Ethiopia wrestled down its mortality rates for children under five by two-thirds from 1990 to 2012 — an impressive feat for a low-income nation.

foggy, fogy

- fog ⓝ 안개(mist)

Crews used county search dogs and a helicopter during the search in rainy and foggy conditions.

foggy ⓐ

- fogy ⓐ 고리타분한(a person with old-fashioned ideas)

The perception of Charles' progressive instincts has always been undermined by his fogy self-presentation.

영국 국왕 찰스

flay, fray

- flay ⓥ 비난하다(to criticize someone very severely)

For all the times that he flayed me in testimony or that I disagreed with an aspect of his views, I deeply honor his long voyage and all that he stood for.

- fray ⓝ 싸움, 전쟁

Jack says deteriorating cross-strait relations are what pushed him into the political fray.

cross-strait relation : 중국과 대만 관계

- fray ⓥ (신경들이) 날카로워지다

Biden must try to improve Washington's frayed relations with regional allies South Korea and Japan, and collectively apply pressure to get Pyongyang back to the negotiating table.

- defray ⓥ (비용을) 지불하다

The rest comes from sponsors, who are reportedly seeking an additional $200 million to defray the estimated $2.8 billion costs of postponing the event.

코로나로 도쿄올림픽 연기
The rest : 연기로 인한 소요비용

fluster, flutter

- fluster ⓝ 허둥지겠함(nervous and confused)   fluster ⓥ
All the yelling on the bus put the driver in a fluster.   in a fluster
- flutter ⓥ ① 빠르고 가볍게 흔들(리)다(펄럭이다) ② (새·곤충이 날개를) 파닥이다
This spring in the East Village, blue and yellow flags flutter in the breeze.

face value, stone-faced

- face value ⓝ 액면가(the apparent worth or implication of something)
There are a handful of studies that have been done on juvenile curfews, and unfortunately the overall conclusion is they don't really have an impact. They tend to be popular at face value.
- stone-faced ⓐ 감정을 드러내지 않는
He stood there stone-faced while the verdict was announced.

forage, foray

- forage ⓥ 먹이를 찾다   forage ⓝ (소·말의) 사료
For three days his family, sleepless, bellies screaming, foraged for fruit and climbed trees for their bitter leaves.
- foray ⓝ
① 급습(a short sudden attack by a group of soldiers)
But in early May, Chinese coast guard vessels glided past Flat Island, part   남중국해 영토분쟁
of an increasingly visible and adventurous maritime foray by the region's   the region's biggest
biggest power.   power : 중국
② (다른 분야에 진입하려는) 시도(a short attempt at doing a particular job or activity)
Jack's first political foray had come a decade earlier, though.

forestall, foretell

- forestall ⓥ 미연에 방지하다
To forestall that possibility, and to bolster its crucial East Asian alliances,   that : 북한의 핵무장
the US may want to consider putting tactical nuclear weapons of its own in South Korea, should Kim insist on continuing his nuclear buildup while refusing to negotiate in good faith.
- foretell ⓥ 예언하다, 예지하다
A snowless future foretold on Europe's tawny slopes   지구온난화 기사 제목

feather, feature

- feather ⓝ 털, 깃털

ⓓ a feather in your cap : 자랑하는 부분

Beating him would be a feather in my cap.

- feature ⓝ

① 영화(a film being shown at a cinema)

Parasite won the top prize at Cannes, and it's South Korea's entry for the Best International Feature Film Oscar.   영화 기생충

② 특징, 특성

Clearly the objection to authority was a central organizing feature of his life.

③ 지세, 지형(a part of the land, especially a part that you can see)

A few days later, on May 10, a US guided-missile destroyer cruised past Fiery Cross Reef, another disputed Spratly feature.

④ (방송이나 언론 등의) 특집

ⓓ feature ⓥ

① ~를(을) 특징으로 하다

The hotel, set to open this spring, will feature no single-use plastic.

② (방송이나 언론에서) 특집으로 다루다

NBC will feature her in prime-time coverage, and blue-chip companies —Nike, Toyota and Procter & Gamble are among the sponsors that make Kim the highest-paid female snowboarder in history — have built ad campaigns around her.

ⓓ featured ⓐ 주연의

Seven years ago, Gauff attended Arthur Ashe Kids' Day at the US Open as a spectator. This year, she'll take the stage and sign autographs in New York as a featured guest before playing in the tournament's main draw.   Gauff : 테니스 선수

flair, flare

- flair ⓝ 스타일(a uniquely attractive quality)

Some of his first acts as King has brought refreshing flair to the stodgy iconography of monarchy.   영국 왕 찰스

- flare ⓝ 확 타오르는 불길

She felt a flare of anger within her.

ⓓ flare ⓥ ① 불길이 확 타오르다 ② (감정이) 갑자기 격화되다

Things came to a head in 2019, when an extradition bill perceived to hand authority to Beijing inspired massive popular protests that flared into several months of violent unrest.

홍콩 사태
come to a head ⓥ 문제가 더 복잡해지다

fix, fixer

● fix ⓥ

① 수리하다, 바로 잡다

Finding a big diamond is a onetime blessing. Learning books can fix your life forever.

② 고정시키다

Essentially, they are slaves : human beings who have been reduced to being possessions with a fixed value.

● fixer ⓝ 해결사

Other guests included Samantha Cohen, the daughter of Michael D. Cohen, the longtime lawyer and fixer for former President Donald J. Trump who turned on him and provided testimony leading to the recent indictment in a hush money case.

윤석열 대통령의 미국 방문 시 만찬

turn on ⓥ 공격하다

● fixture ⓝ (직업이나 장소에) 오래 붙박이는 사람

Jack has been a fixture in the Chicago White Sox lineup for nine seasons.

G

외신으로 보는
대한민국
VOCABULARY

gruff, guff

- gruff ⓐ 깐깐한(rough, brusque, or stern in manner, speech, or aspect)

Mr Yoon is a gruff prosecutor who entered politics less than a year before he was elected.　　Yoon : 윤석열 대통령

- guff ⓝ 실없는 이야기(nonsense, foolish talk or ideas)

His latest book has a lot of guff about conspiracies of one kind or another.

gorge, gorgeous

- gorge ⓝ 협곡(canyon, a deep narrow valley with steep sides)

The plane fell nose-first towards its left and then crashed into the gorge.

ⓓ gorge ⓥ 폭식하다

South Korean kids gorge themselves on studying for one reason : to get into one of the country's top universities.　　우리나라 사교육

- gorgeous ⓐ 아주 멋진

Yet those of us who lived here on 9/11, and continue to live here today, have an advantage : we once saw in our city a smoking hole that also served as a mass grave for lives, and flesh, that had been incinerated in a flash on a gorgeous late-summer day.　　9-11 테러　here : 뉴욕

gaff, gaffe

- gaff ⓝ (큰 물고기를 끌어 올리는 데 쓰는) 갈고리　　gaff ⓥ

It made the boy sad to see the old man come in each day with his skiff empty and he always went down to help him carry either the coiled lines or the gaff and harpoon and the sail that was furled around the mast.

- gaffe ⓝ 실수(blunder)

He realized that he had committed an awful gaffe when he mispronounced her name.

gook, goon

- gook ⓝ (경멸) 아시아인
- goon ⓝ 폭력배(thug, especially one hired to terrorize opposition)

Senior leaders have called the protesters "antinationals" and "goons."

gaggle, giggle

- gaggle ⓝ 시끌벅적한 무리(관광객, 아이들)

the gaggle of photographers that dogged the President's every step

ⓓ 'a gaggle of tourists/children etc'의 형식으로 씀

- giggle ⓝ 킥킥 웃음   giggle ⓥ

Every conversation is peppered with giggles and guffaws.

gargle, gurgle

- gargle ⓥ 입안을 헹구다, 가글링(gargling)하다

He gargled with salt water.

- gurgle ⓥ 물 흐르는 소리가 나다

Underwater sounds gurgle from a pair of speakers.   명상

ⓓ 물 흐르는 소리는 burble도 사용

grandee, guarantee

- grandee ⓝ 고위층 (the highest social class, a lot of influence)

Macron's youth and clean-cut looks set him in contrast to France's political grandees.

Macron : 프랑스 대통령
clean-cut ⓐ 말쑥한

- guarantee ⓥ 보장하다   guarantee ⓝ

And yet education is no guarantee of a job.   대학 졸업 ≠ 직업(대한민국)

grace, grand

- grace ⓝ ① (하느님의) 은총 ② 우아함, 품위

But we can do it with grace, by handling it without a trace of aggression and without being rude ourselves.   it : rudeness

- grand ⓐ 웅장한

the grand State Dining Room of the White House

ⓓ grand jury : 대배심

A grand jury also refused to indict.

ⓓ grand piano : 그랜드 피아노

ⓓ GOP : grand old party (미국 공화당)

ⓓ grandeur ⓝ grand의 명사형

① 그랜저(우리나라의 현대차)

② 웅장함(impressive beauty, power, or size)

the grandeur of the mountains

graceful, gracious

- graceful ⓐ 우아한(attractive and usu, effortlessly fine and smooth)

By the late '60s, though, the couple were creating longer and more graceful silhouettes.

- gracious ⓐ 자애로운(in a polite, kind, and generous way, to people of a lower rank)

Now, amid Paris' gracious boulevards and neighborhoods are pockets that have become a kind of refugee camp on a wide, fragmented scale.

파리로 몰려든 아프리카 난민

grim, grime

- grim ⓐ 암울한

More than 5,700 homes and businesses have been destroyed, and over 40 people have died, a grim toll that is sure to rise.

대형 화재

- grime ⓝ 때, 더께

The labor left her covered in grease and grime and not a little well-earned pride.

grimy ⓐ

2차 대전 당시, 엘리자베스 여왕이 기계공으로 참전

gatekeeper, goalkeeper

- gatekeeper ⓝ 문지기

Today, K-pop is a multibillion-dollar business, but for decades the gatekeepers of the music world — the Western radio moguls, media outlets and number crunchers-treated it as a novelty.

- goalkeeper ⓝ (축구의) 골키퍼

When Saki fired a penalty shot past US goalkeeper Solo in the final of the 2011 World Cup, a tormented nation exhaled, if only for a moment.

㏄ tormented nation : 후쿠시마 쓰나미를 겪은 일본

ghastly, ghost

- ghastly ⓐ 잔인한, 무서운

an effort to bring an end to a ghastly campaign against ethnic Albanians in Kosovo

ghast는 잘 안 씀

- ghost ⓝ 귀신

The city of New Orleans is no stranger to ghost stories.

㏄ ghost ⓥ (사전 연락 없이) 갑자기 연락을 끊다

Being ghosted is one of the toughest ways to be dumped.

ghost kitchen, ghost write

- ghost kitchen ⓝ 배달 전문음식점

Third Ward's newest food hall opened in November 2020 as a group of ghost kitchens, but according to its Instagram the hall is now open for dine-in meals.

- dine-in ⓐ 식당에서 먹는

- ghost write ⓥ 대필하다

She was hired to ghostwrite the mayor's autobiography.

gut, gutter

- gut ⓝ ① (동물의) 내장 ② 배짱 ③ 직감

Once infected, we are more aggressive, less creative and worse at our jobs. The only way to end a strain is to make a conscious decision to do so. We must have the guts to call it out, face to face. We must say, "Just stop."

전염되는 'rude'

'have the guts' 형식을 많이 씀

- gut ⓥ ① (내장을) 제거하다 ② 없애다

The idea was that this little-used pathway would help avoid the months-long wait times typical of more traditional channels like the US Refugee Admission Program(USRAP), which was gutted by former President Trump.

- gutter ⓝ (도로의) 배수로

Water runs off into the gutter as the Las Vegas Valley Water District issues fines and citations for water waste.

gut feeling, gut reaction, gut wrenching

- gut feeling ⓝ 직감

My theory was that the most important years were 0 to 5. It was a gut feeling.

자녀 교육

- gut reaction ⓝ 본능적 반응

When London-based lawyer and women's-rights activist Jane first heard the news of Floyd's killing on May 25, her gut reaction was raw anger.

Floyd : 경찰의 목 눌림으로 죽은 흑인

- gut-wrenching ⓐ 속이 뒤틀리는, 아주 괴로운(making you feel very upset or anxious)

But the most gut-wrenching decision I've faced, by far, is whether to travel across the country to see my sick and immunocompromised mom, potentially exposing her to a virus from which she might not recover.

immunocompromised ⓐ 면역력이 약화된

governance, government

- governance ⓝ 통치   govern ⓥ

Over the past year, citizens in Africa, Asia, Europe, Latin America and the Middle East took to the streets to raise their voices against inequality, corruption and bad governance.

- government ⓝ 정부

I don't think the government of Myanmar deserves any credit for this.

globe, glove

- globe ⓝ ① 지구본 ② 세계   global ⓐ

Music doesn't have to be English to be a global phenomenon.

- glove ⓝ 장갑, (권투, 야구) 글로브

He is wearing boxing gloves.

globalization, glocalization

- globalization ⓝ 세계화   globalize ⓥ

If a company, industry, or economy globalizes or is globalized, it has business activities all over the world.

- cf deglobalize ⓥ 탈세계화하다

Many people blame the coronavirus epidemic on globalization and say the only way to prevent more such outbreaks is to deglobalize the world : build walls, restrict travel, reduce trade.

- glocalization ⓝ 세계화(globalization)와 현지화(localization)의 결합   신조어

gauge, gauze

- gauge ⓝ 게이지, 측정기

The petrol gauge is still on full.

- gauze ⓝ 거즈(보통 면이나 실크로 된 가볍고 투명한 천)
- cf gauzy ⓐ

① 가볍고 투명한

gauzy wings   잠자리나 파리의 날개

② 애매하고 확실하지 않은(marked by vagueness, elusiveness, or fuzziness)

The South's preference for negotiations is grounded in the gauzy ideal of future reunification.   남북관계

garish, garnish

- garish ⓐ 야한, 화려한(Obtrusively bright and showy; lurid)

Both women sport garish red lips, wide eyes that are lusciously over-lashed, and hair that can be unnaturally blond or orange.

- garnish ⓥ

① 고명을 입히다

He garnished each serving with a dollop of sour cream.

② (채권 압류를) 통고하다

If students don't repay federal loans after leaving universities, the government can garnish their wages, tax refunds and Social Security benefits.

grid, grit

- grid ⓝ

① 격자무늬

② (전기·가스 등의 공급용) 배전망

On the ground, nations will also need to build new power plants to keep up with demand or risk an unstable grid.

- gridlock ⓝ 교통 정체

The fumes from decades of gridlock have worsened the damage.

노틀담 대성당 화재사고

- gridiron ⓝ 석쇠

- grit ⓝ 투지, 기개

I've known few men who could match Jack's grit

gill, grill

- gill ⓝ 아가미(gill raker)

아가미가 raker처럼 생김
lactate ⓥ 젖이 나오다

More worryingly, gill raker plates have been marketed as an aid for lactating mothers.

- grill ⓥ

① 그릴(석쇠)에 굽다

They slaughtered all the livestock. All of March the smell of grilled meat hung over the village.

우크라이나 마을을 점령한 러시아 군대

② 다그치다, 닦달하다

Attorney Darrow grilled populist politician Bryan on his interpretation of well-known Bible stories.

창조론과 진화론에 관한 공방

grade, degrade

- grade ⓥ

① 등급을 매기다

The report seeks to grade several companies on their business in China in a uniform way.

② (점차) 변화하다

For the first time since the onset of the coronavirus pandemic, schools in Virginia will be graded on whether students are coming to school.

ⓓ grade ⓝ (학교의) 학년

Taliban cancels education for girls beyond sixth grade, despite its pledge not to.

- degrade ⓥ (질적으로) 저하되다

Dancing can burn up to 300 calories every half hour, and research has linked it to an increase in white matter in the brains of older adults, which tends to degrade with age.

ⓓ bio-degradable : 미생물에 의해 환경친화적으로 분해하는

Guests will be given refillable stainless-steel water bottles when they check in, and rooms will contain bio-degradable bin bags.

ⓓ degradation ⓝ 저하, 악화

The climate crisis is already playing out not just in extreme weather and degradation of the natural environment but also in food insecurity and the displacement of millions.

downgrade, upgrade

- downgrade ⓥ (등급을) 떨어뜨리다, 격하시키다

Japan strengthened restrictions on several high-tech exports to South Korea in July and downgraded South Korea's status as a trusted trading partner in August.

- upgrade ⓥ 개선시키다 (상위 등급으로) 향상시키다

For now, her plans for Beijing include unveiling three new tricks. "I'm so excited," she says. "They're an upgrade from everything I've done."

her : 동계올림픽 참가 snowboarder 선수

gravel, grovel

- gravel ⓝ 자갈

Once, success meant winning races on gravel courses and setting world records on the track.

- grovel ⓥ 굽신거리다(with the body prostrate in token of subservience)

I had to really grovel to the bank manager to get a loan.

grave, gravity

- grave ⓝ 무덤(tomb)

One by one, the graves have been exhumed, the remains analyzed and identified with advances in DNA technology and science.

- grave ⓐ 심각한   graveness ⓝ

North Korea may not rank as urgent, but it is a truly grave peril.

- gravity

① 중력

But fame came fast and hard for Kim, whose gravity-defying twists and flips made her the youngest female Olympic gold medalist in snowboarding history.   Kim : 스노보드 선수

② 중요성

Jack's fellow Olympians recognized the gravity of the moment.   선수들의 스트레스에 관한 내용

gravitas, gravitate

- gravitas ⓝ 엄숙함, 진지함

Kofi Annan's deep well of grace, humility and calm energy set him apart. Such was his seemingly boundless vigor and the gravitas he exuded, that his death at the age of 80 on Aug. 18, shocked all who knew and loved him.   Kofi Annan : 유엔 사무총장을 역임한 아프리카 가나 출신의 외교관

- gravitate ⓥ 인력에 끌리다   gravitation ⓝ 만유인력, 중력

Some of the women gravitated to camp towns to find a living. Others, like Ms. Cho, were abducted, or lured with the promise of work.   대한민국 기지촌 역사

garlic, ginger

- garlic ⓝ 마늘
- ginger ⓝ ① 생강 ② 생강색, 연한 적갈색

goods, goody

- goods ⓝ 상품, 물품

By boosting connectivity, China can spur growth, gain access to valuable natural resources and create new markets for its goods. 　중국의 일대일로 사업

- goody ⓝ 맛있는 것, 매력적인 것(something attractive, pleasant, or desirable)

Living standards are in decline, and though an election later this year has Putin promising all sorts of goodies, his 21 years in power inspire little confidence that better days lie ahead.

gargantuan, gregarious

- gargantuan ⓐ 엄청난(gigantic, enormous)

Clearly, the calculation of precise costs for all support for older people would be a gargantuan task.

- gregarious ⓐ 남과 어울리 좋아하는, 사교적인(sociable)

Where Jack was guarded, introverted, damaged, Jane was gregarious, openhearted, charming.

glow, glower

- glow ⓥ 빛나다

All the lights are off except for one gently glowing lamp. 　명상

- glower ⓥ 노려보다, 쏘아보다

In his most iconic scenes, Jack, a talented physical comedian, often didn't speak, but rather glowered at Jane's love interests — in particular Ross — or endured scratches from her demonic cat.

　cf love interest : (영화·소설에서 주인공의) 애정 상대

growl, prowl

- growl ⓥ 으르렁거리다(it makes a long deep angry sound) 　growl ⓝ

I make a sound at him that is somewhere between a groan and a growl

- prowl ⓥ 돌아다니다(especially because it is hunting another animal) 　prowl ⓝ
　prowl car ⓝ (경찰) 순찰차

Their travel was tough, with traders facing the threats of the terrain and the bands of bandits that prowled the Silk Road.

glimmer, glimpse

- glimmer ⓝ 희미하게 깜빡이는 빛(shimmer)

Despite the backlash, glimmers of institutional change are also appearing.

- glimpse ⓝ

① 잠깐 보기, 일별

Jane stopped to take selfies with her fans, who crowd around a fence to get a glimpse of her.   육상선수

② 짧은 경험, 짧은 접촉

The world once had a "sense of optimism that Hong Kong was a glimpse into China's future, not that Hong Kong would grow into a reflection of China's past."

genesis, genius, genus

- genesis ⓝ 기원(the beginning or origin of something)   제네시스(현대자동차)

This approach examines the historical genesis of a social system and shows how oppressive structures have emerged.

- genius ⓝ 천재

Being a genius is different than merely being supersmart.

- genus ⓝ (생물 분류상의) 속(屬)

genealogy, geology

- genealogy ⓝ 족보학

My paternal grandfather, Jack, had traced our genealogy back to the 1600s in Germany and Sweden.

- geology ⓝ 지질학   geo~ : 지구나 토양

Did he really believe that the whale swallowed Jonah, that Joshua made the sun stand still and that Adam and Eve were the first people? Byran answered yes, but Darrow made him admit he didn't know how these things happened and didn't know any geology or ancient history.

창조론과 진화론 공방
Byran : 창조론자
Darrow : 진화론자

- ⓓ geography ⓝ 지리   geographer ⓝ 지리학자

Geography, meanwhile, no longer affords the US the buffer it once did.

- ⓓ geopolitical ⓐ 지정학적인   goepolitics ⓝ 지정학

Finally, Russia's war in Ukraine has also shifted geopolitics to China's disadvantage.

서방세계의 분열로 이익을 보았는데 전쟁으로 서방세계가 단결함

governess, governor

- governess ⓝ 가정교사 겸 보모

They also stabled, cared for, and learned to train a royal succession of pet ponies, and shared the same nannies and governesses.

they : 엘리자베스 2세 여형제

- governor ⓝ 주지사

At one point, the President stopped in his aide Jack's office to talk about the race with Tom, the former North Carolina governor who had agreed to manage the 1968 campaign.

glory, gory

- glory ⓝ 영광, 영예

Not that the glory comes without drawbacks : namely, lack of free time.

glorious ⓐ

- gory ⓐ 유혈의, 피투성이의

The new series struck familiar themes: a succession drama filled with jealousy, flying dragons and gory human deaths.

grievance, grieve

- grievance ⓝ 불만

Many South Koreans remain wary of great powers, reflecting their deep grievances over Japanese colonial rule and the division of the Korean Peninsula by the Soviet Union and the United States at the end of World War II.

- grieve ⓥ 슬퍼하다

Her mother grieved her brother's death until she died in 2007.

ⓓ grief ⓝ 슬픔

By the time the former President began calling COVID-19 "the Chinese virus," by the time racists began shouting and tweeting (and spray-painting) the term kung flu, my father was gone and my mother's cancer had spread, and the difficult conversations left to us were about our grief and how much we loved and missed one another.

글쓴이 중국계 미국인

gleam, glean

- gleam ⓥ 어슴푸레 빛나다

Kim Jong-un, wearing a black-and-white pinstripe suit, looks at a gleaming warhead.   *사진 설명*

- glean ⓥ

① (추수 후) 이삭 줍다

② (정보나 지식 등을 어렵게 여기저기서) 얻다, 모으다(garner)

Some parents are obsessively tracking every press release, investor report and social media announcement to glean information, and a few have even lied about their kids' ages to get their children vaccinated.

graft, grift

- graft ⓥ 접목(접목은 나무를 접붙임)하다

Hong Kong was grafted back onto China under a "one country, two systems" formula designed to preserve its legal and political systems within an authoritarian state.   *홍콩이 영국에서 중국으로 복귀하는 것을 graft로 표현*

- graft ⓝ 뇌물, 뇌물수수, 부정부패

Aware that rampant graft threatened the legitimacy of the Communist Party, then party Chairman Xi launched an anticorruption campaign in 2012 to target both "tigers and flies," or high and low officials.

- grift ⓥ 사기치다(deceive)

At this point, you may think you have *Parasite* all figured out : it's a dark comedy about grifters using their wiles to get by, a parable about forgotten members of society who manage to squeeze in through the back door — that would have been a good enough movie right there.   *영화 기생충(Parasite)*

gasp, grasp

- gasp ⓥ 숨을 제대로 못 쉬다

Indians gasping for breath are being turned away from overwhelmed hospitals, sometimes simply because they don't' have lab reports confirming COVID-19 infection.

- grasp ⓥ 완전히 이해하다, 파악하다

I don't think people quite grasp the seriousness of the situation.

- grasp ⓝ

Beijing doesn't have a full grasp of how Hong Kong really feels.   *홍콩 문제*

YZABCDEFG

HIJK

외신으로 보는
대한민국
VOCABULARY

LMNOPQRSTUVWX

haven, heaven

- haven ⓝ 안식처, 피난처

The heavily armed DMZ separating North and South Korea has become a wildlife haven.

- heaven ⓝ 천국, 하늘나라

Heaven helps those who help themselves.

hyperbola, hyperbole

- hyperbola ⓝ (수학) 쌍곡선
- hyperbole ⓝ 과장(exaggeration)

To say that he is prone to hyperbole does a disservice to the word.

cf do somebody/something a disservice : 몹쓸 짓을 하다

hyper~ : 과도한, 지나친
he : 김정은

hurl, hurtle

- hurl ⓥ 던지다

Protesters marching through the city's Left Bank ripped up the sidewalk and hurled chunks of concrete at riot police.

- hurtle ⓥ 돌진하다

For days it has seemed as if the country was hurtling toward the brink.

huddle, hurdle

- huddle ⓥ (춥거나 무서워서) 옹송그리며 앉다, 모이다

I just huddled together at home with my two young daughters watching the TV for updates.

- hurdle ⓝ 장애, 장애물

Chinese foreign policy also faces hurdles, beginning with North Korea.

harbinger, harbor

- harbinger ⓝ 조짐

It's a harbinger of things to come.

- harbor ⓥ (계획이나 생각 등을) 마음에 품다

Warming US waters are harboring more bacteria.

cf harbor ⓝ 항구(port)

지구 온난화

hardly, hardy

- **hardly** adv 거의 ~하지 않는다(almost not)

The children were so excited they could hardly speak.

- **hardy** a (척박한 환경에도) 튼튼한, 잘 견디는(able to bear difficult living conditions)

Hardy juniper clings to the ancient rock.

juniper n 향나무, 노간주나무

hub, hubris

- **hub** n

① (바퀴의) 중심축

② 허브, 중심지

By bringing Hong Kong International Airport, one of the world's busiest transit hubs, to a standstill.

- **hubris** n 자만심, 거만

We also could have done much better in marshaling and accounting for our resources and guarding against corruption and waste. We could have checked our hubris and optimism at the door.

아프간 전쟁 반성

hangry, hanker, hungry

- **hangry** a 배고파 화나는

hungry+angry

- **hanker** v 갈망하다

With Lady Gaga playing in her earbuds, Jane won gold with a score that was more than eight points higher than silver medalist Liu of China. In between her runs, Jane tweeted about her hankering for ice cream and lamented her decision to leave a breakfast sandwich unfinished, making her "hangry."

Jane : 평창동계올림픽 Snowboard 선수

- **hungry** a ① 배고파하는

Strangers took in refugees ; restaurateurs fed the hungry ; doctors flew in to help the wounded.

우크라이나 사태

② ~을 갈구하는

There are girls locked out of school who are hungry to learn and who need support to continue their education, online or in underground schools.

아프간 여성

- cf **power-hungry** a 권력을 갈망하는
- cf **Hungary** n 헝가리

Democracy is wilting in Hungary.

heterogenous, homogeneous

- **heterogeneous** ⓐ 다른 종류로 이뤄진

Jack notes that in a heterogenous market like India, all other media, including TV and print, is segmented by language.

- **homogeneous** ⓐ 동종의

Politicians hoped an influx of foreign spectators would help prepare this homogenous society for the relaxed immigration laws necessary to address a severe low-skilled labor shortage.

- cf **homogenize** ⓥ 균질화하다, 통일하다

They are trying to mix in a culture that is famously homogenized, orderly and keenly aware of its unwelcoming past.

시리아 난민의 독일 정착
its unwelcoming past :
히틀러의 만행

hone, honk

- **hone** ⓥ ① (칼 등을) 날카롭게 갈다 ② (기술을) 연마하다

Her competitiveness was honed in fierce board games with her parents and two older sisters.

- **honk** ⓥ (자동차의) 경적을 울리다

But in the predawn streets of the city, there are no honking cars, bustling markets, or even people.

harass, harness

- **harass** ⓥ (계속해서) 괴롭히다(harry)

It's been eight years since Jane says she was sexually harassed.

- **harness** ⓝ

① 마구(馬具)

② (사람 몸에 매는 마구 비슷한) 벨트 또는 용구

반려견도 harness 사용

One of his first tasks at the Doha Oasis construction site, the luxury residential and entertainment complex in downtown Doha that was his place of employment for six years, was in scaffolding — an assignment that required a heavy harness and a hard hat, which sent rivulets of sweat cascading down his body within minutes of going outside.

카타르 월드컵 공사 현장

scaffold ⓝ (건설 현장) 비계

- cf **harness** ⓥ 이용하다, 활용하다

But… that anger is actually being harnessed into something, which is going to create real change.

habit, habitat

• habit ⓝ

① 습관

Friends explained that the man was in the habit of swallowing slugs to relieve his arthritic joint pain.

② (수도사·수녀가 입는) 의복

ⓓ habituation ⓝ 습관화

Thanks to a growing population and a high level of habituation to humans, visitors have a good chance of spotting the elusive animals inside the National Park(the second most popular park in the country with more than 300,000 visitors per year) or on privately owned ranch-land surrounding the park.

puma에 관한 내용

ⓓ riding habit : (여성용) 승마복

• habitat ⓝ 서식지

Much of their traditional habitat has been turned over to rubber plantations.

hot air, hot spot

• hot air

① 뜨거운 열기

When Jack's massive cargo plane landed, the doors opened and a gush of hot air rushed over the evacuees.

Jack : 아프간을 탈출하는 아프간인

② 허풍(empty talk)

He dismissed the theory as a load of hot air.

• hot spot

① 분쟁 발생 가능 지역

The Korean Peninsula has been a hot spot for decades.

② '와이파이 통신을 통해 인터넷을 할 수 있는 구역'을 말한다

A : This problem precedes the current moment?

B : In the past, before COVID, because there's no access, do you know many of these communities were putting hot spots on school buses and parking them in their community?

this problem : 와이파이 (wi-fi)가 안되는 것
current moment : COVID-19

initial, initiative

- initial ⓐ 처음의, 초기의

the $540 million initial cost of the project

- initiative ⓝ 주도권

An initiative documenting incidents against Asian Americans and Pacific Islanders, Stop AAPI Hate, received more than 2,800 reports of racism and discrimination from March 19 to Dec. 31.

AAPI : Asian American and Pacific Islander

ICU, IUD, DUI

- ICU ⓝ 중환자실(intensive care unit)

ICU doctors

- IUD ⓝ 자궁 안 피임 기구(intrauterine device)

uterus ⓝ 자궁
uterine ⓐ

- DUI(driving under the influence) ⓝ 음주운전

He was arrested for DUI.

interfere, intervene

- interfere ⓥ 참견하다(where you are not wanted or needed)

interference ⓝ

Both generals of these two warring sides had been warned in no uncertain terms, do not interfere.

- intervene ⓥ (상황 개선을 돕기 위해) 개입하다

intervention ⓝ

After a series of short hospital stays, former U.S. President Jimmy Carter today decided to spend his remaining time at home with his family and receive hospice care instead of additional medical intervention.

cf intervening ⓐ (두 사건·날짜·사물 등의) 사이에 오는(있는)

In the intervening years, Jack had revolutionized the travel industry.

irony, ivory

- irony ⓝ 아이러니, 역설

We have to see the irony in taking down a statue of slave owner and replacing it with work by an artist whose ancestors have benefited from slavery.

- ivory ⓝ

① (코끼리) 상아

② 아이보리색

irrigate, irritate

- **irrigate** ⓥ 관개하다(to supply land or crops with water)   irrigation ⓝ

Do not go out to check rice paddies for irrigation.

- **irritate** ⓥ 신경 쓰게 한다(annoyed, impatient)   irritation ⓝ

While larger particles may irritate your eyes, nose and throat, smaller particles pose an even greater threat.

inter, intra

- **inter** ⓥ 매장하다(to bury a dead person)   interment ⓝ

cf **inter** ⓟᵣₑ 사이의, 상호 간의

Following his election to the presidency in 2017, Moon has made dramatic moves with regard to North Korea : hosting Kim Jong Un's sister at the Winter Olympics, agreeing to an inter-Korean summit and brokering what could be a first-ever US-North Korea summit between President Trump and Kim.

cf **disinter** ⓥ 시신을 꺼내다

But in 2015, the Pentagon instructed the caskets be disinterred, and the exhumation took place that year.

- **intra** ⓟᵣₑ 안에, 내부(안쪽)에의 뜻   pref는 접두사

intrastate commerce   주내(intrastate)에서의 상업

icon, idol, scion

- **icon** ⓝ 아이콘   iconic ⓐ

And so the leader of more than 50 million South Koreans began belting out one of the most iconic American songs of the modern age to the delight of a crowd of diplomats and celebrities cheering him on.   윤석열 대통령의 백악관 만찬

cf **iconoclastic** ⓐ 우상 파괴적인

Kahlo channeled this turmoil into breathtaking, iconoclastic art.   Kahlo : 멕시코 국민 화가

- **idol** ⓝ 우상(someone or something that you love or admire very much)

cf **idolatrous** ⓐ 우상을 숭배하는

Rioting Huguenots damaged parts of the building they believed to be idolatrous in the mid-16th century.   파리 Notre Dame 대성당

- **scion** ⓝ 명문가의 자손(a young member of a famous or important family)

Park may be the nation's first female President, but she has always been more a dynastic scion than trailblazing feminist.   박근혜 대통령

idea, ideal

- **idea** ⓝ 아이디어

Macron has repeatedly floated the idea of the EU's developing armed forces to feasibly mobilize in battle.

Macron : 프랑스 대통령

⒞ have no idea : 모른다

In 2006, he was acquitted of raping a woman in a case that revealed he had no idea how AIDS was transmitted in a country battling an HIV epidemic.

- **ideal** ⓝ 이상

The West has long seen Hong Kong, where English is widely spoken and Western ideals embraced, as "a catalyst of democratic values" in China, as President Clinton put it in 1993.

⒞ ideal ⓐ 이상적인

Experiments show that the traditional onggi pots "breathe" carbon dioxide to create ideal conditions for probiotic microbes to thrive.

김치 기사

inhabit, inhibit

- **inhabit** ⓥ (특정 지역에) 살다, 거주하다

Google released street view images of the DMZ for the first time this week, offering a rare glimpse into the flora and fauna that inhabit this no man's land.

한반도의 DMZ

⒞ inhabitant ⓝ 거주민

inhibition ⓝ

- **inhibit** ⓥ 못하게 하다, 억제하다

Its leaves and roots inhibit the growth of other species, creating a mono-thicket that spreads rapidly.

isle, islet

- **isle** ⓝ (문학적인 표현) 섬

A rising China, meanwhile, is more assertively pursuing what it considers its birthright : a Monroe Doctrine-like sway over nearly the entire South China Sea and indisputable sovereignty over its sprinkling of reefs, rocks and isles.

- **islet** ⓝ 아주 작은 섬(a very small island)

A leisurely stroll around the second smallest islet of the Spratlys — a scattering of rocks, reefs, shoals and island flung across the South China Sea — takes just minutes.

Spratlys : 남사군도

incubate, intubate

- **incubate** ⓥ 알을 품다, 배양하다

As HYBE has evolved, it has grown from a small artist incubator — Bang handpicked the seven performers of BTS from around Korea — into what he calls "360-degree business," in the mode of brands like Disney that own and operate a catalog of intellectual properties (IPs).

incubation ⓝ

HYBE : 방시혁(BTS의 총감독)의 연예기획사

- **intubate** ⓥ (의료) (기관 내에) 삽관술을 하다

After she was intubated and spent four days on a ventilator, she went home to rest for less than two weeks before returning to work.

intubation ⓝ

inmate, innate

- **inmate** ⓝ 수감자, 재소자

According to his family, Jack has lost more than 50 lb. subsisting on the prison's diet of uncooked chicken and raw pasta, meals his former prison inmates have claimed are mixed with feces.

- **innate** ⓐ 타고난, 선천적인(inherent)

Children have an innate ability to learn language.

inchoate, incoherent

- **inchoate** ⓐ 이제 시작단계인

Just the inchoate resentment of British voters who felt cheated and estranged from the European project

영국의 Brexit 문장은 아님

- **incoherent** ⓐ 앞뒤가 안 맞는 말을 하는, 일관성이 없는

After his detainment, Jack remained in an agitated state, which included speaking, yelling and making incoherent noises.

inappropriate, misappropriate

- **inappropriate** ⓐ 부적절한

His comments were wholly inappropriate on such a solemn occasion.

- **misappropriate** ⓥ (특히 공금을) 멋대로 사용하다

Lee had to apologize after his son was caught gambling illegally, and has faced allegations that he illegally hired a provincial government employee to serve as his wife's personal assistant, who then misappropriated state funds via his corporate credit card.

Lee : 이재명

inherent, inherit

- inherent ⓐ 내재하는　　　　　　　　　　　　　　　　inherence ⓝ

We all want to live the life of a decent human being with inherent dignity.

- inherit ⓥ 상속받다, 물려받다　　　　　　　　　　　　inheritance ⓝ

So South Korea's next President will inherit a deepening crisis with an irascible dictator on one side and a geopolitical neophyte on the other.

문재인 대통령

incite, indict

- incite ⓥ 선동하다　　　　　　　　　　　　　　　　incitement ⓝ

In addition, the Supreme Court has placed Jack under investigation for inciting the violence, a charge he denies.

- indict ⓥ 기소하다　　　　　　　　　　　　　　　　indictment ⓝ

When officers are indicted, convictions are rare.

미국 경찰이야기

interlock, interlude

- interlock ⓥ 서로 맞물리다

Mr. Yoon's pursuit of diplomacy in tandem with the Biden administration collides with the reality of South Korea's interlocking trade ties with China, said Jack, a senior analyst at the Sejong Institute, a think tank in South Korea.

- interlude ⓝ (연극·영화 등의 중간) 막간

Each night is a marathon of sharp dance choreography, music — video interludes and indoor pyrotechnics — all backgrounded, of course, by the roars of screaming fans.

BTS

impassable, impasse

- impassable ⓐ 통행할 수 없는

Around 15 cities and 280 towns felt the quake, and several roads were rendered impassable.

- impasse ⓝ 교착상태

If the US is serious about reaching a diplomatic solution to the Korean impasse, it may well have to stomach a nuclear Pyongyang.

stomach ⓥ 참다, 견디다

impassive, impressive

- **impassive** ⓐ 감정이 없는

Her face is impassive, with the slightest hint of a smirk.

- **impressive** ⓐ 인상적인, 감명 깊은　　　　　　　　　　　　　　　impression ⓝ 인상, 감명

Ethiopia wrestled down its mortality rates for children under five by two-thirds from 1990 to 2012 — an impressive feat for a low-income nation.

infest, infidelity

- **infest** ⓥ 들끓다, 우글거리다

However, people typically are not affected by swimming in waters infested with red tide.

- **infidelity** ⓝ (배우자나 애인에 대한) 부정　　　　　　　　　　　　영국의 찰스와 다이애나비

But infidelity would intrude on both sides, and the ability to maintain the pretense of marriage for the sake of appearances became impossible.

ⓓ **infidel** ⓐ 다른 종교를 믿는

The spokesman made no mention of the peace talks, but Taliban delegates there have refused to recognize the U.S.-backed Afghan government's legitimacy to negotiate, calling it an infidel foreign puppet.

implicate, imply

- **implicate** ⓥ (죄나 범죄에) 연루되었음을 보여주다　　　　　　　implication ⓝ

He and others implicated in the investigation all deny having anything to do with the murders.

- **imply** ⓥ 암시하다　　　　　　　　　　　　　　　　　　　　　implication ⓝ

What does this history teach us for the current coronavirus epidemic? First, it implies that you cannot protect yourself by permanently closing your borders.

impart, impartial

- **impart** ⓥ 주다, 전달하다 (a particular quality to something)　　impartment ⓝ

Those are among the lessons I think he would have liked to impart to all Americans.

- **impartial** ⓐ 공정한, 공평한　　　　　　　　　　　　　　　　　partial ⓪⑨

We offer impartial advice on tax and insurance.

inculcate, inoculate

- inculcate ⓥ (사상 따위를) 심어주다   inculcation ⓝ

The North Korean regime has inculcated every strata of society with the need of nuclear weapons to keep them safe and complete the revolution in the South.

- inoculate ⓥ 예방주사를 놓다, 접종하다   inoculation ⓝ

The Javits Center had become a key hub of a New York City vaccination effort inoculating close to 100,000 people a day.

inundate, inured

- inundate ⓥ 감당 못할 정도로 주다   inundation ⓝ

So many Cubans wanted to leave the country that in 1980, Castro, in a typical fit of pique at the US, let 125,000 of them inundate Florida in the Mariel boatlift — a move that helped sweep Jimmy Carter from the White House.

Castro : 쿠바의 일인자
Carter : 미국 대통령

- inured ⓐ 익숙한, 단련된

Nurses soon become inured to the sight of suffering.

implacable, implausible

- implacable ⓐ 달랠 수 없는   placable ⟺ placate ⓥ

Supporters of the bill must deal with a powerful religious lobby implacably opposed to greater freedoms for the LGBTQ community.

차별금지법

- implausible ⓐ 믿기 어려운   plausible ⟺

Implausible is the adjective which best befits the Babe.

Babe : 전설적인 미국의 육상선수이자 골프 선수

ill-conceived, ill-equipped, ill-gotten

- ill-conceived ⓐ 계획이 잘못된

The policy was ill-conceived and misguided.

- ill-equipped ⓐ 장비를 제대로 갖추지 않는

Chronic underfunding of the health system over decades has also left hospitals ill-equipped to deal with the surge.

코로나 사태

- ill-gotten ⓐ 부정하게 얻은

The rebel has pledged to get out of the cocaine-smuggling business, help the army locate and destroy land mines, apologize to its victims and use some of the organization's ill-gotten earnings to compensate them.

impeachment, impediment

- **impeachment** ⓝ 탄핵

But with impeachment proceedings imminent, that's merely an offer to jump the moment before she is pushed.

- **impediment** ⓝ 장애

It's China's only province without 4G cell-phone coverage, which, say officials, has been deliberately held up to impede the download of jihad propaganda.

impeach ⓥ
탄핵 직전에 물러나겠겠다는 박근혜 대통령

impede ⓥ
위구르 신장 지역

impinge, impish

- **impinge** ⓥ 나쁜 영향을 미치다

Jack was determined that the tragedy would impinge as litte as possible on his son's life.

- **impish** ⓐ 장난의(mischievous)

He captivated audiences with his ability to inject both deep pathos and impish humor into a repertoire spanning jazz, folk, and even chain-gang chants.

impingement ⓝ

imp ⓝ a mischievous child
He : Harry Belafonte(가수, 인권운동가)

impracticable, impractical

- **impracticable** ⓐ 실행 불가능한

It was an appealing plan but quite impracticable.

- **impractical** ⓐ 터무니없는, 비현실적인

In response to these developments, some in Hong Kong are calling for an impractical solution : the territory's independence.

practicable ⓐ

practical ⓐ

imperil, imperial

- **imperil** ⓥ 위험에 빠뜨리게 하다(endanger)

The toxic fumes imperiled the lives of the trapped miners.

- **imperial** ⓐ 제국의

She railed against capitalism and imperialism.

imperil : im + peril
imperilment ⓝ

imperialism ⓝ 제국주의

imperious, impervious

- imperious ⓐ 고압적인

Less than a third of South Koreans view him favourably. Though many dislike his policies, especially on education and the economy, they loathe the imperious way he presents them.

him : 윤석열 대통령

- impervious ⓐ 영향을 받지 않는

The material for this coat is supposed to be impervious to rain.

impending, imposing

- impending ⓐ 곧 닥칠, 임박한

She had a sense of impending disaster.

- imposing ⓐ 인상적인

an imposing 17th-century manor house

cf impose ⓥ 부과하다, 강요하다

That same year, 2019, Japan imposed restrictions on exporting chemicals essential to South Korea's semiconductor industry. Seoul filed a complaint against Tokyo with the World Trade Organization.

cf imposition ⓝ 부과, 강요

Those who oppose equal rights for women in Afghanistan may claim this agenda is a Western imposition.

impertinent, imperturbability

- impertinent ⓐ 무례한, 버릇없는(insolent rudeness)

Father Jack got up, exchanged words with the impertinent young man, and returned to his seat.

pertinent ⓐ 관련 있는

- imperturbable ⓐ 차분한, 쉽게 동요하지 않는(remaining calm and unworried)

I'm not guaranteeing you bulletproof imperturbability, but short daily doses of meditation can make you meaningfully less likely to do things you will later regret.

imperturbability ⓝ
명상

cf perturb ⓥ (심리적으로) 동요하게 하다

Initially, he was perturbed by the fact that the front door was not aligned with the center of the entrance hall.

improbable, impromptu

- **improbable** ⓐ 사실일 것 같지 않은(not likely to happen)

Jack's tragic murder and the injustice of the case galvanized a national civil rights movement, one led by Asian Americans, with Detroit as its improbable epicenter.   Jack : Detroit 자동차 공장 직원

- **impromptu** ⓐ (사전 준비 없이) 즉흥적인(extemporaneous)

She capped our interview in the city's hulking Metropolitan Government Building with an impromptu tour of the rooftop view gallery, where tourists browsed caps and tees emblazoned with the Tokyo 2020 emblem.   She : 도쿄 도지사

improvise, extemporize, extemporaneous

- **improvise** ⓥ (준비 없이) 즉석에서 처리하다(forced to do this by unexpected events)

IED(사제폭탄) : improvised explosive device

- **extemporize** ⓥ (연주나 연설 등을) 즉흥적으로 하다

A good talk show host has to be able to extemporize the interviews when things don't go as planned.

cf **extemporaneous** ⓐ (사전 준비 없이) 즉석에서

Trump has gone his own way, extemporaneously threatening "fire and fury like the world has never seen," while also tweeting an inchoate mix of insults and offers of friendship at Kim.   김정은

intense, intensive

- **intense** ⓐ 극심한, 강렬한(having a very strong effect or felt very strongly)

But efforts to come to terms with the brutalities from one of the bloodiest wars in modern history have triggered intense emotions in both the United States and South Korea.   베트남전 양민 학살

cf **intensity** ⓝ 강렬함   intensify ⓥ

But numerous studies have shown that virtually any amount of physical activity, done at any intensity, can help prevent chronic disease, boost longevity and improve mental health.

- **intensive** ⓐ 집중적인(a lot of activity, effort, or careful attention in a short period)   intensiveness ⓝ

That process has proved to be incredibly energy-intensive.

ignoble, ignominious

- **ignoble** ⓐ 비열한 (base)(not deserving respect; not noble or honorable)

Torturing the House Republican leadership and holding the GOP agenda hostage has become an ignoble strategy for these rabble rousers.

- **ignominious** ⓐ 불명예스러운 (public disgrace or shame)

Such was the fear of ignominy that only one patient, a 32-year-old named Jack, agreed to be photographed with Diana, and only on condition that the picture be taken from behind.

noble ⓟ
rabble rouser ⓝ 대중 선동가
ignominy ⓝ
one patient : AIDS 환자
Diana : (영국) 다이애나 왕세자 비

incalculable, incurable

- **incalculable** ⓐ 헤아릴 수 없는, 막대한

Her contribution to our work is incalculable.

- **incurable** ⓐ 치료 불가능한

Jack was diagnosed with a degenerative, incurable spinal cord condition in 2019.

calculate ⓥ
cure ⓥ

incarcerate, incantation, incarnate

- **incantation** ⓝ (마술을 걸기 위한) 주문

Two women lose all control as they approach the Dalai Lama's throne and are carried away shaking in rapture, clutching prayer beads and muttering incantations.

- **incarcerate** ⓥ 감금하다

For instance, millions of formerly incarcerated people in states like Alabama have lost the right to vote and are therefore shut out of the democratic process.

- **carceral** ⓐ 감옥의

Jack worked tirelessly to challenge the violence of the carceral state

- **incarnation** ⓝ 생애

The Dalai Lama is considered a living Buddha of compassion, a reincarnation of the bodhisattva Chenrezig, who renounced Nirvana in order to help mankind.

incarceration ⓝ

reincarnation ⓝ 환생
bodhisattva ⓝ (불교) 보살
Nirvana ⓝ (불교) 열반

irascible, ire

- irascible ⓐ 화를 잘 내는

There had been on official dialogue between North and South since 2013, and caught between an irascible dictator and a geopolitical neophyte, Moon feared the worst : "We were actually on the brink of war."

- ire ⓝ 노여움, 분노(wrath)

Demonstrators are now increasingly directing their ire at the mainland, taking to the streets in sneakers and black clothing to call for the end of China's Communist Party. — 홍콩사태

indigenous, indignant, indignity

- indignant ⓐ 분개하는

Melville was so struck by the drama of the Essex (deliberately battered by an indignant and maddened whale, which at last brained itself by sinking the ship) that he used it as the end of Moby-Dick. — Melville : Moby-Dick의 작가

- indigenous ⓐ 토착의, 본래부터 있어 온(native)

Air strikes on nuclear facilities, coupled with cyberattacks and perhaps commando raids, could do some damage, but since the program is now entirely indigenous, it could be repaired soon enough. — 북핵

- indignity ⓝ 수모, 모욕

Conditions for the team have vastly improved since the 1990s, and US Soccer has invested far more in women's soccer than most other countries. But plenty of indignities linger. — 미국 여자 축구

install, instate

- install ⓥ 설치하다 — installation ⓝ

The village well, installed by an NGO a decade ago, had dried up, and women and children trekked almost a mile to fetch water from a stream for their daily needs.

- instate ⓥ 사람을 임명시키다, 취임시키다 — instatement ⓝ

The response to the removal of Colston's statue has been to ask : Whom do we put there instead? There's currently a petition to instate a statue of a Black person. — 노예 상인(slave trader) 동상 제거

jug, jut

- jug ⓝ 주전자, 항아리 (a large deep container)

a milk jug

a jug of water

- jut ⓥ 내밀다, 돌출시키다

The President turned to the handful of senior advisers and jutted out his chin in what aides have come to recognize as a sign that he's about to say something provocative. — 트럼프

jet lag, jetway

- jet lag ⓝ 시차로 인한 피로 — jet-lagged ⓐ

But for now, at least, they may need sleep. "I'm still trying to get over my jet lag," deadpans Suga, one of the group's three rappers.

- jetway ⓝ (항공기의) 이동식 탑승교

When the passengers filed off the jetway, ~.

jangle, jingle

- jangle ⓥ

① 쨍그랑거리다 (typically a discordant one)

Jack stood on the terrace jangling his keys.

② (신경에) 거슬리게 하다

a forty-eight point game that jangled the nerves

- jingle ⓥ (듣기 좋게) 딸랑거리다 (a light metallic ringing sound) — 크리스마스 캐롤 징글벨

What to Consider: The large metal zippers tend to jingle constantly, which can become annoying.

jungle, jumble

- jungle ⓝ 정글

Without a university education, or fear, she headed into the jungle with a notebook, sat atop a grassy knoll or climbed a tree, and waited. — 침팬지의 대모 제인 구달

ⓓ jungle gym ⓝ 정글짐

Occasionally he uses the jungle gym in his local park to do pull-ups.

- jumble ⓝ 뒤섞임, 뒤죽박죽

The two young Asian women dissolved seamlessly into this jumble. — 국제공항에서 김정남 암살범

jubilation, jubilee

- **jubilation** ⓝ 환호

As word spread, so did jubilation, shock, religious awe and anger.

cf **jubilant** ⓐ 승리에 젖어있는, 자축하는

His wife shared his jubilant reaction video on TikTok, and it has been viewed more than 7 million times.

- **jubilee** ⓝ 기념일

cf **platinum jubilee** : 70주년

However it proceeds, it has already thrown a shadow over the Queen's platinum jubilee — her 70-year anniversary on the British throne.

> word : 노예해방 소식
>
> golden jubilee : 50주년
> silver jubilee : 25주년
> platinum : 백금

jiggle, juggle

- **jiggle** ⓥ (아래위·양 옆으로 빠르게) 움직이다(흔들다)

She jiggled the handle of the pram to make the baby stop crying.

- **juggle** ⓥ

① 저글링 하다(공 같은 물건을 세 개 이상 들고 공중으로 던져 가며 다양한 묘기를 보이다)

② (두 가지 이상의 일을 동시에) 곡예하듯 하다

Russia juggles a shrinking economy, an aggressive military and an expanding role in the Middle East.

jaw, maw, paw

- **jaw** ⓝ 턱

When you're a rabbit caught in the jaws of a lion, going limp at least gives you a chance of survival.

cf **jaw-dropping** ⓐ 입을 떡 벌리게 만드는(being surprised)

Maradona netted that most jaw-dropping goal in World Cup history minutes after scoring the most controversial one.

- **maw** ⓝ (뭐든지 집어삼킬 듯 쩍 벌어진 동물의) 구멍(an animal's mouth or throat)

He felt the maw heavy and slippery in his hands and he slit it open.

- **paw** ⓝ (동물의 발톱 달린) 발(an animal's foot that has nails or claws)

The cat sits on the floor in the room's middle, calmly licking one paw.

jump-start, kick-start

- jump-start ⓥ

① (차의 배터리가 다 됐을 때) 다른 차의 배터리에 연결시켜 시동을 걸다

② …의 시작에 많은 힘을 기울이다(rapidly or forcefully)

He has tried to increase the housing supply and jump-start the economy.

cf. jump cable(jump lead)로 시동을 거는 것

- kick-start(v)

① (오토바이처럼 발로 힘껏 밟는) 시동을 걸다

② 촉진시키다

Her words resonated. Today, Seo's interview is widely credited with kick-starting South Korea's own #MeToo movement, triggering a wave of women speaking out against film directors, actors, a poet and others.

Seo : 서지현 검사

ajar, jar, jarring

- ajar ⓐⓓⓥ 문이 반쯤 열린

In 2019 the palace announced the prince was stepping back for the foreseeable future, leaving the door ajar for his return.

- jar ⓝ (잼이나 꿀을 담아두는) 병

Even more revolutionary was his vision for a diversified namesake brand; Cardin licensed his name on everything from fragrances and furniture to pickle jars and car interiors.

- jarring ⓐ 혼란스럽다, 충격적이다

But his lightning ascent has also been jarring.

jaunty, jumpy

- jaunty ⓐ 의기양양한, 쾌활한(confident, happy)

There was a jaunty red scarf around her neck, pinned with a large jeweled brooch.

- jumpy ⓐ 조마조마한(worried or nervous)

The gun salute had started nearby, and the dogs in the park were jumpy.

knock out, knockout

- knock out ⓥ 패배시키다, 뿌리 뽑다(to damage something so that it does not work)

But four months later, after national election brought in a new government that won largely on a campaign to knock out corruption, work in the village has begun in earnest. 　　다이아몬드 채굴

- knockout ⓝ 뿅 가게 만드는 엄청 멋진 것(혹은 사람)

Her dress was a knockout.

knee, kneel, knell

- knee ⓝ 무릎

Those who take a knee in Tokyo may face the same sanctions as US sprinters Smith and Carlos, who were expelled from the 1968 Mexico Olympics for raising a fist on the podium to protest racism. 　　take a knee : 저항의 표시로 한쪽 무릎을 꿇다

- kneel ⓥ 무릎을 꿇다

Every night for 20 years, Jack knelt beside his three daughters' beds and whispered an incantation.

- knell ⓝ 조종(because someone has died)

For more than half a century, observers have been pronouncing the end of Hong Kong — most recently, US Secretary of State Pompeo, who on May 22 called the national-security law a "death knell" for the city.

kite, kitten

- kite ⓝ ① 연 ② 솔개

Einstein proved, by flying a kite, that lightning is electricity, and he invented a rod to tame it. 　　fly a kite : to tell people about an idea, plan etc in order to get their opinion

- kitten ⓝ 새끼 고양이(kitty)
- kittenish ⓐ 아양을 부리는, 교태를 부리는

In unguarded moments, the usually austere Queen was, in the words of one observer, "kittenish" when interacting with her husband. 　　엘리자베스 여왕

kennel, kernel

- kennel ⓝ 개집
- kernel ⓝ ① (견과류·씨앗의) 알맹이 ② (사상·주제의) 핵심(알맹이)(core)

I didn't realize what I'd done until I looked down to see my feet surrounded by stray kernels.

ABCDEFGHIJK
L
외신으로 보는
대한민국
VOCABULARY

MNOPQRSTUVWXYZ

lockdown, lockstep

- **lockdown** ⓝ 봉쇄

If you discover 100 coronavirus cases in your country, would you immediately lock down entire cities and regions?

- **lockstep** ⓝ 발을 맞추어 걷기

A joint statement agreed "to coordinate our approaches to the DPRK in lockstep.

DPRK : democratic people's republic of Korea(북한)
한미대통령 정상회담 후 공동성명

loyal, royal

- **loyal** ⓐ 충성스러운, 충실한

But some experts say the law could be used against candidates who do not demonstrate loyalty to Beijing, since anyone convicted under the new legislation will be barred from office.

loyalty ⓝ
홍콩 보안법

- **royal** ⓐ 왕의

Being a royal is not easy. There is still something of the medieval court about royal life, but Markle will catch on quickly.

영국 왕자 Harry의 약혼
Markle : 해리의 약혼자

ⓓ royalty ⓝ (책의) 인세, (음악 작품 등의) 저작권 사용료

ludicrous, lugubrious

- **ludicrous** ⓐ 터무니없는(completely unreasonable, stupid, or wrong)

Some of this censorship is trivial, some is ludicrous, and some is breathtaking in its power to dumb down what children learn in school.

- **lugubrious** ⓐ 과장된(exaggeratedly or affectedly)

Too often, performances of this selection are lugubrious and heavy.

lascivious, luscious

- **lascivious** ⓐ 음탕한(lewd)

Jack was jailed on three counts of lewd and lascivious behavior.

- **luscious** ⓐ

① (음식) 감미로운

This vegan pumpkin pie recipe is every bit as silky and luscious as a traditional slice.

② 섹시한 (very sexually attractive)

He'll fall for a luscious Spanish girl who can match him in passion.

lewd, lurid

- lewd ⓐ 음탕한

But currently, Miss Jane has her hands full asking people not to post insulting rhetoric and lewd propositions.

have one's hands full : 바쁘다

- lurid ⓐ 충격적인, 끔찍한

Convictions found commonly among Americans are described in this memo with lurid alarm.

liquid, liquidation

- liquid ⓝ 액체(a substance that is not a solid or a gas, for example water or milk)

Add a little more liquid to the sauce.

- liquidation ⓝ 청산(서로 간에 채무·채권 관계를 셈하여 깨끗이 해결함)

Thomas Cook collapsed into liquidation on Sept. 23, having failed to secure the $1.37 billion it needed to stay afloat.

leech, lurch

- leech ⓝ 거머리

The family began to see him as a leech.

- lurch ⓥ (갑자기) 휘청거리다

China's recent history has lurched from quasi-colonization to devastating war and then collectivized economic turmoil, poverty and political strife.

limelight, limestone

- limelight ⓝ 집중 조명(spotlight)

Whether performing in rock concerts or starring in a kung fu movie, Jack Ma has always relished the limelight.

- limestone ⓝ (광물) 석회석

legacy, legend

- legacy ⓝ 유산

Moon is so invested in rapprochement and consumed by a waning legacy that he has lost support from those who put him in power in the first place.

남북관계가 좋아지지 않는 상황

- legend ⓝ 전설

She orchestrated a funeral based on Lincoln's that gave a ritual and pageantry, cementing her husband's legend.

She : 암살당한 케네디 대통령 부인

lore, lure

- **lore** ⓝ 전승적인 지식, 구전(by words of mouth)

Her winning goal in the semifinal against Canada — a header seconds before time expired — has become soccer lore.

ⓓ **folklore** ⓝ 민속(the traditional stories, customs etc of a particular area or country)

- **lure** ⓥ 유혹하다

He believes Paris should try to lure British financial institutions after Brexit.

He : Macron

lift, list

- **lift** ⓥ

① (다른 위치로 옮기기 위해) 들어 올리다, 들어 올려 옮기다

But the time they are lifted from the sea, they are, at least, once again human beings.

② (제재를) 풀다(해제/폐지하다)

Mr. Yoon said that with Japan moving to lift the export restrictions on important technology, and with Japanese and Korean tourists visiting each other's countries, "mutual benefit will be significant, and that is national interest to me."

ⓓ lift : (영국 영어) 엘리베이트(elevator)

지중해에서 구조된 아프리카 난민

- **list** ⓥ

① 배가 기울다

Jack, the man elected four years ago to right a listing economy ship, can hope~.

② 상장하다

Initially founded as Big Hit Entertainment in 2005 by musical mastermind Bang Si-hyuk, the company listed publicly on the Korean exchange in 2020 as HYBE ; it's valued at $9.5 billion today.

livid, vivid

- **livid** ⓐ 매우 화가 난(extremely angry)

Trump had grown livid as he watched Canadian Prime Minister Trudeau declare that the new US trade tariffs were unfair.

- **vivid** ⓐ 생생한

I look at the calendar in my neighbourhood in suburban Nara, and almost every event seems to speak for an agrarian, long-ago Japan that hovers around us as vividly as my late father-in-law does.

Nara : 일본의 나라 지방

landscape, moonscape, seascape

- landscape ⓝ 풍경

The entrepreneur, who supplements his income with a variety of off-farm business, says drought has always been a part of the landscape.

- moonscape ⓝ ① 달의 표면 모습 ② 황량한 지역

More than 4,450 air-strikes by the US-led military coalition and others have left its streets a moonscape of shattered buildings and mountains of detritus.

- seascape ⓝ 바다 경치

Trade brought the continents together and created a seascape around the Pacific basin that included places like Acapulco, Manila and the coast of California.

미국의 아시아와의 교역

ladder, lard, larder

- ladder ⓝ 사다리

He who would climb the ladder must begin at the bottom.

천 리 길도 한 걸음부터

- lard ⓝ 라드(돼지비계를 정제하여 하얗게 굳힌 것. 요리에 이용함)

My husband, not wanting to waste any pork, started experimenting with soap and the lard.

- larder ⓝ 식품저장소(for storing food in a house, pantry)

So it was with armored fighting vehicles, with France and Germany opening up their larders once the Biden administration signaled in January that it would send Bradleys.

larder는 비유적 표현

Bradley : 장갑차

laboratory, lavatory

- laboratory ⓝ 실험실(lab)

Indians gasping for breath are being turned away from overwhelmed hospitals, sometimes simply because they don't have lab reports confirming COVID-19 infection.

- lavatory ⓝ 화장실, 변기

Last May, a woman gave birth to a healthy baby boy in a lavatory on board a Frontier Airlines flight from Denver to Colorado, with assistance from a flight attendant.

lull, lullaby

- lull ⓝ (활동 사이의) 잠잠한 시기, 소강상태

On March 13, weeks after the US and the Taliban signed a peace agreement, Kabul-based photographer Jack and his colleagues took advantage of the lull in fighting to visit insurgents in the eastern province.

cf lull ⓥ 달래다, 안심시키다

But don't let the jobs boom lull you into a false sense of employment security.

- lullaby ⓝ 자장가

It's taught to Korean children from a young age and is sung as a lullaby, in festivals, on holidays and during moments of grief.

log, logo

- log ⓝ ① 통나무 ② (항해·비행 등의) 일지(기록)

According to rescue logs made later, each boat was stuffed well beyond capacity ; none was up to the rigors of the open sea.

the rigors : 혹독함
(the problems and difficulties of a situation)

cf log ⓥ (나무를) 베다

Logging and flooding had damaged North Korean land, while urban development and pollution had fragmented habitats in South Korea.

- logo ⓝ 로고

The kids ran up the pitch dressed in a mix of traditional tunics and flashy donated jackets and sneakers stamped with American logos.

미국으로 이주한 아프칸 난민 아이들

limb, limbo, limp

- limb ⓝ (하나의) 팔, 다리

Criminals had limbs amputated and cauterized in boiling butter.

cf torso ⓝ (팔, 다리를 포함하지 않는) 몸통

- limbo ⓝ (다른 사람의 결정을 기다리는) 불확실한 상태

Doctors across the country are caught in legal limbo about how to advise patients.

미국에서 낙태가 불법이 된 대법원 판결 이후의 상황

- limp ⓐ 힘없는 (not firm or strong)

a limp handshake

limply ⓐⓥ

facelift, powerlift, uplift

'lift'의 '올라가다'에서 유추하면 됨

- facelift ⓝ 주름살 제거 수술
- powerlifting ⓝ 역도

For many, the phrase *physical activity* conjures sweaty runs or powerlifting sessions at the gym.

- uplift ⓥ 업되다(to improve the spiritual, social, or intellectual condition of)

Hope in Somalia has always been a fragile thing, uplifted by the waves of refugees who have returned to make something of their homeland after decades of civil war and deflated by the attacks from terrorist groups.

loop, loophole

- loop ⓝ (올가미나 동그라미 모양의) 고리
- ⓓ in the loop : (중요한 일을 다루는) 핵심(중추)의 일원인, 특정한 문제에 대해 잘 아는

No one in the loop — including, almost surely, the man himself — was sure he would really do it.

- ⓓ out of the loop : 특정한 문제에 대해 잘 모르는

He claims that he was kept out of the loop when the decision to sell the company was being made.

- loophole ⓝ (법률이나 계약서 등에서) 빠져나갈 구멍

China and Russia, which have sought to make the North a more useful partner in their rivalry with the United States, have become loopholes in enforcing the U.N. ban, helping the North earn badly needed cash as it deals with the fallout of international sanctions and the pandemic.

liter, litter

- liter ⓝ 리터

The product will be sold by the liter, retailing at $20.

- ⓓ milliliter ⓝ 밀리리터(1/1,000 리터)

milli~ : 1/1,000

- litter ⓥ 흩어져 어지럽히다(scattered in an untidy way)

Its outskirts were littered with mines.

MN

외신으로 보는
대한민국
VOCABULARY

mangle, mingle

• mangle ⓥ 짓이기다, 심하게 훼손하다

Mr Yoon is, to mangle a handy Korean phrase, getting his clothes soaked in a drizzle of unforced errors.

가랑비에 옷이 젖는다는 우리 속담을 비꼰 내용

• mingle ⓥ 섞다, 어우러지다

Some people may have thought that, having been prevented from mingling with other humans for a period, folks would greet the return of social activity with hugs, revelry and fellowship.

mislead, misread

• mislead ⓥ 호도하다, 오도하다(잘못 인도하다)

On June 16, exactly a week before the referendum, the noisy, rancorous and often misleading campaign for the country to leave the EU nearly fell apart.

영국의 EU 탈퇴

• misread ⓥ 잘못 읽다, 오해하다

The issue of nukes turns Trump's potential misreading of the peninsula into a matter of life and death for each of them, and millions more.

북핵

mediate, meditate

• mediate ⓥ 중재하다

The posting underscores Beijing's determination to mediate issues on the Korean Peninsula.

mediation ⓝ

ⓒf mediator ⓝ 중재자(intermediary)

• meditate ⓥ 깊이 생각하다

Meditation can help in the era of angry politics.

meditation ⓝ 명상

ⓒf meditative ⓐ 깊은 생각에 잠긴

Those abstract paintings have a stillness that draws the viewer in with an almost meditative quality, often with soft colors and a three-dimensional look.

medicine, medication

- medicine ⓝ 약

If a medicine is taken again too soon, it may undo all the good that has been done.

- medication ⓝ 약물치료

I take three different allergy medications just to share a home with her.   her : 반려견

medical, medicinal

- medical ⓐ 의학의, 의학적인

He was denied medical care for bronchitis, a kidney stone and pneumonia.

- medicinal ⓐ 약효가 있는 (having healing properites)

medicinal sea cucumbers

cf sea cucumber : 해삼

mussel, muzzle

- mussel ⓝ 홍합
- muzzle ⓝ

① (개나 말의) 주둥이 부분

② (개의) 입마개

③ (총) 총구

mantle, mental

- mantle ⓝ ① 망토 ② 역할, 책임

He has donned the mantle of modernizer, associating himself with a decree ending a ban on women drivers.

cf don the mantle of something : 중요 직책을 맡다

cf dismantle ⓥ 분해하다, 해체하다   dismantlement ⓝ

For North Korea, it has always been about dismantling the US-East Asian   it : 비핵화
alliance system, removing American troops from South Korea and Japan and dismantling the US "nuclear umbrella."

- mental ⓐ 정신의

But numerous studies have shown that virtually any amount of physical activity, done at any intensity, can help prevent chronic disease, boost longevity and improve mental health.

mass, landmass, massive

• mass ⓝ 대규모, 다중

mass arrests

America was formed from huddled masses yearning to breathe free.

㏅ mass ⓥ 집결하다

He's referring to the Russian troops who have massed along that border during the past two weeks, forcing the world to guess at the intentions of President Putin.

• landmass ⓝ 광활한 땅덩어리

The shoal has been transformed into a 680-acre (275 hectare) landmass, one of seven artificial islands the Chinese have constructed in the South China Sea since 2014.

• massive ⓐ 대규모의

The massive $10.8 billion base in Pyeongtaek is America's largest overseas military base as a more than decade-long expansion project draws to an end.

mess, morass

• mess ⓝ 엉망인 상황

Two weeks ago, Jack, a former professor of constitution law who had clearly decided he'd seen enough of Tunisia's political mess, fired Prime Minister Jane and suspended parliament for 30 days.

㏅ mess ⓥ 엉망으로 되다

If life wanted to mess with you, it couldn't have come up with a better way than death.

㏅ messy ⓐ 엉망인

The road to democracy is often messy.

• morass ⓝ ① 늪 ② 난국(빠져나가기 어려운 상황)

Lee's hopes appear to rest on the liberal voters' consolidating behind him in response, on ordinary people's seeing through the morass to focus on the issues that truly matter, and on his promise that he has the vision and track record to push real change.

Lee : 이재명

in response : 윤석열 대통령과 안철수 단일화 여파

mean, means

• **mean** ⓥ

① 의미하다

This means it is out of range of most of North Korea's conventional artillery installations — though the distance hasn't halted threats.　　　This : 평택 미군기지

② 의도하다

Closer to home, China's leaders mean for their country to tighten control of Hong Kong, to pressure Taiwan to stop resisting Beijing's push for unification with the mainland, and to build military strength in the South China Sea.　　　Closer to home : 속내는

ⓓ **mean** ⓐ 인색한, 친절하지 못한 (cruel, not kind)

Meditation is by no means a cure-all for our era of mean tweets and mindless tribalism.

ⓓ **mean** ⓝ ① 평균 ② 방법

Abe wants very much to amend Article Nine of Japan's constitution — which repudiates war as a mean to resolve global disputes — to affirm once and for all Japan's right to maintain a military.　　　Abe : 일본 총리

ⓓ **meaningful** ⓐ 의미있는

Without more data we cannot make a meaningful comparison of the two systems.

• **means** ⓝ 수단, 방법

Before long, and by dishonest means, he gets every member of his family employed in the Park household.　　　영화 기생충

moderate, modest

• **moderate** ⓥ 완화하다, 누그러뜨리다　　　moderation ⓝ

In their eyes, if internet companies didn't moderate any content, then terrible things could happen.

• **modest** ⓐ (크기·가격·중요성 등이) 그다지 대단하지는 않은, 보통의

There was no internet on board, and the amenities were modest.　　　대통령 전용 기차

metabolism, metastasize

- **metabolism** ⓝ 신진대사

China is, of course, big enough to metabolize a few white elephants.

cf white elephant : 막상 많은 돈을 들여 설치했으나 유용하지도 않고 유지비용도 부담이 됨. 그렇다고 철거하기도 쉽지 않을 때 쓰는 표현(a property requiring much care and expense and yielding little profit)

- **metastasize** ⓥ (의학 용어) 전이하다

Some outsiders wonder whether the nation's lack of introspection could cause militarism to metastasize again.

metabolize ⓥ

metastasis ⓝ
일본의 과거사 반성

mandate, mandatory

- **mandate** ⓥ 명령하다, 지시하다

All able-bodied men in South Korea are mandated to start 21 months of military service before age 28.

- **mandatory** ⓐ 법에 정해진, 의무적인

But organizers will not yet explain entry requirements for Japan, whether vaccinations will be mandatory, how many spectators allowed into stadia.

2021년 도쿄올림픽

morbid, moribund

- **morbid** ⓐ 병적인(of, relating to disease)

He is also, at 32, relatively young, morbidly obese, possibly addicted to opioids and possessed of a really bad haircut.

- **moribund** ⓐ 빈사 상태의, 죽음 직전의(being in the state of dying)

Millions of tons of poured concrete and smelted steel encouraged banks to lend and helped jump-start a moribund economy.

cf 메멘토 모리(Memento mori) : "자신의 죽음을 기억하라"를 뜻하는 라틴어

He : 김정은

'mori'의 흔적

matchmaking, matchup

- **matchmaking** ⓝ 중매

The matchmaking service Shaadi.com stopped letting users sort by skin tone.

- **matchup** ⓝ 대결

Many experts and voters had predicted a Macron-Le Pen matchup in next year's presidential second-round runoff.

프랑스 선거

memorialize, memorize

• **memorialize** ⓥ 기념하다, 추모하다

His life has already been memorialized by the party he leads.

• **memorize** ⓥ 암기하다

Why would a father ask his ever-expanding brood of what became 11 children to memorize a poem about war and slaughter?

memorialization ⓝ

memorization ⓝ

가정교육

manhandle, mishandle

• **manhandle** ⓥ 사람을 거칠게 다루다

We were spat on, sworn at, and manhandled.

• **mishandle** ⓥ 잘못 처리하다

Now, anger has mounted over his mishandling of the COVID-19 pandemic (he dubbed it a "psychosis" that could be cured by vodka).

misfire, surefire

• **misfire** ⓥ 제대로 점화되지 않다

Nerve cells misfire, leading waves with daytime temperatures of 38°C to 39°C turn deadly when humidity exceeds 50%.

• **surefire** ⓐ 확실한, 틀림없는

A former artist himself, nicknamed Hitman for his surefire musical instincts, Bang is thoughtful and earnest in his answers — even as he is bold in his goals.

misfire ⓝ

지구 온난화

Bang : BTS 감독 방시혁

militant, militia

• **militant** ⓝ 투사(to use strong or violent action to achieve political or social change)

Schools are a prime target of militants in the Sahel.

cf **militant** ⓐ 투쟁적인

Six of those who died there were members of the Palestinian militant group, which emerged in the city last year.

• **militia** ⓝ 민병대, 의용대

It was here where the last ISIS fighters staged their final stand as the city they once styled as their capital was recaptured in October by an alliance of Syrian militias backed by US airpower.

mutual, mutate

- mutual ⓐ 상호의, 서로의

The meeting is historic, even if they have little in common beyond a mutual need for regional stability and a shared antipathy toward Iran.

mutuality ⓝ

- mutate ⓥ 돌연변이가 되다

Simple organisms like bacteria mutate rapidly.

mutation ⓝ

major, minor

- major ⓐ 주요한, 중대한

Few recalled major rifts between their parents.

cf major ⓝ ① (군대) 소령 ② (음악) 장조 ③ 전공

- minor ⓐ 경미한, 작은, 가벼운

a relatively minor error

cf minor ⓝ ① 미성년자 ② (음악) 단조 ③ 부전공

majority, minority

- majority ⓝ 대다수

A majority of singles reported being eager to be off the market — the sooner, the better.

cf off the market : 임자가 있는, 연애 중인

cf majoritarian ⓐ 다수결주의의

The voices of women and minorities were being systematically drowned out by the majoritarian politics of the regime.

cf silent majority : 침묵하는 다수

He also pulled off a strategic victory by calling for surprise regional elections on Dec.21, paralyzing the *independistas* and emboldening the so-called silent majority in Catalonia that favors staying in Spain.

분리 독립문제로 시끄러운 스페인의 카탈로니아

- minority ⓝ 소수, 소수집단

A minority is even calling for Japan to develop its own nuclear weapons.

maximum, maximize

- maximization ⓝ 최대화함

A corporation's main goal is the maximization of profit.

maximize ⓥ 최대화하다

- maximum ⓝ 최대

The car has a maximum speed of 120 mph.

miniature, minimum

- miniature ⓐ 아주 작은, 축소된
- ⓓ miniaturize ⓥ 소형화하다

Worse, unlike in earlier tests the bomb was described as a "nuclear device," which suggests the North is moving closer to being able to miniaturize a nuclear weapon and put it in a missile. 북핵

- minimum ⓝ 최소한도

At a minimum, Western governments should impose targeted sanctions against military officials for human-rights abuses.

- ⓓ minimize ⓥ 최소화하다

More important, it is in minimizing the resulting human misery—and in investing in the future of other developing countries to minimize the risk of future conflicts—that the UN plays its crucial role.

- ⓓ minimal ⓝ 아주 적은, 최소

If we don't keep that curve flat, and try to keep the critical cases down to a minimal, we're going to get to a point where we just don't have enough resources. 코로나

mound, mount

- mound ⓝ 흙더미, 언덕

Gyeongju's abundant archaeological sites include temple and palace ruins and nobility burial mounds.

- mount ⓥ (강도가) 증가하다

On June 8, as pressure mounted, France announced a ban choke-hold arrest tactics.

mechanical, methodical

- mechanical ⓐ 기계로 작동되는

Perhaps more worrisome, a 2010 survey estimated that the US had just 62,000 mechanical ventilators-breathing assistance machines required to treat severe cases of COVID-19.

- methodical ⓐ 체계적인

In a recent cartoon, the daily *Berliner Zeitung* depicted the Chancellor as a shapeless amoeba, methodically swallowing and digesting its prey.

muddle, muffle

- muddle ⓝ 혼란, 엉망진창, 뒤죽박죽

There was one winner from this muddle : Jack of the center-right Les Republicains has emerged as a serious challenger for President's next year.

- muffle ⓥ 소리를 죽이다, 소리를 약하게 하다

"I now have freedom. Freedom is the only thing that matters," she says between muffled sobs. — 아프간 탈출 난민

cf muffler ⓝ 머플러

mob, mobster

- mob ⓝ 군중, 무리

Jurors began hearing attorneys' opening statements for the trial more than two years after members of the far-right extremist group joined a pro-Trump mob in storming the U.S. Capitol on Jan. 6, 2021.

cf mob ⓥ (사람 주위로) 떼지어 몰려들다

His agent says that when he goes out in Seoul, he wears a cap and a surgical mask—commonly worn here when people are sick—to avoid being mobbed by fans. — His : 손흥민

- mobster ⓝ 조직 폭력배

The mobster threatened to break his legs if he didn't pay up.

module, modulate, mold

- module ⓝ 모듈(과정이 분할된 이수 단위)

They went to a high school with an open-module system, which meant that sometimes they went to class only two days a week.

- modulate ⓥ (목소리의 크기·강도 등을) 조절하다(바꾸다) — modulation ⓝ

Additionally, fluctuating levels of testosterone, estrogens and progesterone can modulate brain function in adults.

- mold ⓝ 곰팡이(mould) — moldy ⓐ

Some of the bread was moldy, the rest was dirty, but the mothers still ran to the wheelbarrow, grabbed the slices of bread, and dusted them off to feed their children. — 피난민 상황

mute, mutter

- mute ⓐ 말 없는

mute ⓥ 소리 죽이다

For instance, one of the stories is based on a mute character called Jane who is a young mother with mental health challenges.

- mutter ⓥ 중얼거리다

Two women lose all control as they approach the Dalai Lama's throne and are carried away shaking in rapture, clutching prayer beads and muttering incantations.

marrow, mellow

- marrow ⓝ (의학) 골수(bone marrow)
- mellow ⓥ (연륜을 쌓으면서, 술이 들어가면서) 부드러워지다

After five years in power, there are no signs that the mercurial and corpulent Kim is mellowing.

Kim : 김정은

mercenary, mercurial

- mercenary ⓝ 용병

They sometimes clash, as when Turkey shot down a Russian fighter jet in 2015, or when Russian mercenaries attacked US Marines last year near a gas plant in Syria.

- mercurial

mercury ⓝ

① 수은이 함유된

② 변덕스러운

Rather rely on a mercurial US President, Seoul recognizes that it must be proactive in determining what happens on the Korean Peninsula.

marital, martial

- marital ⓐ 결혼의

Marital rape isn't a crime in India, one of three dozen countries — including Bangladesh, Iran, Nigeria, and Libya — where it's still legal for a man to have nonconsensual sex with his wife.

부부강간

- martial ⓐ 싸움의, 전쟁의

Throughout her 12 years in office, she has shown a martial artist's touch for turning the strengths of her opponents against them.

독일 여성 총리

them : 나치를 연상시키는 행동들

cf martial art(무술), martial law(계엄령)

malinger, malice

- malinger ⓥ 꾀병을 부리다

But when workers take advantage of the manager's kindly nature to malinger or disrupt operations, the entire business is threatened.

- malice ⓝ 악의　　　　　　　　　　　　　　　　　　　malicious ⓐ

His father, Jack, was convicted on eight counts, but found not guilty of malice murder.

cf malice murder : 고의 살인(done with express or implied malice)

mobile, mobilize

- mobile ⓐ 이동하는　　　　　　　　　　　　　　　　　mobility ⓝ

To be a young Hong Kong person today is to face falling incomes, unaffordable housing and diminishing upward mobility, which used to be astonishingly rapid.

cf mobile phone ⓝ 휴대폰

cf automobile ⓝ 자동차　　　　　　　　　　　　　　　automotive ⓐ

the automobile industry

- mobilize ⓥ　　　　　　　　　　　　　　　　　　　　mobilization ⓝ

① (군대를) 동원하다

The past year has demonstrated that a mobilized army is no match against a mobilized society.

우크라이나-러시아 전쟁
the past year : 전쟁 발발 연도(2022년)

② (물자·수단 등을) 동원하다

To mobilize the kind of response that's needed, you not only need to get the attention of governments, you have to get the attention of the public.

가뭄으로 고생하는 아프리카

metrics, meteoric

- metric ⓐ 미터법의, 미터법으로 측정된

cf metrics ⓝ 메트릭스(업무 수행 결과를 보여주는 계량적 분석)　　meter ⓝ

This new strategy means using different metrics as the basis for COVID-19 restrictions.

- meteoric ⓐ 일약(happening very suddenly and quickly)

She held the position for only a brief period, resigning in June after further electoral losses, but her meteoric rise made her one of the most visible politicians in South Korea.

She : 박지현(민주당 비상대책위원장을 역임했던 정치인)

marine, maritime

- marine ⓐ 바다의

As of now, nobody knows for sure how the oil spill will affect the abundant marine life living on the rig itself.

- maritime ⓐ 바다의

The Commander of the US Navy's 7th Fleet, which is based on Japan, oversees America's largest forward-deployed maritime force.

marine ⓝ 해병대
submarine ⓝ 잠수함

rig ⓝ 석유 등의 굴착 장치

mode, model

- mode ⓝ 방식(a particular way or style of behaving, living, or doing something)

Nor did companies drilling for undersea oil create noise pollution everywhere, making life increasingly difficult for social creatures whose sense of hearing is their primary mode of communication.

- model ⓝ 모델

This model is no longer sustainable.

cf model ⓥ 모방하다, 따라하다(be modeled on)

The new cooperation agreement is closely modeled on how NATO nations plan for possible nuclear conflict,.

윤석열 대통령과 미국 대통령 사이의 워싱턴 선언

magnanimous, magnificent, magnify

- magnanimous ⓐ 도량이 넓은(kind and generous)

a magnanimous donation to the town's animal shelter

- magnificent ⓐ 참으로 아름다운, 훌륭한

Many of readers said that the sky was so magnificent that their photos couldn't do it justice.

- magnify ⓥ 확대하다

Her decision, magnified by a global spotlight, created a rare opportunity to move the discussion from raising awareness to taking action.

magnifying glass(확대경)

maize, maze

발음이 같음

- maize ⓝ 옥수수 (corn)
- maze ⓝ 미로(a puzzle through which one has to find a way, labyrinth)

For the past year, Time has been following Jack and his family as they navigate the bewildering maze of the European asylum system in search of a home.

중동 난민(Jack)의 유럽 정착
Time : 잡지 이름

melt, smelt

- **melt** ⓥ (열 때문에 액체가 되도록) 녹다

In India, where crematoriums have been burning so long that their metal structures have started to melt   코로나로 사망자가 늘어나 감당하기 힘든 화장장

ⓓ crematorium ⓝ 화장장   cremate ⓥ 화장하다

ⓓ meltdown ⓝ

① 원자로 노심의 용융(유독 방사능 유출로 이어지는 심각한 사고)

② (경제의) 어려움(badly affected by a lot of problems within a short period of time)

Angry protesters camp out in the Sri Lankan presidential palace in Colombo on July 11 following months of demonstrations over the country's economic meltdown amid soaring food and fuel prices.

- **smelt** ⓥ (광석을) 제련하다

ⓓ steel smelter ⓝ 용광로

Increasing numbers of Chinese engineers, crane operators and steel smelters stand to reap the benefits of maturing projects.

margin, marshal

- **margin** ⓝ (시간·득표 수 등의) 차이

Gallup polled 5,167 adults online between Feb. 21 and 28, with an error margin of +/- 2%.   error margin : 오차 범위

ⓓ marginal ⓐ 미미한, 중요하지 않은

A common theory holds that summer vacation was created for farm kids who needed to work. That's only marginally true. : students at rural schools did get time off for harvests, but those breaks fell in the spring and the fall.   여름방학 기원

ⓓ marginalize ⓥ 하찮은 기분이 들다, 소외되다

But Xinjiang is also China's most volatile region, prone to convulsions of strife from a predominantly ethnic Uighur Muslim population that feels marginalized and persecuted under Beijing's rule.

- **marshal** ⓥ (특정 목적을 위해 사람·사물·생각 등을) 모으다(결집시키다)   marshall도 씀

But instead of marshalling global unity against Tehran's malign activities, Trump abandoned the nuclear agreement the UN reported Iran had been adhering to.

moon, moot

- **moon** ⓥ

① 엉덩이를 보이면서 놀리다, 비웃다

Jack, meanwhile, makes a statement by pulling down his leather and denim trousers to moon the audience.

② 멍청하게 시간을 보내다(to spend in idle reverie)

I don't want her mooning about in the morning.

- **moot** ⓐ (가능성이 적으므로) 고려할 가치가 없는

The question is no longer whether his own principles have been sacrificed in pursuit of reconciliation, but whether any success is rendered moot. 　남북관계
　his : 문재인 대통령

cf **moot** ⓥ (의견 등을) 제기하다(move)

That such a plan could even be mooted reflects the fact that, again, Trump does not understand the cure.

million, millennial

- **million**(수사)　　　　　　　　　　　　　　　　　　　수사(數詞) : 사물의 수량을 나타내는 품사

① 수많은

There were a million reasons to say no, and~.

② 백만

Yet the Spanish state refuses to formally notify the European Parliament of my election in Catalonia in May, ignoring the will of more than a million voters.

- **millennial** ⓐ 1980년대 혹은 1990년대 생인

She became a Hail Mary candidate for Prime Minister, a millennial woman thrown into an election at the last minute to resurrect the fortunes of her slumping party in a Pacific Island nation of 4.8 million people.　뉴질랜드

cf **millennium** ⓝ 천년(a period of 1,000 years)　　　　　　　millennia(pl)

people who have inhabited this land for millennia

nebulous, nefarious

- nebulous ⓐ 애매모호하다

The revolutionary guerrilla Kim Il Sung seized power in 1948 and built the state ideology around the nebulous concept of juche, which is loosely defined as ultra-nationalist self-reliance.

- nefarious ⓐ 범죄의, 비도덕적인

TCM's resurgence has spawned unregulated quackery that, in turn, is related to an uptick in wildlife trafficking — a nefarious global trade that, the UN says, already generates $19 billion a year.

TCM : Traditional Chinese Medicine
중국의 야생동물 불법거래

needle, noodle

- needle ⓝ 바늘

a needle in a haystack : 건초 더미에서 바늘 찾기(거의 불가능한 일)

- noodle ⓝ 국수

Biden and Xi have spent considerable time together, including eating at a noodle shop in Beijing in 2011, when both were Vice Presidents.

ⓓ noodle ⓥ 즉흥적으로 악기를 연주하다

He noodles around, testing out chords and muttering softly to himself, silver hoop earrings glinting in the light.

navel, novel

- navel ⓝ 배꼽(belly button), 중간

a city that likes to regard itself as the nation's navel of art and culture

- novel ⓐ 신기한, 새로운

The novel coronavirus was spreading beyond mainland China, and all three were hit early.

novelty ⓝ
novel ⓝ 소설
all three : 홍콩, 대만, 싱가포르

nonage, nonbinary

- nonage ⓝ 미성년, 미성숙

The short stories of the novelist's nonage have only recently been discovered by scholars.

- nonbinary ⓝ 제3의 성(이분법적인 성별에 속하지 아니한 사람)

an effort to create more equality for nonbinary and transgender students across campus

non+binary(두 부분으로 이루어진)

nuance, nuisance

- nuance ⓝ 뉘앙스, 미묘한 차이

On those, her voice was luscious, pure and full of nuance.

cf. luscious ⓐ 섹시한(very sexually attractive)

- nuisance ⓝ 성가신 것, 귀찮은 것

This April, nine leaders of the Umbrella Movement were charged with "public nuisance" offenses.

홍콩의 민주화 운동

nevertheless, nonetheless

동의어

- nevertheless ⓐⓓⓥ 그렇기는 하지만, 그럼에도 불구하고

Nevertheless, resistance to equal opportunities and fair pay for female athletes remained strong.

- nonetheless ⓐⓓⓥ 그렇기는 하지만, 그럼에도 불구하고

But the demonstrators are nonetheless bracing for a lethal blow as the government's patience wears thin.

nada, nadir

- nada ⓝ 아무것도 아닌 것(nothing)

"No gasoline, no water, no nada" says Jack, driving through a San Juan that looks as though it's been raked.

강력한 태풍 후의 풍경
San Juan : 푸에르토리코 수도
마지막 'no'는 강조 용법

- nadir ⓝ 최악의 순간

He is also eager to promote a "two-track strategy" to restore relations with Japan, which reached a nadir during the Moon administration because of South Korea's pressing the Japanese on human-rights abuses during World War II.

He : 이재명

nibble, nimble

- nibble ⓥ 조금씩 먹다

This is for dark chocolate lovers and people who prefer to nibble on chocolate, which is not me.

- nimble ⓐ 빠른, 민첩한(agile)

The Indiana Chamber of Commerce, which historically has sided with Republicans, has been vocal about its opposition to bills that would limit Indiana businesses' ability to be nimble.

normalcy, normality

- normalcy ⓝ 정상 상태

Finding a semblance of normalcy became harder for Jack and his brother after their parents divorced.

- normality ⓝ 정상 상태

When does a pandemic end? Is it when life regains a semblance of normality?

동의어

normal, abnormal

- normal ⓐ 정상적인, 평범한, 보통의

Wuhan strives to return to normal, but coronavirus scars run deep.

- abnormal ⓐ 비정상적인, 기형의

Now she is seeking re-election on Oct. 17 in a campaign that's showing how some political normality can endure an abnormal time.

Wuhan : coronavirus 진원지

she : Arden 뉴질랜드 총리

abnormal time : 코로나 정국

negligence, negotiate

- negligence ⓝ 부주의, 태만

Most of the officers were accused of contributing to the deaths through negligence of official duty or fabricating or trying to destroy official documents that may include criminal evidence.

- negotiate ⓥ (힘든 부분을) 통과하다, 넘다

To take a train at the Urumqi's railway station requires negotiating four ranks of X-ray machines and metal detectors.

negligent ⓐ
neglect ⓥ
이태원 사고

negotiation ⓝ
우루무치 : 중국 신장 자치구의 도시

nozzle, nuzzle

- nozzle ⓝ 노즐, 분사구(fitted to the end of a hose, pipe etc)

He twisted the nozzle of the shower head.

- nuzzle ⓥ (애정 표시로 코를) 비비다

Mother bears nuzzle muzzles with their cubs to demonstrate affection and strengthen bonds.

- nuzzle in : get involved

Sacrifice in the pursuit of excellence defined the Olympics long before politicians and sponsors nuzzled in.

두 단어 모두 코(nose)에서 유래

natural, nurture

- natural ⓐ ① 자연적인 ② 정상적인

ⓓ nature ⓝ 성질, 모습

The increasingly radical nature of the protests has not, as authorities expected, diminished their popular support.

ⓓ natural gas ⓝ 천연가스

The economic toll grew heavier when the pandemic forced down the global prices of oil and natural gas, vital Iranian exports

- nurture ⓥ 잘 자라도록 보살피다   nurtur ⓝ

Prime Minister Fumio Kishida of Japan arrived in Seoul to meet President Yoon Suk Yeol and to nurture a fledgling détente.

neuter, neutral

- neuter ⓥ 거세하다

She had her dog neutered by the veterinarian.

- neutral ⓐ ① 중립의 ② 영향이 없는   neutrality ⓝ

with an ambitious plan to make Iceland carbon neutral by 2040

naturalist, naturalize, neutralize

- naturalist ⓝ 동식물 연구가, 박물학자   박물 : 동물학, 식물학, 광물학, 지질학을 통칭하는 말

In the rest of the house, wooden shelves are crammed with books, figurines and photographs — souvenirs from Goodall's life as the world's best-known naturalist.   침팬지 박사 제인 구달 (Goodall)

- naturalize ⓥ (외국인을) 귀화시키다   naturalization ⓝ

After Korean-American pop star Yoo avoided military service by becoming a naturalized US citizen in 2002, he was banned from re-entering South Korea.   Yoo : 가수 유승준

ⓓ 'be naturalized'의 형식으로 씀

- neutralize ⓥ 무효화시키다 (to prevent something from having any effect)

The US and its allies have various motivations for engaging with Kim, but all would benefit from neutralizing a rogue nuclear state.

O

외신으로 보는
대한민국
VOCABULARY

omnipotent, omnipresent

omni~ : 모든 곳, 모든

- **omnipotent** ⓐ 전능한

potent ⓐ

For them, Putin was the guarantor of omnipotence, and they put tremendous pressure on him at that time to hold on to power.

them : 러시아 국민

ⓓ **impotent** ⓐ 무기력한

impotence ⓝ

A : How do you deal with your anger at people for not getting vaccinated?
B : Anger is a strong word. It's more frustration and the feeling of impotence over the situation

B : 코로나 전담 치료 의사

- **omnipresent** ⓐ 편재하는, 어디에나 있는

The omnipresent smoke may affect the flavors of fruit left on the vine.

포도밭 화재

order, ordor

- **order** ⓝ

order ⓥ

① (음식) 주문

A : But isn't ordering takeout unethical too?
B : I think you can still order ; just have the delivery person leave the food at the door and go.

코로나 상황에서 비대면 식사

② (종교) 교단

the Benedictine Order

③ (사회적) 질서

law and order : 법과 질서

④ 순서

He talked about the philosophy behind truth and reconciliation — about his deep belief that they have to happen in that order. Only after the truth has its way can a clenched fist become an open hand.

He : 남아프리카 공화국의 Tutu 신부

⑥ (야구) 타순

The middle of the order is particularly intimidating with stars like Paul Goldschmidt, Mike Trout, Nolan Arenado and Pete Alonso.

미국 야구대표팀

⑦ (동식물 분류상의) 목

ⓓ in order : 적당한, 알맞은(appropriate, suitable)

an apology is in order.

- **ordor** ⓝ 악취

ordour도 씀

Hikers eventually noticed a strange odor in the Santa Monica Mountains of Mulholland Highway on Oct. 3.

outage, outrage

- **outage** ⓝ 정전(power cut)

a power outage

- **outrage** ⓝ 분노

outrage ⓥ

When you're blinded by outrage, you're unable to understand the views of people with whom you disagree.

- cf **outrageous** ⓐ 아주 별난

She's known for her wild hairdos and outrageous costumes.

oppression, opprobrium

- **oppression** ⓝ 탄압

oppress ⓥ

There won't be stability if a peace agreement ushers in a new era of injustice and oppression of women.

- **opprobrium** ⓝ 맹비난

Others who manage to avoid service also meet with opprobrium. Nineties K-pop sensation Yoo Seung-jun was due to be drafted in 2002, but he renounced his citizenship just before his call up.

Yoo Seung-jun : 가수 유승준

overwhelm, underwhelm

- **overwhelm**

① (격한 감정) 압도하다(overcome)

Jack was overwhelmed by a feeling of homesickness.

② (너무 많은 일 등으로) 어쩔 줄 모르게 만들다

And the court system is so overwhelmed by appeals to asylum rejections that it is struggling to process legitimate deportation orders.

③ 이기다, 승리하다

In 1532 the Spaniards finally overwhelmed the armies of Peru.

- cf **overwhelming** ⓐ 압도적인

If North Korea attacks the US or its allies, the overwhelming response will mean the end of Kim's regime.

- **underwhelm** ⓥ 감명을 주지 못하다, 인상적이지 못하다

Xi continued to underwhelm in his next appointments in southern Fujian province, where he was tasked with attracting foreign investment to help fuel China's export-powered economic revival.

overstate, understate

- **overstate** ⓥ 과장해서 말하다 — overstatement ⓝ

It's no overstatement to call Jack the most influential African-American architect of his generation.

- **understate** ⓥ 축소해서 말하다 — understatement ⓝ

The press have tended to understate the extent of the problem.

outmaneuver, outnumber

- **outmaneuver** ⓥ (책략으로) 이기다

Although the Finns outmaneuvered the Soviets on land, they also outmaneuvered them with regard to time.

> out~ : ~보다 더 크다, 많다, 길다 등
> Finn : 핀란드 사람
> Finnish : 핀란드의
> fin : (생선) 지느러미

ⓓ **maneuver** ⓝ 묘책(a skilful or careful movement that you make)

With a quick maneuver, she avoided an accident.

- **outnumber** ⓥ 수적으로 우세하다

It reached the "dead cross," when deaths outnumbered births, in 2020, nearly a decade earlier than expected.

> 저출산의 대한민국

outride, override

> out~과 over~의 구별

- **outride** ⓥ 더 빠르다(to ride faster or further than someone else)

I can outride him on a bicycle.

- **override** ⓥ 무력화시키다

First, it would allow the Knesset, Israel's parliament, to override court decisions with a simple majority vote.

> it : 이스라엘 정부의 개혁안

ongoing, outgoing

- **ongoing** ⓐ 현재 진행 중인

He faces several ongoing corruption cases.

- **outgoing** ⓐ ⓐⓓⓥ

①외향적인, 사교적인

What I found very different about him than other Chinese leaders I met with was that he's much more outgoing and inquisitive.

> him : 시진핑

②(임기를 마치고) 떠나는(departing)

outgoing President Yeltsin shakes hands with his successor in 1999.

ⓓ **outgoings** ⓝ 정기적으로 나가는 지출

Before taking a loan out, calculate your monthly outgoings.

officer, official, officious

- officer

① 장교

We listened aghast to the story of a group of soldiers whose commanding officer orders them to ride into an ambush, knowing they will be slaughtered — yet they still obey the command.

'The charge of the light brigade'(영시)의 내용으로 용감함을 노래

② 경찰관(constable)

③ (고위) 공무원, 임원(in a position of authority in an organization)

- official ⓐ 공식적인

It wasn't until the middle of 1920 that the pandemic was finally over in many places, though there was no official declaration that the coast was clear.

1920년대 스페인 독감

ⓓ the coast is clear : 더 이상 붙잡히거나 들킬 위험이 없다

ⓓ official ⓝ (고위) 공무원, 임원(in a position of authority in an organization)

The contest had almost been canceled, as baseball officials planned to nix the whole thing out of deference to soldiers fighting in World War Ⅰ.

nix ⓥ 거부하다, 퇴짜 놓다

- officious ⓐ 거들먹거리는, 위세를 부리는(too eager to tell people what to do)

Officious doormen and security guards hold you up only to point the temperature gun at your coat sleeve.

코로나 방역

outlier, outlandish

- outlier ⓝ (통계) 특이값, 이상치

These efforts are really outliers, in part because they are completely going against the grain of the body language that both governments are sending to their people.

미국의 자선단체나 종교계의 북한 지원

ⓓ go against the grain : 자연스럽지 못하다

- outlandish ⓐ 이상한

The outlier was Psy, a South Korean rapper whose "Gangnam Style" became a viral hit in 2012, though his comic, outlandish persona was an unlikely (some critics argue, problematic) herald for the genre.

Psy : 가수 싸이

onset, outset

- **onset** ⓝ (좋지 않은 것의) 시작, 출발(bad, unpleasant)

the onset of winter | 겨울은 추우니까

- **outset** ⓝ 착수, 시작(start, beginning)

Key to successful coronavirus responses so far have been decisions to respond aggressively from the outset. | 언뜻 보면 have가 틀린 것 같은데, 문장이 도치되었다고 생각하면 have가 맞음

ⓓ **set out** : (일·과제 등에) 착수하다[나서다]

We might even be able to set out a plan to find the killers — and discover who they answered to. | answer to : 자신(the killers)의 행동에 대해 누구의 탓(who)이라고 말하다

out, outing, ouster

- **out** ⓐ 게이(gay)임을 밝힌

As an out gay woman who have overcome bullying, hate, and alienation, she has served as inspiration, especially to fellow members of the LGBTQ+community, for how to live out loud and proud.

- **ouster** ⓝ 추방 | oust ⓥ

Crowds estimated from 500,000 to 1,5 million have thronged central Seoul to demand Park's ouster. | 박근혜 대통령 탄핵 당시

- **outing** ⓝ

① (잠깐의) 외출, 소풍

During a quarantine outing to our local park this week, my toddler son ran around kicking his big red ball.

② (스포츠 대회) 출전

South Korean soccer's big outing on the world stage

overhead, overhear

- **overhead** ⓐ | overhead ⓐⓓ

① (비용) 간접비의

SOC(Social Overhead Capital) : 사회간접자본

② 머리 위의

An hour after the fire broke out, a helicopter hovered overhead.

- **overhear** ⓥ 우연히 엿듣다

I overheard part of their conversation.

ⓓ **eavesdrop** ⓥ 고의로 엿듣다 | eaves ⓝ (집) 처마

offline, online

- **offline** ⓐ 작동이 되지 않는

At the moment, 26 of the country's 56 reactors are offline for maintenance, either routine or a result of corrosion, leaving output at its lowest point since the 1990s.

ⓓ go offline : 작동되지 않는

Across Texas, natural gas pipelines ill equipped to handle winter weather went offline.

- **online** ⓐ (컴퓨터) 온라인의

ⓓ go online : 컴퓨터를 접속하여

Whenever I was feeling particularly low, which was often, I would go online and start looking for supplies and puppy toys.

offline은 컴퓨터 관련된 용어였으나 지금은 의미가 확장되어 보기와 같이 씀

outpost, outpouring

- **outpost** ⓝ 전초 기지

This craggy outpost on the South China Sea, home to 7.3 million people, is known as "Asia's World City" because of its cosmopolitan nature.

- **outpouring** ⓝ 분출, 터져 나옴.

Yet amid the outpouring of grief, questions will rumble louder about why King Charles Ⅲ should now be their head of state from a distance of thousands of miles.

this craggy outpost : 홍콩

grief : 영국 여왕의 죽음 카리브해(Caribbean)에 있는 바하마(Bahama)가 영연방이 되어야 함에 대한 의문

orient, disorientate, reorient

- **orient** ⓥ 자기 위치를 알다

The ceilings are marked with numbers and QR codes to help the robots orient themselves.

ⓓ Orient ⓝ 동양. Occident ⓝ 서양

- **disorient** ⓥ (…의 방향 감각을) 혼란시키다(disorientate)

The fact that his first year as Commander in Chief disoriented and distressed members of the media and political establishment is not a bug but a feature.

- **reorient** ⓥ 방향을 바꾸다(change the focus or direction of)

Our aim must be to reorient Kim's paranoia, making him fear losing an opportunity for security in the eyes of his own people more than he is afraid of dependence on China.

orientation ⓝ

Trump
not a bug but a feature : 버그가 아니라 본래 그런 의도야

북한

oversee, overseas

- **oversee** ⓥ 감독하다(supervise)

Much of my 33-year career was spent as a nuclear warrior — I later oversaw the U.S. intercontinental ballistic missile fleet and served as deputy commander of American military forces in the Pacific — experience that informs my deep alarm over the growing risk of nuclear conflict with North Korea.

cf **overseership** ⓝ 감독의 역할, 감독의 지위(the role or office of overseer)

The school was a hotbed of radical, sometimes violent ideas competing to reform Cuba's corrupt and chaotic society, which had only shaken off US overseership of the island a decade earlier.

cf **oversighht** ⓝ 감독

On March 12, the EU's executive body published a paper branding China a "systemic rival" and urging stronger oversight of its investment in Europe.

- **overseas** ⓐ 해외의

The safety and security of US citizens overseas is one of our highest priorities.

overtone, overture, overtures

- **overtone** ⓝ 함축

The choreography is often slow and ritualistic, and some scenes include tribal drums, adding an overtone of spiritualism.

cf **choreography** ⓝ 안무

- **overture** ⓝ (음악) 서곡
- **overtures** ⓝ 제안(proposal)

After the diplomatic overtures of recent years fell apart, Mr. Kim has only become more belligerent and the risk of conflict is more acute.

김정은

outlaw, outlay

- **outlaw** ⓥ 불법화하다

Indonesia is on the verge of outlawing all sexual intercourse outside marriage.

on the verge of ~ : ~하기 직전의

- **outlay** ⓥ 지출하다

Farmers have to outlay massive amounts of money at the beginning of the season to pay for everything.

'lay out'로 쓰이기도 함
outlay ⓝ 비용

outreach, overreach

- outreach ⓝ 팔을 뻗음(the extent or limit of reach)

Even after Mr. Trump's outreach to Mr. Kim collapsed in 2019, Mr. Kim indicated he was still open to diplomacy.

- overreach ⓥ (자신의 능력, 힘) 이상으로 하다

The Church overreached itself in securing a territory that would prove impossible to hold.

overreach oneself 형식

outbreak, outburst

- outbreak ⓝ 발병

break out의 변형

South Korea won plaudits abroad for stamping out an initial COVID-19 outbreak in February and keeping case numbers low without imposing harsh lockdowns.

- outburst ⓝ (특정 활동의) 급격한 증가

burst out의 변형

But his refusal to fully withdraw it, coupled with allegations of police brutality, triggered an even bigger outburst : organizers say some 2 million people marched the very next day.

홍콩 시위
his : 시위 주도자
it : 시위

outflank, out-flatter

- outflank(v)

① 측면(flank)에서 공격하다
② 앞지르다, 선수 치다(outwit)

That arrival of mercenaries in Mali is seen as Russia attempting to outflank the Americans in Africa.

- outflatter ⓥ (상대방보다 더) 듣기 좋은 말을 하다

In the case of Mr. Biden and Mr. Yoon, the two leaders were trying to out-flatter each other throughout the evening.

outtalk, out-touch

- outtalk ⓥ 보다 많이 말하다(outdo or overcome in talking)

She outtalked the prince and even stopped him short when he was about to let slip who introduced them.

She : prince 약혼자
them : 기자들

- out-touch ⓥ (수영에서) 먼저 도달하다

Singapore's Joseph Schooling out-touched Phelps for gold in the 100-m butterfly.

PQ

외신으로 보는
대한민국
VOCABULARY

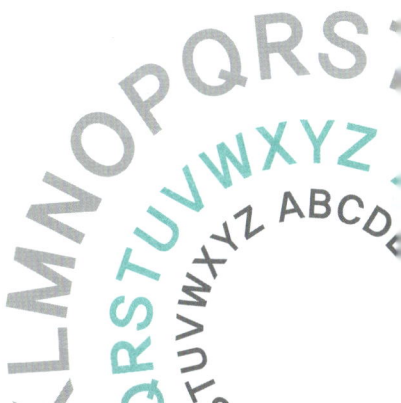

pertinacity, pertinent

- pertinacity ⓝ 끈덕짐

He continually astonished me by his powers of comprehension, his pertinacity and his industry.

- pertinent ⓐ 적절한

But there are so many sorts of things that are pertinent to his story today.

cf impertinent ⓐ 무례한, 버릇없는(cheeky)

pertinacious ⓐ
He : 달라이 라마

phenom, phenomenon

- phenom ⓝ 경이(驚異)(unusual because of a rare quality or ability that they have)

The pioneer in the women's snowboard slopestyle event congratulated the young phenom on her first-ever gold.

- phenomenon ⓝ 현상

South Korean philosopher and author Jack describes the passion of BTS's fandom as a phenomenon called "horizontality," a mutual exchange between artists and their fans.

경이로운 사람

peddle, puddle

- peddle ⓥ 팔러 다니다, 행상하다

people who peddle cigarettes to young children

- puddle ⓝ 물웅덩이(a small pool of liquid, especially rainwater)

The basement wasn't heated, but the air was hot from the hundreds of bodies. The walls remained cold and condensation from people breathing ran down them, so that the people by the walls sat in puddles.

우크라이나-러시아 전쟁 피난민 상황

pad, paddy

- pad ⓥ

① 조용히 걷다, 소리없이 걷다

I rose and padded silently into Mama and Papa's room.

② 패드를 대다(a soft material in order to protect it or make it more comfortable)

cf launchpad ⓝ 발사대

This was a primary launchpad for the Vietnam and where, on Aug. 7, seven B-1B bombers took off to fly sortie over the Korean Peninsula.

cf fad ⓝ (일시적) 유행(craze)

Interest in organic food is not a fad, it's here to stay.

padding ⓝ

this : 괌의 미군 기지

'for a day'의 줄임말

- paddy ⓝ 논

Military hardware aside, Camp Humphreys could be a suburban slice of Anytown USA laid over Pyeongtaek's rice paddies.

평택 미군기지

permanent, perma-smile

- permanent ⓐ 항구적인

Current Secretary-General Ban Ki-moon is most often accused of timidity and eagerness to please the permanent members — the US in particular.

perma~: 영구적인, 지속적인

cf permanent wave : 파마

cf impermanence ⓝ 덧없음, 일시성

But a time of national tumult, a felt sense of impermanence can also be deeply comforting.

명상

- perma-smile ⓝ (약물 등의 영향으로) 항구적인 미소

But four years of growing up in the spotlight have both hardened her exterior and made her willing to reveal what's going on behind the perma-smile.

permasmile 붙여쓰기도 함
올림픽 메달리스트

paradox, paragon

- paradox ⓝ 역설

It may seem a paradox that gun manufactures have suffered during the Trump era.

- paragon ⓝ 귀감, 모범

Lincoln did not bring about heaven on earth, nor does he stand as a paragon of equality and justice for all.

perk, perky

- perk ⓝ 특혜, 특전 (perguisite)

Researchers are only beginning to understand how singlehood affects health and happiness, and the solo life comes with surprising perks

본래의 의미는 봉급 외 차, 집 등의 특혜

- perky ⓐ 활기찬, 생기 넘치는

a perky salesgirl

peek, peep

- peek ⓥ 살짝 비치다

Then the sun peeks through the tall pines.

- peep ⓥ 훔쳐보다

his door was ajar and she couldn't resist peeping in.

plague, plaque

- plague ⓝ

① 전염병

We should therefore have expected to live in an infectious hell, with one deadly plague after another.

② 흑사병(black death)

ⓓ plague ⓥ 괴롭히다

Voters are demanding that whoever ends up in the presidential Blue House dismantle the rampant inequality that plagues South Korean society, a condition underscored by a series of scandals that emerged during the tenure of incumbent President Moon Jae-in, such as local officials using insider knowledge to speculate on property while housing prices soar.

우리나라 대통령 선거

- plaque ⓝ

① (이빨) 플라크

② 명판(名板: 사람·사건 등을 기려 이름과 날짜를 적어 벽에 붙여 놓은 물건)

On his desk was a plaque that read "The Buck Stops Here," a gift from President Biden when he came to Seoul in May.

his : 윤석열 대통령

pain, painstaking

- pain ⓝ 아픔, 고통

They can also be used to examine changes in a person's breasts, such as a new lump, pain and more.

painful ⓐ

ⓓ pains ⓝ 노력, 노고

My mom and dad went to great pains to make sure my upbringing was as "normal" — or at least similar to my nondisabled brother's — as possible.

my : 장애인

- painstaking ⓐ 공들인

Executing on such a policy will be a painstaking balancing act for Mr. Yoon. All of his recent predecessors have tried and failed to roll back the North's nuclear program.

such a policy : 북한의 위협에 맞서 미국과 일본과의 협력 강화

plait, plate

- plait ⓝ (머리나 밧줄을) 땋은 것 (braid)

Jane is keen on emphasizing that each plait is done by hand to call attention to the time and care put into these hairstyles.

- plate ⓝ

① 작은 접시 (a round or oval flat dish that is used to hold food)   platter ⓝ 큰접시

"I hated life," Kim, now 21, recalls over plates of pad thai in the airy four-bedroom home in the west side of Los Angeles she shares with her boyfriend, skateboarder Berle.   pad thai : 태국의 국수 요리

② (금속으로 된) 판

③ (자동차) 번호판

ⓓ plate ⓥ (철판 같은) 판을 두르다

At around 45 m.p.h., it's faster than older tanks and has specialized armor plating designed to withstand direct hits with antitank weapons.   it : (미국의) Abrams tank

protein, protean

- protein ⓝ 단백질

ⓓ fat ⓝ 지방, carbohydrate ⓝ 탄수화물

- protean ⓐ 변화무쌍한 (to change frequently or easily)

The global executive's leadership style will need to be protean, changing from situation to situation.

peal, peel

- peal ⓥ (종) 크게 울리다

Cheers of "God Save the Queen" filled the abbey as trumpets blared; outside, and across the British Empire, bells pealed and cannons roared.   엘리자베스 여왕 즉위 당시

- peel ⓥ 껍질을 벗기다, 벗겨지다

She got sunburned and her back is peeling.

periodic, periodical

- periodic ⓐ 주기적인

North Korea's relationship with the US has always been rooted in bitter acrimony, with its periodic threats of annihilating America sounding almost quaint, coming, as they do, from an impoverished nation of 25 million.

- periodical ⓝ 정기 간행물

prologue, prolong

- **prologue** ⓝ 프롤로그(연극·책 영화의 도입부)

The past is not always prologue, but history suggests that our divisions are as deep as they have been since Lincoln's time-and thus his experience repays consideration.

- **prolong** ⓥ 연장시키다

Now, months in, the prolonged mix of stress, anxiety, isolation and disrupted routines has left many feeling drained.

prostate, prostrate

- **prostate** ⓝ 전립선

Jack's doctor diagnosed his prostate cancer during a routine checkup in 2018, and he dedicated the last year of his life to spreading awareness about cancer screenings.

prostate cancer : 전립선암

- **prostrate** ⓐ 바닥에 엎드린

Jack then stood over the prostrate Tom and fired two more times into his head, prosecutors said.

prior, priority

- **prior** ⓐ 사전의

North Korea loathes Japan because of its colonization of the Korean Peninsula prior to World War Ⅱ.

- **priority** ⓝ 우선순위

I could afford to change our priorities in Latin America where the probability of hard combat was low.

ⓓ **prioritize** ⓥ 우선시하다

Investing in people's skills, putting gender equality at the forefront, and prioritizing energy security are the vital underlying conditions for enabling a just transition where everyone can thrive.

prioritization ⓝ 지구 온난화

pull-up, push-up

- **pull-up** ⓝ 턱걸이(chin-up)

Think sit-ups, pull-ups, push-ups, crunches or squats, as examples.

- **push-up** ⓝ 푸쉬업(엎드려 팔굽히기)

Norwegian wrestler Jack did push-ups with his baby on his back.

puppet, puppy

- **puppet** ⓝ 꼭두각시, 꼭두각시   puppeteer ⓝ puppet을 부리는 사람

But North Korea's founding father Kim Il Sung's guiding principle of juche, or patriotic self-reliance, meant that his nation would never be anyone's puppet.

- **puppy** ⓝ 강아지

Whenever I was feeling particularly low, which was often, I would go online and start looking for supplies and puppy toys.

propensity, prosperity

- **propensity** ⓝ 경향, 성향

Japan's history and propensity for severe seismic activity means disaster preparedness is treated with the utmost seriousness.

- **prosperity** ⓝ 번영, 번성   prosper ⓥ

American leadership is still seen as vital to the stability and prosperity of the entire region, the cockpit of the global economy.

personable, presentable

- **personable** ⓐ (잘생기고 성격이 좋아서) 매력적인

Jane's physicality on the court belies her more personable nature.   Jane : 운동선수

- **presentable** ⓐ (모습이) 남 앞에 내놓을 만한

We've gone beyond using leaves. It's about being clean and presentable and social and not smelling bad.   팬데믹(pandemic) 때 화장지 사재기(hoarding)

preclude, prelude

- **preclude** ⓥ 못하게 하다, 불가능하게 하다   preclusion ⓝ

The constitution of the US's other major regional partner, Japan, largely precludes it from taking an active role in security matters.

- **prelude** ⓝ (음악에서의) 서곡, 전주곡

All of that is a prelude to Kim's planned summit with Trump in May.   that : 김정은과 시진핑의 만남

PDA

- **PDA** ⓝ 개인정보단말기(Personal Digital Assistants)
- **PDA** ⓝ 공개적인 애정 표현(Public Display of Affection)

pamper, pepper

- **pamper** ⓥ 애지중지하다, 소중히 보살피다

The lapdogs were too small, too useless for any work, but ladies liked to pamper them.

- **pepper** ⓥ ① 후추를 뿌리다 ② 많은 양을 뿌리다

pepper ⓝ 후추

He had begun his daughters' education long before they were peppering Standford physicists with questions about nuclear particles.

He : Standford 대학교수

penetrate, perpetrate

- **penetrate** ⓥ 뚫고 들어가다, 관통하다

penetration ⓝ

If a dangerous virus manages to penetrate this border anywhere on earth, it puts the whole human species in danger.

- **perpetrate** ⓥ (나쁜 짓을) 저지르다

perpetration ⓝ
Me Too

Many end up denounced as "gold diggers", receiving a torrent of online abuses and even being countersued by alleged perpetrators of harassment or assault.

ⓓ perp-walk ⓝ 범죄인 포토라인 세우기

Since perp-walking his uncle out of a party meeting and having him shot soon after, Kim has been on a murder spree, executing more than 300 people, often in public with firing squads.

his uncle : 김정은의 고모부 장성택

pronounce, pronouncement, pronunciation

- **pronounce** ⓥ

① 표명하다

Jack was transported to Sharp Mercy Hospital, where he was later pronounced dead, according to the Sheriff's Department.

② 발음하다

There's even some confusion over how to pronounce his last name.

- **pronouncement** ⓝ 발표, 성명

His pronouncement caught the U.S. public health community, and even some administration officials, off guard.

- **pronunciation** ⓝ 발음

What is the correct pronunciation of his name?

pinch, punch

- pinch ⓥ (손가락으로) 꼬집다

The hit satirical-news puppet show *Les Guignol* depicted Hollande pinching the cheeks of his infant protégé, and cooing, "He's cute."

Hollande : 마크롱의 전임 대통령

- punch ⓝ 효과(a strong effective way of expressing things that makes people interested)

Kimchi has come into vogue as a superfood, due in part to the gut-healthy bacteria that help deliver its distinctive punch and sour taste.

cf punch ⓥ (주먹으로) 치다

History is clay and can be pummeled or punched, corralled or even caressed, into a whole new shape.

러시아를 개혁·개방으로 이끈 고르바초프의 관련 글

produce, productivity, production

- produce ⓝ 농산물

Instead, every morning at 1:30, Mr. Oonami, 73, wakes up and drives an hour to a fresh produce market on an islet in Tokyo Bay.

- production ⓝ

① 생산

② (영화 연극 등의) 제작

In February 2021, the movie was forced to halt production in Italy, days before its planned shoot in Venice, as the country contended with one of the highest COVID death rates in Europe.

- productivity ⓝ 생산성

It's in the middle — our 40s and 50s, when our power, potential and productivity are the greatest and we should be feeling our happiness — that life satisfaction bottoms out.

cf productive ⓐ 생산성 있는

More than 55% of the Ukraine's land area is "farmable," and it has some of the most productive soils on the globe.

patent, patient

- patent ⓝ 특허
- patient ⓝ 환자

inpatient : 입원환자
outpatient : 외래환자

parcel, particle

• parcel

① 소포, 꾸러미

The parcel was delivered last week.

② (땅의) 구획(a tract or plot of land)

The second parcel would be a coffee tenant with a 2,200-square-foot building, 41 parking spaces and a single drive-thru lane.

• particle ⓝ ① (아주 작은) 입자(조각) ② (물리) 미립자

The dangers of air pollution are sharply felt in South Korea, where masks are a common line of defense on days when fine dust particles form a gray haze in the sky. — 미세먼지

cf particulate ⓝ 입자성 물질

pack, pact, peck

• pack ⓥ

① (짐을) 싸다, 챙기다

He packed a knitted beanie because he had heard it was cold in Canada, and extra supplies of toothpaste, deodorant and acne cream, in case they were too costly abroad. — 캐나다로 어학연수 떠나는 아프리카 청년

② 가득 채우다

There's so much focus on togetherness during the holidays that those without a packed calendar might feel isolated and sad. — 연말 일정이 빠듯한 상황

cf jam-packed ⓐ 빽빽이 찬

Photos from inside the jam-packed flight spoke volumes about what had been at stake during two decades of war. — 아프간 탈출 비행기

• pact ⓝ 약속, 협정, 조약

Just a week earlier, the US and the UK announced plans to equip their ally with tools for the job : the AUKUS pact will see Australia acquire Tomahawk cruise missiles and technology to build nuclear submarines. — AUKUS : A(Australia) UK(United Kingdom) US(United States)

• peck ⓥ (새가 부리로) 쪼다

Weakened by heat and thirst, sheep and cattle become vulnerable. When they venture into dried-up creeks, they get trapped in the mud. Crows peck out their eyes and monitor lizards — known in Australia as goanna — eat them alive.

persist, pester

• persist ⓥ 집요하게 계속하다　　　　　　　　　　　　　　persistence ⓝ

While the US has become more diverse over time, this has obscured the persistence of segregation.

• pester ⓥ 성가시게 하다, 조르다(harass)

Tight supplies, higher prices and limited selections are likely to continue to pester the market, dealers and economists say.

package, packet

• package ⓝ 일괄(a set of ideas or services that are suggested or offered all together as a group)

The package of legislation would give Israel's parliament, the Knesset, the power to overrule Supreme Court decisions with a simple majority.

• packet ⓝ 꾸러미(parcel)

At a grocery store one day, the man in front of me holds a Kalashnikov rifle, a grenade launcher — and a packet of sausage.

pock, pocket

• pock ⓝ 마맛자국　　　　　　　　　　　　　　　　　　　pock ⓥ 마맛자국을 남기다

The devastation of the war soon appeared on both sides of the highway : bus stops pocked with shrapnel gashes, twisted shells of bombed-out buildings, a family restaurant in the shape of a castle that looked as if it had been strafed with a chain gun.

• pocket ⓝ (주변과는 이질적인) 집단(지역)

Before Kabul fell, a usual day for Jack would include visiting the gym after a day at the office, or meeting friends for coffee inside one of the country's trendy cafes, pockets of calm and sanctuary where young women could　　calm ⓝ
freely socialize.

ⓓ pocket ⓥ (돈을) 착복하다

Jack has been accused of stealing settlement money from the Satterfield children and pocketing it for himself.

ⓓ pocket money : 용돈

Before the pandemic, there were millions of people like Jack who could make a living, or at least earn decent pocket money, off gig work.

pregnant, progeny

- pregnancy ⓝ 임신

I was 13 weeks pregnant with my first child when I felt a sharp, tearing pain in my groin.

- progeny ⓝ 자손

Although he was the son and grandson of four-star admirals, when he was grilling you in testimony, you would swear he was the progeny of drill sergeants.

pregnant ⓐ
groin ⓝ 사타구니

he : 국회의원

primal, primary

- primal ⓐ 원시의, 태고의 (ancient and animal-like)

Toilet paper has primal — even infantile — associations, connected with what is arguably the body's least agreeable function in a way we've been taught from toddlerhood.

- primary ⓐ 주된, 주요한

As one of Time's White House photographers for nearly two decades, she says her primary goal with politicians was to "show you how human they were."

preeminent, prominent

- preeminent ⓐ 탁월한, 발굴의

And his drawing of Vitruvian Man — a work of anatomical exactitude combined with stunning beauty — became the preeminent icon of the connection of art and science.

- prominent ⓐ 유명한

Moon grew to prominence as a pro-democracy student activist, passing the state bar exam in 1980.

preeminence
his : 레오나르도 다 빈치

prominence ⓝ
Moon : 문재인 대통령

peach, preach

- peach ⓝ 복숭아
- preach ⓥ 설교하다

The resulting stew of negativity makes me worry that the future — my kid's future — will be grimmer. Yet how can I expect them to practice what I barely manage to preach?

Raising optimistic kids in an era of pessinism (기사 제목)

pallet, pellet, pullet

- **pallet** ⓝ 화물 운반대. '팔레트'라고도 함

wooden pallets

- **pellet** ⓝ 총알

She died with 10 shotgun pellets in her back

- **pullet** ⓝ (1년 미만의) 어린 닭

mallet ⓝ 나무망치

praise, prize

- **praise** ⓥ 칭찬하다

The truly adoring reviews praise the film's sincerity and social messages.

- **prize** ⓝ 상

She has been named one of the most powerful women internationally, mentioned in connection with a Nobel Peace Prize and profiled in glossy media around the world.

praise ⓝ

She : 뉴질랜드 총리 Arden

press, pressure

- **press** ⓥ (무엇에 대고) 누르다

As he lingered by the check-in-kiosks, one woman grabbed the man from behind and the other pressed a small cloth to his face.

cf **press** ⓝ 언론

This unpopularity could undermine his agenda. A perception of incompetence and arrogance makes the people — and the press — predisposed to think the worst of him.

- **pressure** ⓥ 압박(압력)을 가하다

At the same time, residents are pressuring city governments to use the disruption of COVID-19 to impose new rules on the industry.

he : 김정은 이복형 김정남

his : 윤석열 대통령

경기회복 기대

prospect, prospectus

- **prospect** ⓝ 가망, 가능성(possibility)

"The Chinese people and Chinese nation embrace brilliant prospects."

- **prospectus** ⓝ ① (학교·대학 등의) 안내서 ② (기업의) 투자(사업) 설명서

China International Capital Corporation, one of the three investment banks listed in the prospectus alongside Citi and BofA Securities, didn't respond to requests for comment.

시진핑 연설문

parlor, parole, patrol

- parlor ⓝ 영업점 (ice-cream / funeral / tattoo parlor)

Ob-Gyn clinics are closing, and funeral parlors are opening.

저출산의 대한민국

- parole ⓝ 가석방

Under the terms of his parole, any travel required special permission from South Korea's justice ministry.

humanitarian parole : (미국의) 인도적 임시 입국 허가

- patrol ⓥ 순찰하다

Accurate information is hard to come by, but analysts say there has been a Chinese buildup of military hardware behind the "line of actual control" in some areas, with troops patrolling on the Indian side.

patrol ⓝ

pageantry, peasant, pheasant

- pageantry ⓝ 화려한 행사(예 : 올림픽 입장식)

In summer 2008, the Beijing Olympics marked a big moment in China's progress toward global power. With that spotlight came controversy; activists used the event to highlight the government's human-rights abuses, but the event's triumphalist pageantry illustrated the story of China's rise toward prosperity and prestige for a world audience.

- peasant ⓝ 소작농 (poor farmer who owns or rents a small amount of land)

Still, the raid made Castro a hero to downtrodden Cuban peasants when he stood trial that September.

- pheasant ⓝ 꿩

proliferate, prolific

- proliferate ⓥ 급증하다, 확산하다

cf nonproliferation ⓝ 비확산

Time and again, nuclear-nonproliferation negotiations have fallen apart or deals have been broken, with tensions spiking, though they have recently receded since North Korea stopped testing missiles in mid-August.

proliferation ⓝ

- prolific ⓐ 다작의, 다산의

After Goodall shifted from research to activism in the 1980s, her steady, non-confrontational approach allowed her to become one of the most prolific environmentalists in modern history.

persecute, prosecute

- **persecute** ⓥ 박해하다(religious or political beliefs, race)   persecution ⓝ

I stand with people fleeing war and persecution.

- **prosecute** ⓥ 기소하다   prosecution ⓝ

The unrest began in response to a proposed law that would allow Hong Kong to extradite its citizens to face prosecution in mainland China's court system.

- cf prosecutor ⓝ 검사, 검찰

He previously served as the nation's top prosecutor.

precipitate, precipitous, propitiate

- **precipitate** ⓥ 촉발시키다, 가속화시키다

What I can bring is only the memories precipitated by love.   Steve Jobs의 유언

- cf precipitation ⓝ 강수량, 강설량

The previous record for precipitation in a 24-hour period was 1.14 inches in 2017.

- **precipitous** ⓐ 가파른   precipitously ⓐⓓⓥ

The main issue in last year's report regarded a precipitous 30 percent drop in the U.S. bird population over the past 50 years.

- **propitiate** ⓝ ⓥ 달래다, 비위를 맞추다   propitiation ⓝ

Bonfires to propitiate the gods in the hope of a good harvest

pane, panel

- **pane** ⓝ 유리창(a piece of glass used in a window)

frost on a window pane

- **panel** ⓝ

① 패널(a group of people with skills or specialist knowledge)

In fact, on the Intergovernmental Panel on Climate Change, 195 countries signed on to a document that accepts the climate crisis as man-made.

② 판(a flat piece of wood, glass etc with straight sides)

The solar panels that run fans during the day don't work at night.

proceedings, proceeds

• proceedings ⓝ 법적 절차, 소송 절차

She has begun divorce proceedings.

• proceeds ⓝ 수익금

In handing the diamond over to the government, which by law had the right to 60% of the proceeds from its sale,

process, procedure

• process ⓝ 과정, 절차(a series of actions, to achieve a particular result)

There is new pressure on the UN this year to make election process more transparent.

ⓓ in the process : 과정에 있다

The rope of desperation has replaced their iron chains. Now Africans are sending themselves to Europe and becoming slaves in the process.

rope : a continuous stream

ⓓ process ⓥ

① (원자재 식품 등을) 가공 처리하다

The buffalo then emerge on an overhead conveyer belt that spans the length of the adjacent processing room.

도축장

② (문서 등을) 처리하다

Although the number of asylum seekers reaching Germany has declined by two-thirds since 2015, federal and state agencies tasked with processing their arrival are still swamped.

③ 행진하다(walk or march in procession)

procession ⓝ

• procedure ⓝ

① 절차

the standard procedure for informing new employees about conditions of work

② 수술

I went with them to medical appointments and discovered that my mother was not supposed to be eating sugar and my father was supposed to have a procedure.

them : parents

precede, proceed

- precede ⓥ 앞에(앞서) 가다

The warm welcome Zelensky received in Washington in December preceded the authorization of a record aid package and the deployment of Patriot missiles.

- proceed ⓥ (시작된 일을) 진행하다

As the parade proceeded down Pennsylvania Avenue, my great-grandmother took advantage of the chaos, "got lost" in the crowd, then inserted herself front and center of the Illinois delegation.

precedence, precedent

- precedence ⓝ 우선

Making things tougher is that stability has taken precedence over reform.

- precedent ⓝ 선례

When asked whether South Korea planned to lodge a protest or demand an explanation from Washington, he said the government would study precedents from the past and similar cases involving other nations.   대통령실 도청

ⓓ unprecedented ⓐ 선례가 없는

The WHO has made unprecedented investment in immunization in poorer countries.

potent, potential

- potent ⓐ 강력한   potency ⓝ

Even with the awareness of America's history of colonial expansion and white supremacy, the promise of life, liberty and the pursuit of happiness is still a potent lure.

- potential ⓐ 잠재적인, 가능성 있는

We have no diplomatic contact, we have no commercial contact, so some kind of humanitarian contact as a potential bridge to improve the relationship would be helpful.   북미 관계

punishing punitive

- punishing ⓐ 극도로 힘든

A thousand miles south of the Rio Grande, Jane plodded along a Mexican road comforting her year-old son Sam, her partner holding up an umbrella to shield them from the punishing sun.

- punitive ⓐ 처벌을 위한

Other critics say that the takedowns can be too punitive.

takedown : 학폭 가해자들이 현역에서 물러남

cf impunity ⓝ 처벌을 받지 않음

Opponents of the peace deal claim that it amounts to impunity for war criminals.

proactive, provocative

- proactive ⓐ 상황을 앞서서 주도하는

By Feb. 1, Singapore, Taiwan and Hong Kong had all proactively implemented travel restrictions on passengers coming from mainland China.

- provocative ⓐ 도발적인

provocation ⓝ
provoke ⓥ

His erratic provocations are seen to be making a bad situation far worse.

pretence, pretension

- pretence ⓝ 구실, 핑계(pretense)

So when President Biden welcomes President Yoon Suk Yeol of South Korea to the White House on Wednesday, only the second state visit of Mr. Biden's presidency, there will be few pretenses that disarming North Korea remains a plausible goal.

- pretend ⓥ ~인 체하다

pretension ⓝ
윔블던 테니스 우승자 인터뷰

"How did you feel at Wimbledon with all those eyes on you?" asked a boy. Jane's reply : "I tried to pretend I was here."

portion, potion

- portion ⓝ ① 부분 ② (음식) 1인분

And vast portions of the region were untouched by the flames.

- potion ⓝ 묘약(a drink intended to have a special or magical effect on the person)

a magic potion

a love potion

passel, tassel

- **passel** ⓝ 많은 수 — 'passel of'의 형식으로 씀

The young couple had a passel of babies in the span of a few years.

- **tassel** ⓥ (쿠션이나 옷에) 술을 달다(fringe)

In a green military cap with a red star, signaling political fealty to the party, and tasseled leather boots

proportion, proposition

- **proportion** ⓝ (전체의) 부분, 비율 — 대한민국 정치 상황

In April 2020, a record 57 women were elected to the 300-seat parliament; though just 19%, the proportion was the highest ever since democratization in 1987.

- cf **disproportion** ⓝ 불균형 — disproportionate ⓐ

Critics have also questioned whether the harm done to reputations is disproportionate to the offenses.

the offense : 학폭
harm : 학폭 피해자의 고발로 학폭 가해자가 받는 피해

- **proposition** ⓝ 명제 — 링컨의 게티스버그 연설

He spoke of the past, of the "proposition that all men are created equal" on which the Republic was founded.

- cf **proposition** ⓥ (단도직입적으로) 섹스하자고 하다

Actress who have been propositioned — or worse — by moguls have long opted to remain silent for fear of losing parts.

영화계
Actress : 성폭력 피해자

pure, purge

- **pure** ⓐ — purity ⓝ

① 순수한

② 완전한, 순전한(sheer)

Those moments when an audience inside a dark theater laughs together or is surprised together are moments of pure joy and timeless happiness.

- cf **purify** ⓥ 정화하다

Whatever the true cause of her disappearance, Fan appears to be the highest-profile victim of Beijing's attempt to purify what it sees as a runaway, corrupt industry.

Fan : 영화배우

- **purge** ⓥ 제거하다, 숙청하다

Just two weeks earlier, Jack, the head of state security, was mysteriously purged.

propaganda, propagate

- propaganda ⓝ 선전, 선동   propagandist ⓝ 선전원

After Moon banned activists from sending propaganda balloons into the North, a bipartisan group of 13 former US officials accused his government of "undermining North Korea's human-rights movement" in an open letter.

대북 전단 발송

- propagate ⓥ   propagation ⓝ

① (사상·신조·정보를) 전파하다(disseminate)

Split into three branches, each sector is designed to check the others' power and balance it out so that no one branch can propagate tyranny.

② (동물이나 식물이) 번식하다

pat, pet, pot

pat과 pet는 동의어

- pat ⓥ (애정을 담아) 토닥거리다

He patted the dog affectionately.

- pet ⓥ (사랑스럽게) 어루만지다

Why would my kids want her "self-soothing" in a room by herself when she could be sitting at their knees, ready to be stealthily petted whenever they get frustrated or bored with school Zooms?

her : 반려견

- pot ⓝ

① 그릇, 용기

But I am like the frog who has jumped into the pot and noticed how murky the water is.

② 마리화나

Jane admitted — in discussion of a referendum to legalize marijuana — that she had smoked pot "a long time ago."

pip, pit

- pip ⓝ (과일의) 씨(a small hard seed in a fruit)

Jack picked the melon pips from his teeth.

- pit ⓝ

① 구덩이

We still live in townships, we still have pit latrines, the electricity is nonexistent, and most of my friends are unemployed.

latrine ⓝ 변소

② 복숭아씨(영국영어 : stone)

physiology, psychology

- physiology ⓝ 생리학

We're going through a time where physiologically, people's threat system is at a heightened level.

physiological ⓐ
physiologist ⓝ 생리학자

- psychology ⓝ 심리학

In a personal statement appended to her application, Jane addressed her past, explaining that she had a psychological breakdown after experiencing abandonment and domestic violence and that she had repeated those patterns with her son.

psychological ⓐ
psychologist ⓝ 심리학자
아들을 살해하고 교도소에서 공부하여 하버드 입학

prone, prune

- prone ⓐ 하기 쉬운

One newspaper was widely criticized for articles that depicted gay men as promiscuous and prone to risky sexual behavior.

- prune ⓥ (나무를) 전지하다, (가지를) 잘라 내다

pruning ⓝ

Currently, Jack estimates most jobs to maintain or prune trees and shrubs fall between $200 and $760 and average $460.

principal, principle

- principal ⓐ 주요한, 주된

These refugees come principally from Asia, Africa and Latin America, which is to say they often come from countries the President has frequently disparaged.

트럼프 대통령

cf principal ⓝ ① 교장 ② (은행의) 원금

- principle ⓝ 원리, 원칙

We also know that some laws, like the segregation statute, contravene basic principles of the Constitution.

presumptive, presumptuous

- presumptive ⓐ 추정되는 (based on a reasonable belief about what is likely to be true)

A Cold-War style showdown is now coalescing in the South China Sea, between the world's established superpower and its presumptive one.

- presumptuous ⓐ 주제넘는, 건방진

I am afraid only that I may seem presumptuous to have broached a question so vast and so important.

'역사란 무엇인가?'의 첫 문장

pantheon, pathogen

- **pantheon** ⓝ (한 나라나 지역에 있는 모든) 신들

Xi joins Mao Zedong and Deng Xiaoping in the pantheon of modern China's most powerful men.

- **pathogen** ⓝ 병균, 병원체(germ)

However, when the attack comes not from a human enemy but from a virus or other pathogen, moral stress-cracks form in the community.

- cf **pathology** ⓝ 병리학

Jack's suffering combined with his relentless exposure of corruption — something Putin's own lieutenants have described as a pathology eating away at the nation — have won him admirers in the unlikeliest precincts.

pan~ : 전체를 뜻하는 접두사
마오쩌둥, 덩샤오핑

Jack : 양심수
첫 번째 his : Putin
두 번째 him : Jack

precursor, procure

- **precursor** ⓝ 선구자(before something else and influenced its development)

The far-right National Front leader Le Pen — a strong Trump fan who sees his victory as a precursor to her own — could win the most votes in the French presidential election in the first round.

- **procure** ⓥ (어렵게) 구하다, 구입하다

The delivery of the Abrams tanks will take several months, given the time needed to procure them and train Ukrainian troops on their use.

National Front : 프랑스 정당의 이름

우크라이나-러시아 전쟁
the Abrams : 미국 탱크

porter, portal

- **portal** ⓝ ① (건물) 웅장한 정문 ② (인터넷) 포털(사이트)

They risk the city's status as a financial portal, as the unrest begins to take a toll on the economy.

- **porter** ⓝ (기차역, 공항 등) 짐꾼

There aren't any porters, so we'll have to find a trolley for the luggage.

홍콩 민주화

protocol, protract

- **protocol** ⓝ (치료에 관한) 일반원칙

Breaches of its coronavirus protocols have led to a permanent resident's losing his status.

- **protract** ⓥ (시간을) 길게 끌다, 연장하다

If such a downturn is prolonged and protracted, months after the fact it is labeled a recession.

pinpoint, pinprick

• pinpoint ⓥ 딱 집어내다

Experts say the approach helped pinpoint outbreak hot spots, allocate resources and isolate infections.

• pinprick ⓝ ① (특히 핀으로 뚫은 것 같은) 아주 작은 구멍 ② (아주 작고 사소한) 성가신 것

These problems were pinpricks compared with what was to come.

parameter, barometer, paramedic

• parameter ⓝ (일정하게 정한) 한도, 제한

Summits normally follows a series of lower-level meetings, where policy specialists thrash out parameters in painstaking, coffee-soaked sessions.

cf barometer ⓝ 지표

The skin is an accurate barometer of emotional and physical health.

• paramedic ⓝ 준의료 활동 종사자

The paramedics showed up to wheel her out of our house on a stretcher.

para~: 준(準, 공식적이거나 완전히 자격을 갖추지는 않은)

predate, predator

• predate ⓥ ~보다 앞서다

But persistent drug shortages predate the pandemic.

• predator ⓝ 포식자

The death unnerved a region unaccustomed to the presence of these storied predators.

상어(shark)

premier, premiere

발음이 같음

• premier ⓐ 최고의

He is considered one of the premier scientists studying the tiny owls in the U.S. and Mexico.

cf premier ⓝ 총리, 수상

The scale of challenges facing Britain obscures the historic nature of Sunak's premiership.

premiership ⓝ

Sunak : 유색인종으로 영국 총리가 된 인도 출신 이민자

cf Premier League : 영국 프로 축구의 최상위 리그

• premiere ⓝ 첫 공연, 초연

Ahead of the premiere of the show's sixth run in January, Jane stepped down from her role after being charged with assaulting her boyfriend.

quarry, quarter

- **quarry** ⓝ 사냥감

We no longer need slavers going into Africa to capture their quarry.

- **quarter** ⓝ 1/4(3개월마다)　　　　　　　　　　　　　　　　quart~ : 4개의

A cornerstone of his stint as mayor of Seongnam was paying "youth dividends" of 250,000 won ($200) per quarter to 24-year-old residents, which became so successful that he expanded the program across Gyeonggi Province when he became governor in 2018.

한국 대통령 선거

- ⓓ **quarterfinal** ⓝ 준준결승　　　　　　　　　　　　　　　semifinal ⓝ 준결승

The top two teams from each group advance to knockout quarterfinals.

- ⓓ **quartet** ⓝ (음악) 사중주

A quartet of stars made Rio a celebration.

Rio 올림픽 4명의 스타선수

quality, quantity

- **quality** ⓝ 자질, 특성

Emotional maturity tops the list of what US singles are looking for, beating out all other qualities, according to a new study by the dating site Match released on Nov. 9.

- ⓓ **quality** ⓐ 양질의

Nor should we ignore the need for a Secretary-General who can provide quality leadership for the entire organization.

UN 사무총장 선거

- ⓓ **qualify** ⓥ 자격을 부여하다, 자격이 있다　　　　　　　qualification ⓝ

In May, the Washington-based rights group Freedom House said Hungary no longer qualifies as a full democracy.

- ⓓ **disqualify** ⓥ 자격을 박탈하다　　　　　　　　　　　　bullet : Khan에 대한 저격 시도

In addition to bullets, Khan has also been hit by charges — 143 over the past 11 months, by his count, including corruption, sedition, blasphemy, and terrorism — which he claims have been concocted in an attempt to disqualify him from politics

- **quantity** ⓝ 양

To spend time with Jane, who died on June 17 at 92, was to be bowled over by the sheer quantity of positive energy she brought to this world.

- ⓓ **quantify** ⓥ 수량으로 나타내다　　　　　　　　　　　　quantification ⓝ

And Ethiopia is not the only country where such progress is quantifiable

qualitative, quantitative

- qualitative ⓐ 질적인
- quantitative ⓐ 양적인

Technologies like these enable a more rigorous approach to interpreting both quantitative and qualitative data.

TCM : Traditional Chinese Medicine

quack, whack

- quack ⓝ 돌팔이 의사

It was just like allowing a quack to do diagnosis and administer drugs on a patient.

- whack ⓝ 세게 후려치기

Trying to knock out fringe sites will also create a never-ending game of whack-a-mole.

quackery : 돌팔이 의사 의 짓
quack ⓥ 오리가 꽥꽥거리다

불법 온라인 단속

quadruple, quadriplegia, quadrennial

quad~ : 4의

- quadrennial ⓐ 4년마다의

Those moments, the embraces on ice and the magic in the air, will likely serve as the legacy of these Games. They are our quadrennial reminder that barriers — physical, mental, social, even political — are of our own making. And they're just waiting to be broken.

동계 올림픽의 figure-skating duo 게임

- quadriplegia ⓝ 사지 마비

a 10-year-old girl with cerebral palsy, who suffered from spastic quadriplegia that made her unable to stand or sit

- quadruple ⓥ 4배가 되다

quadruple ⓝ

When wind speed doubles, the force exerted on homes, power lines and other infrastructure quadruples.

R

외신으로 보는
대한민국
VOCABULARY

rapport, rapprochement

• rapport ⓝ 친밀한 관계

Carter had some conventional assets. Although he was a southerner, he had an easy rapport with blacks and the early support of some key black leaders in his home state.

• rapprochement ⓝ 관계 회복 (after a period of unfriendly relations)

Yet what might be even more worrying than a Chinese-North Korean rapprochement is the possibility that even Beijing's influence over Pyongyang is limited.

Carter : 미국 남부출신 Jimmy Carter 대통령

rickets, rickety

• rickets ⓝ 구루병

• rickety ⓐ 곧 부서질 듯한, 곧 무너질 듯한

On the morning of April 8, Jack boarded a rickety Antonov plane and flew to the edge of the war zone with a coterie of generals, some of whom looked more nervous than their commander in chief.

reconnaissance, renaissance

• reconnaissance ⓝ 정찰, 정찰 활동

US military vessels and aircraft frequently carry out reconnaissance in Chinese coastal waters.

• renaissance ⓝ 르네상스, 문예 부흥

Even as Buffalo has enjoyed a renaissance over the past decade, city hall has neglected the working-class Black neighborhoods on the East Side.

Buffalo : (미국) 뉴욕주의 도시

raze, razor

• raze ⓥ 완전히 파괴하다

The remains of burnt villages in Myanmar's Rakhine state, on Oct. 10 ; hundreds have been razed since the conflict began.

사진 설명

• razor ⓝ 면도칼

ⓓ razor-thin ⓐ 면도칼의 날처럼 아주 근소한

Before winning the presidential election with a razor-thin margin in March, Mr. Yoon had been a prosecutor for 26 years and never held elected office.

relieve, relive

• **relieve** ⓥ (고통 따위를) 덜어주다, 완화하다

The progress is a source of relief for Jack, who has been assured by government officials that construction will ramp up further in September, at the end of the rainy season.

ramp up : 증가하다

ⓒ **reliever** ⓝ (야구) 구원 투수

There are no Shohei Ohtanis on the Czech team, but the homegrown squad does have a 37-year-old firefighter on its pitching staff (who has been a two-way star for his team) and a reliever who doubles as the team's publicity director.

Shohei Ohtanis : 일본의 세계적인 야구 선수

two-way : (야구) 투수와 타자가 가능

ⓒ **relief** ⓝ

① (조각) 양각

a piece of sculpture in relief

intaglio ⓝ (조각) 음각

② 구원, 구원 물품

relief pitcher(reliever) : 구원 투수

③ 완화

Marijuana can provide pain relief for some cancer patients.

• **relive** ⓥ (과거의 일을) 다시 체험을 하다

In China, where I now live, Japanese atrocities are relived in textbooks.

과거 일본의 만행

reckless, ruthless

• **reckless** ⓐ 무모한, 난폭한

Given Kim's reckless habits — drinking and driving are two of his favorite pastimes — a self-inflicted biological solution is more than possible.

Kim : 김정은

• **ruthless** ⓐ 인정사정없는, 무자비한

a ruthless use of force

render, rendition

• **render** ⓥ (어떤 상태가) 되게 하다(make)

It's especially frustrating as COVID-19 can spread while people are asymptomatic, rendering these tests mostly pointless.

• **rendition** ⓝ (음악) 연주

It was at Game 1 that Red Sox third baseman and furloughed Navy sailor Fred offered a rendition of the patriotic song.

(스포츠) 국가제창의 연원

evolve revolt, revolution

- **evolve** ⓥ 진화하다   evolution ⓝ

She has often said that to survive, the monarchy has to evolve, and she will be confident this couple can begin their new life with love and togetherness.

영국 왕실의 약혼자

- **revolt** ⓝ 반란, 저항   revolt ⓥ

For now, the regional and wider reverberations of Iranian girls' revolt could not be more seismic.

이란에서 일어난 여성들의 히잡(hijab) 착용 거부사태

- **revolution**

① 회전

The last rider of his event, he landed a back-to-back 1440-four full revolutions in the air-to steal gold from Hirano of Japan at the buzzer.

he : 동계올림픽 snowboard 선수, 1440은 4바퀴 회전

② 혁명

He decided to annex Crimea in response to a revolution in Ukraine that he believed to be part of a global anti-Russia conspiracy.

He : Putin

㏄ **revolutionary** ⓐ 혁명적인

Citing the revolutionary days of 1917, he was now forced to protect his own capital and power against thousands of Prigozhin's mercenaries.

프리고진 : 러시아 용병그룹의 우두머리, 1917년 러시아 혁명

㏄ **revolutionize** ⓥ 대변혁을 일으키다

Einstein revolutionized our understanding of the universe by coming up with the two pillars of contemporary physics : relativity theory and quantum theory.

㏄ **revolve** ⓥ (축을 중심으로) 돌다, 회전하다

resident, residual

- **resident** ⓝ ① 거주민 ② 수련의(의사)   residential ⓐ reside ⓥ

Another choice is Seoul's popular mayor, Park Won-soon (no relation to the President), a former left-wing activist who would wield the backing of a large proportion the capital's residents.

- **residual** ⓐ 나머지의, 잔여의

Owing to residual support among diehard conservatives, her approval rating across all ages stands at a paltry 4%.

her : 박근혜 대통령
diehard conservatives : 태극기 부대

rabid, rabies

• **rabid** ⓐ 광적인(very extreme and unreasonable opinions)

Her husband is a rabid baseball fan.

• **rabies** ⓝ 광견병

Raccoons are also one of the main carriers of rabies, second to only bats, according to the CDC.

CDC : Centers for Disease Control(질병관리본부)

rural, urban

• **rural** ⓐ 시골의

How concerned are you about lack of access to broadband in rural areas?

broadband : 고속 데이터 통신망

• **urban** ⓐ 도시의

Much of the low-hanging fruit, including moving people from rural to urban areas, has been picked.

중국 경제
low-hanging fruit : 쉽게 구할 수 있는 직업
urbanite ⓝ 도시인
urbanist ⓝ 도시계획전문가
ubanity ⓝ
김정은

ⓒf **urbane** ⓐ 세련된, 자신 있는

But it's not Kim that the urbane population of this capital is most worried about. It is Trump's seeming indifference to the value of Washington's alliance with their city that confuses the citizens of Seoul.

resolve, resolute, solve

• **resolve** ⓥ

① 문제를 해결하다

resolution ⓝ

Both internally and externally, North Korea always resolves any kind of political dispute through violence or the threat of violence.

ⓒf **unresolved** ⓐ 문제를 해결하지 못하고

Despite ongoing nationwide protests and court cases still unresolved for the victims of the strongman's martial law, the laundering of the dictator's legacy is nearly complete.

② 굳게 결심하다(to make a definite decision to do something)

We here highly resolve that these dead shall not have died in vain.

Gettysburg 연설문

ⓒf **resolve** ⓝ (단호한) 결심

He ordered the tree completely cut down as a symbolic act of resolve.

1976년 판문점 도끼 만행
He : 당시 주한미군 사령관

• **resolute** ⓐ 단호한, 확고한

He remained resolute in his belief that the situation would improve.

solution ⓝ

• **solve** ⓥ 문제를 해결하다

They are working to solve the traffic problem.

renegade, renege

- renegade ⓝ 배반자, 이탈자

They were formed by Bang Si-hyuk, a K-pop renegade who left a major label to start his own enterprise.

- renege ⓥ (약속, 합의 등을) 어기다(on)

Pyongyang has signed five denuclearization agreements in the past but reneged on all.

runaway, runway

- runaway ⓝ 가출한 사람(특히 청소년)

Many runaway youths she works with are denied service for "the most ridiculous reasons."

df runaway ⓐ 고삐 풀린, 통제가 안되는

a runaway, corrupt industry

df run away ⓥ 가출하다, 도망가다

children who run away from home normally go to big cities

- runway

① catwalk ⓝ (패션쇼장에서 모델들이 걸어 다니는) 무대

② (비행기) 활주로

the runway of Havana's International Airport

차별금지법에 관한 기사, 동성애자들 이야기

rash, rush

- rash ⓝ

① (피부) 발진

② (짧은 시간에) 많음

One person was killed and five people were wounded in a rash of overnight shootings in Indianapolis.

a rash of

df rash ⓐ 성급한, 경솔한

The French government suggested Trump had acted rashly and out of anger, and criticized his inconsistency.

rashly ⓐⓓ

- rush ⓥ 급히 서두르다

rush ⓝ

After Phelps heard on May 31 that Naomi Osaka had pulled out of the French Open and he read her Instagram message explaining why, a bunch of thoughts rushed into his head.

rag, rig

• rag ⓐ 옷이 누더기가 된, 다 해진(torn and in bad condition)

ⓓ (from) rags to riches : 무일푼에서 부자로

In many ways, Lee's rags-to-riches success story finds parallels in the story of South Korea itself. — Lee : 이재명

• rig ⓥ 조작하다

The game is especially rigged against women. — 여성 차별

vote rigging

ⓓ rig ⓝ (특정한 용도의) 장치

At the Craggy Wash BLM campground in Lake Havasu City Ariz, where Jack and Jane traveled in February, groups helped one another build out their rigs and organized a socially distanced pig roast. — BLM : Bureau of Land Management(토지관리국)

remission, remittance

• remission ⓝ (병의) 차도

Months after my dad's death in 2018, my mom was diagnosed with cancer. She was in remission for a short time, but then it came roaring back, Stage IV. — remit ⓥ ① (부채·의무·처벌 등을) 면제해 주다 ② 송금하다

• remittance ⓝ 송금

Jack had been sending the bulk of his $400-a-month salary home to his family, part of a $10 billion river of remittances that flows into Nepal every year from Nepali migrant workers employed abroad ; it accounts for nearly a third of the nation's GDP. — 월드컵 개최지 카타르(Qatar)에서 일하는 네팔 근로자(Jack)

ⓓ unremitting ⓐ 끊임없는(constant, incessant)

But across this country, indignation is only intensifying amid an unremitting conflict that has no end in sight.

ramble, rumble, rumple

• ramble ⓥ 장황하게 지껄이다(talk for a long time, not seem clearly organized)

Fidel tried to remain relevant by penning rambling op-eds on world affairs.

• rumble ⓥ 덜커덩거리며 가다

The daily caravan of trucks rumbling over Dandong's iron bridge from the North Korea has slowed to a trickle. — Dandong : 북한에 인접한 중국의 도시

• rumple ⓥ 헝클다

In his rumpled T-shirts and designer jeans, Jack, 51, is hardly the model of a modern political consultant.

rife, ripe

- **rife** ⓐ 가득하다, 만연하다

Over the course of 40 interviews, seamstresses, cutters and cleaners at Hippo Knitting factory allege that verbal abuse and harassment have been rife for years.

- **ripe** ⓐ 익은

Closer to the coast, the wind and dry air are creating ripe conditions for fires to spread.

- **ripen** ⓥ 익다

Altitudes above 1,600 feet are generally considered too cold to ripen grapes reliably.

raft, rift

- **raft** ⓝ ① 뗏목 ② 고무보트

Soon the plywood floor that had been nailed to the bottom of the raft took on water and started to buckle.

- **a raft of** : 많은

China's major stock indexes rose on their first trading day of 2023, despite a raft of weak economic data released over the long weekend.

- **rift** ⓝ (사람들 사이의) 균열

Few recalled major rifts between their parents.

run down, rundown

- **run down**

① ~를 치다

the boy was run down by joyriders.

② (추적 끝에) 잡아내다

A hound who had served his master well for years, and had run down many a quarry in his time, began to lose his strength and speed owing to age.

③ (규모나 수치를) 줄이다

He has criticized the government for running down the Armed Forces.

- **rundown** ⓐ 고물의(in very bad condition because of age or lack of care)

The island was better known for all the rusty 1950s-vintage cars still prowling Havana's rundown streets.

the island : Cuba

resurge, resurrect

- resurge ⓥ 다시 나타나다

They were "pristine prey," as Jack puts it, when the virus resurged this spring.

- resurrect ⓥ 부활시키다

To stave off war with the North, Lee wants to continue with the "sunshine policy" resurrected by Moon, who over the course of 18 months navigated an astonishing process of engagement.

resurgence ⓝ

resurrection ⓝ

Lee : 이재명
Moon : 문재인 대통령

reinstall, reinstate

- reinstall ⓥ 다시 설치하다(to install something or someone again)

Lawmakers will reinstall Abe as Prime Minister in time for Trump's visit to Japan on Nov. 5.

- reinstate ⓥ 복귀시키다, 회복시키다

He is now set to invoke a never-before-used constitutional provision, Article 155, to reinstate home rule over the region.

reinstallation ⓝ
Abe : 일본 총리

reinstatement ⓝ

rage, enrage

- rage ⓥ 맹위를 떨치다

Debate raged for decades.

- enrage ⓥ 화나게 하다

National Security Adviser John Bolton had particularly enraged North Korean leadership by suggesting the regime should follow the "Libya model" of nuclear disarmament.

rage ⓝ a strong feeling of uncontrollable anger

Bolton : 트럼프 시절 안보 보좌관

rot, rug, rut

- rot ⓝ 썩음, 부패(decay)

It seems to be everywhere, like rot in the walls.

- rug ⓝ 작은 깔개같은 양탄자

But our living-room rug and nearly every piece of furniture we own should probably be replaced.

- rut ⓝ (흙길에서 생긴) 바퀴 자국
- rut ⓥ 바퀴 자국을 내다

The village, a small scattering of concrete huts with palm-leaf roofs, lies at the end of a severely rutted road that is all but impassable during the rainy season.

직장 내 성추행

respectable, respectful

- **respectable** ⓐ ① 존경할 만한 ② 꽤 괜찮은

America's GDP grew by a respectable 2.6 per cent.

a perfectly respectable pair of pajamas

- **respectful** ⓐ 존경심을 보이는

I realize now I should have been more tolerant and respectful to people that are different from me.

respective, irrespective

- **respective** ⓐ 각각의

Jack, left, and Tom pictured after their respective arrests in 1965.   사진 설명

- **irrespective** ⓐ 관계없이

The strictest measure has been found in Morocco, where all people travelling from China have been banned from entering the country outright — irrespective of their nationality.

raid, rail

- **raid** ⓥ (경찰) 급습하다, 불시에 들이닥치다

Investigators raided the offices of Samsung after accusations that a controversial merger was approved by the government in return for a "donation" to one of Choi's foundations.   박근혜 대통령 탄핵 당시

- cf **air-raid** ⓝ 공습

- **rail** ⓥ 격분하다(complain or protest, angrily, strongly, persistently)

He railed at capitalism as the source of the world's miseries.

- cf **rail** ⓝ 기차, 철도

China has the most solar panels, wind turbines and high-speed rail in the world.

- cf **derail** ⓥ (기차) 탈선시키다, (계획을) 좌절시키다

As things stand, neither diplomacy nor sanctions seem likely to derail the North's nuclear program.

resume, résumé

- **resume** ⓥ 다시 시작하다   resumption ⓝ

Pyongyang's resumption of rancor means the Singapore summit risks turning into embarrassment.   싱가포르에서 있었던 미북 정상회담의 실패

- résumé ⓝ 이력서(CV, curriculum vitae) — superlative ⓝ (문법) 최상급

His résumé was already peppered with superlatives and onlys.

rambunctious, rowdy

- rambunctious ⓐ 사납게 구는(in a way that cannot be controlled)

a pensive introvert whose quiet calm visibly separates him from his more rambunctious siblings — quiet ⓝ

- rowdy ⓐ 소란을 벌이는(in a noisy rough way, to cause arguments and fighting)

Some of the rowdy behavior sounds like normal, run-of-the-mill mischief.

responsible, responsive

- responsible ⓐ 책임이 있는 — responsibility ⓝ

Police believe that the same man is responsible for three other murders in the area.

- responsive ⓐ 관심을 보이는, 반응하는 — response ⓝ

TCM has been responsive to the plight of threatened animals. — TCM(traditional Chinese medicine)

riffle, ripple

- riffle ⓥ (종이나 책장을 휙휙) 넘기다(quickly, casually)

He then riffled through a stack of old photographs and gave the chef a black-and-white picture of himself when he was 11 years old.

- ripple ⓥ 물결 모양을 이루다, 파문이 생기다

When the bomb lands nearby, the whole building shudders and solid walls can ripple like water.

resilience, resistance

- resilient ⓐ 회복력 있는

If the 40 million Americans in poverty have one common characteristic, it's vulnerability. If they have one common virtue, it's resilience. — resilience ⓝ

- resist ⓥ 저항하다 — resistance ⓝ

Islamic State fighters had taken over the ancient town, toppling its monuments and executing anyone who resisted their draconian rules.

- cf. bullet-resistant : 방탄의(bullet-proof)

rile, roil

- rile ⓥ 안달하게 하다 (to make someone extremely angry)

Since taking China's top job in 2013, he has launched an unprecedented anticorruption drive within the Communist Party and riled Asian neighbors by embarking on military expansions.   *he : 시진핑*

- roil ⓥ 요동치게 하다 (to make turbid by stirring up the sediment or dregs of)

With the US decision to stop playing a global leadership role and mediating disputes, the world will face more grievances between countries that roil economies and trade.   *한국과 일본의 갈등*

rankle, rattle

- rankle ⓥ 마음속에 오래 남아있다

But the experience rankled him — he was especially annoyed by how Medvedev responded to the Arab Spring protests in 2011

he : Putin
Medvedev : 푸틴이 권력을 이양했던 이인자
Arab Spring : (중동) 민주화 바람

- rattle ⓥ

① 덜거덕(달가닥)거리다

The window rattled in the wind.

② 불안하게 만들다 (to make someone lose confidence or become nervous)

Today the 32-year-old is the heir to the throne and author of an ongoing shake-up in the kingdom that has rattled the entire regime.   *사우디아라비아*

ⓓ saber rattling : 무력시위

Putin's nuclear saber-rattling will escalate.

refer, referee

- refer ⓥ 언급하다, 말하다 (to)

Although she didn't mention any names, everyone knew who she was referring to.

ⓓ reference ⓝ 참고 (the act of looking at something for information)

For reference, a breakfast of $\frac{2}{3}$ cup of oats, a cup of berries, and a cup of fruit juice gives you 100 grams of carbs.   *carb ⓝ 탄수화물 (carbohydrate)*

- referee ⓝ (스포츠 경기의) 심판 (football, basketball, or boxing)

ⓓ referee ⓥ 심판보다

But the three daughters of Puerto Rican parents were kept safe, spending most of their time in school or at the boxing gym where their father refereed.

umpire ⓝ 심판 (tennis, baseball, and cricket)
가정교육

retrograde, retrospect

retro~ : 뒤로, 거꾸로

- **retrograde** ⓐ 역행하는, 시대를 거스르는(backward)

In Beijing's eyes, minorities must fall into neat stereotypes : Uighurs are entertainers, pickpockets and extremists. Tibetans are ruddy-cheeked religious fanatics. Mongolians are backward ger-dwelling nomads. Each, in their own way, are retrograde and requiring correction.

- **retrospect** ⓝ 회고, 회상

retrospective ⓐ

In retrospect, the signs that trouble was brewing for Bitwise Industries had been piling up for months.

In retrospect 형식으로 많이 씀

relax, relay

- **relax** ⓥ (법, 규칙 등을) 완화하다

도쿄올림픽

Politicians hoped an influx of foreign spectators would help prepare this homogenous society for the relaxed immigration laws necessary to address a severe low-skilled labor shortage.

- **relay** ⓥ 전달하다, 중계하다

Many young Afghan women, especially those who are educated, grew up listening with horror as their mothers and grandmothers relayed stories from the times of the Taliban.

raven, ravenous, ravine

- **raven** ⓝ 큰 까마귀

magpie ⓝ 까치
crow ⓝ 까마귀
lustrous ⓐ 윤기가 흐르는

Hair as lustrous as a raven's wing has been the dominant aesthetic of late.

- **ravenous** ⓐ 배고파 죽을 지경인

feeling ravenous after a hard day's work.

- **ravine** ⓝ 협곡(canyon, gorge)

Rescuers could be seen climbing into the deep gorge and ravine to try and rescue anyone still alive.

road hog, road rage

- **road hog** ⓝ 길 중앙으로 몰아서 다른 자동차가 앞서지 못하게 하는 운전수
- **road rage** ⓝ violence and angry behavior by car drivers towards other car drivers

hog ⓝ 돼지(밥 먹을 때 동료 돼지를 못오게 하는 습성이 있음)

retrograde, retrospect

retro~ : 뒤로, 거꾸로

- **retrograde** ⓐ 역행하는, 시대를 거스르는(backward)

In Beijing's eyes, minorities must fall into neat stereotypes : Uighurs are entertainers, pickpockets and extremists. Tibetans are ruddy-cheeked religious fanatics. Mongolians are backward ger-dwelling nomads. Each, in their own way, are retrograde and requiring correction.

- **retrospect** ⓝ 회고, 회상

retrospective ⓐ

In retrospect, the signs that trouble was brewing for Bitwise Industries had been piling up for months.

In retrospect 형식으로 많이 씀

relax, relay

- **relax** ⓥ (법, 규칙 등을) 완화하다

Politicians hoped an influx of foreign spectators would help prepare this homogenous society for the relaxed immigration laws necessary to address a severe low-skilled labor shortage.

도쿄올림픽

- **relay** ⓥ 전달하다, 중계하다

Many young Afghan women, especially those who are educated, grew up listening with horror as their mothers and grandmothers relayed stories from the times of the Taliban.

raven, ravenous, ravine

- **raven** ⓝ 큰 까마귀

magpie ⓝ 까치
crow ⓝ 까마귀
lustrous ⓐ 윤기가 흐르는

Hair as lustrous as a raven's wing has been the dominant aesthetic of late.

- **ravenous** ⓐ 배고파 죽을 지경인

feeling ravenous after a hard day's work.

- **ravine** ⓝ 협곡(canyon, gorge)

Rescuers could be seen climbing into the deep gorge and ravine to try and rescue anyone still alive.

road hog, road rage

- **road hog** ⓝ 길 중앙으로 몰아서 다른 자동차가 앞서지 못하게 하는 운전수
- **road rage** ⓝ violence and angry behavior by car drivers towards other car drivers

hog ⓝ 돼지(밥 먹을 때 동료 돼지를 못오게 하는 습성이 있음)

rack, racket

- rack ⓝ 받침대, 선반, 시렁(luggage rack)
- rack up ⓥ 획득하다

No one "went over the wall" (as in, violated curfew) more than Midshipman McCain. No one racked up more demerits. No one dated more women.

- racket ⓥ 시끄러운 소리를 내다

I was struck most by the trendy girls in fishnet stockings, the ubiquitous burger joints, the sound of pinball racketing through fluorescent shopping arcades.

사관학교 기숙사 생활
demerit ⓝ 벌점
racket ⓝ (배드민턴 등의) 라켓

reprisal, reproach

- reprisal ⓝ 보복, 앙갚음

For security concerns, including the possibility of reprisals against family members of migrants still at home, Time has agreed not to use any of the migrants' last names.

- reproach ⓝ 비난, 책망

'You don't need me,' she said quietly, without reproach.

- irreproachable ⓐ 비난할 수 없는, 책망할 수 없는

All of them were irreproachably polite yet turned pale each time I began to demand answers to the most elementary questions.

retail, retaliate, wholesale

- retail ⓝ 소매

Everyone is beholden to online retail giant Alibaba's new Health Code app, which rates users green, yellow, or red, depending on travel history and possible contact with infected people.

be beholden to : 신세지다

- retaliate ⓥ 보복하다, 앙갚음하다

Their refusal to be "baby-making machines," according to protest banners I've seen, is retaliation.

retaliation ⓝ
retaliatory ⓐ
우리나라 저출산

- wholesale ⓝ 도매
- wholesale ⓐ 전반적인

Confronting the compulsory hijab is such a deft way of rejecting the wholesale failures of Iran's system that I often wonder why my generation didn't take the same path.

I : 여성 운동을 지지하는 여성 이란인

S

외신으로 보는
대한민국
VOCABULARY

sag, shag

• **sag** ⓥ 축 처지다, 늘어지다 (because of the weight of something)

North Korea will sell more of its nuclear and ICBM technology to rogue states or terrorist and criminal groups to boost its sagging economy and gain further bargaining power.

ⓓ **saggy** ⓐ 축 처진

The bed was saggy in the middle.

• **shag** ⓝ (머리) 샤기 컷

Her hair was cut short in a boyish shag.

ⓓ **shaggy** ⓐ (머리털이) 텁수룩한

His appearance is ever modern : the shaggy hair, the skinny tie, the suit jacket off, the shirt sleeves rolled.

sure-footed, underfoot

• **sure-footed** ⓐ 틀림없는, 확실한

Ardern was already a figure of global interest, thanks to her age, gender and baby, but her sure-footedness after a disaster of that magnitude really pushed her into the spotlight.

Ardern : 뉴질랜드 총리

• **underfoot** ⓐ 발밑에

They now argue that China must do more to keep Kim Jong Un underfoot or at least at heel.

they : 트럼프 행정부

scrutiny, security

• **scrutiny** ⓝ 정밀조사, 철저한 검토

Applicants for conscientious objector status endure intense scrutiny of their private lives—having to satisfy investigators, for example, that they have never played violent video games.

scrutinize ⓥ
양심적 병역거부

• **security** ⓝ 보안, 안보

A new security law in Hong Kong unveiled this summer is designed to crush pro-democracy activism and compromise what's left of the city's autonomy.

ⓓ **secure** ⓥ (힘들여) 얻어내다, 확보하다

Trump also secured the return of the remains of 5,300 service members who died during the Korean War.

sap, seep

- sap ⓝ (나무) 수액

The sap which courses through the trees carries the memories of the redman.   redman : 인디언

- ⓓ sap ⓥ 점진적으로 파괴하다, 약화시키다

For now Macron will hope that the tax cancellation and the violence begin to dampen public support for the protests and that the holidays sap turnout.

- seep ⓥ (액체가) 스미다, 배다

Salty water can seep through and evaporate, leaving "salt flowers" on the outside of the vessel.   장독

stiff, steep

- stiff ⓐ 심한(great or severe)

In March, he threatened to impose stiff trade tariffs on China and Europe, then enacted them two months later after global markets generally bounced back from initial losses.

- ⓓ stiffen ⓥ 경직시키다, 뻣뻣하게 하다

But they seemingly stiffened his resolve.   they : 미국의 제재

- steep ⓐ

① 가파르다

Those first years in Europe were tough, he says, and though he now speaks German and English, the learning curve was steep.   손흥민

② 급격한(involving a big increase or decrease)

The Western world reacted with dismay, and the US and Europe imposed steep sanctions on Russia.

swell, swelter

- swell ⓥ 부풀다, 부어오르다

Yet each still has fewer than 250 confirmed COVID-19 cases, even as global infection numbers swelled to upwards of 180,000.   코로나
each : 대만, 싱가포르, 홍콩

- ⓓ groundswell ⓝ (갑작스런) 고조, 급증

There is a groundswell of opinion that tougher laws are needed.

- swelter ⓥ 날씨가 더워 짜증나다, 무더위에 시달리다

Jack sweltered in his doorman's uniform.

surge, swarm

• surge ⓥ 급등하다

Average temperatures are surging across the globe.

cf surge ⓝ 급등

In a normal season, Mother's Day or Thanksgiving and Christmas are the times you have a surge in butter demand.

• swarm ⓥ (무리를 지어) 다니다

Hundreds of migrants, hailing from across Africa and the Middle East, were swarming the dock.

systematic, systemic

• systematic ⓐ 체계적인, 조직적인

The voices of women and minorities were being systematically drowned out by the majoritarian politics of the regime.

• systemic ⓐ 전신의, 전체의

The Jacks brothers grew up closer to raw, systemic violence than most families in this story.

교육

ship, sip

• ship ⓥ (배나 다른 수단으로) 실어나르다

On Thursday, the White House also accused Moscow of discussing a deal in which Pyongyang would ship weapons for Russia's war in Ukraine in exchange for food and other commodities.

• sip ⓥ (음료를) 찔끔찔끔 마시다

sipping on a Diet Coke in his spacious office overlooking the Seine.

spat, spate

• spat ⓝ 승강이, 옥신각신함

But it's the trade spat between Japan and South Korea that signals the larger troubles ahead for the world.

spat은 spit의 과거형이기도 함

• spate ⓝ (안 좋은 일의) 계속적 발생

The first American shark panic began in the hot summer of 1916, when a spate of attacks off the Jersey Shore killed four in two weeks.

a spate of 형식으로 많이 씀

schism, schtick

• schism ⓝ (집단 사이의) 대립(chasm)

A death reopens a schism in France. 　　　무슬림과의 대립

• schtick(shtick) ⓝ 자신만의 자질(one's special trait)

Yet as president, the schtick has been exposed as reality : his lack of political skill has become a liability. 　　　his : 윤석열 대통령

spit, spite, split

• spit ⓥ (입에 든 음식 등을) 뱉다 　　　spit-spat-spat

He chewed it carefully and then spat out the skin.

cf spit ⓝ 갑(岬), 곶(cape)

Yet this spit of sand outfitted with nothing more than a pair of concrete garrisons and a wooden hut is claimed by four governments : China's, Vietnam's, Taiwan's and that of the Philippines, which occupies it. 　　　영토분쟁지역

• spite ⓝ 악의, 앙심

Contempt, spite and insult are felt in every encounter.

• split ⓥ 쪼개지다, 나뉘다

No matter what happens, we won't split.

stoned, stony

• stoned ⓐ (마리화나, 술에) 취한

He's in the local pubs getting stoned.

• stony ⓐ ① 돌멩이가 많은 ② 냉담한(not showing any friendliness or pity)

Minutes later, when Vice President Pence delivered a greeting from his boss, President Trump, the room full of European diplomats responded with stony silence.

cf stone ⓥ 돌을 던지다

They were flogged, beaten, mutilated and stoned to death for supposed immorality. 　　　they : 아프간 여성

cf stone-faced ⓐ (돌처럼) 표정을 드러내지 않은

The judge sat stone-faced as the defendant pleaded with him to show mercy.

surf, surface

- surf ⓥ

① 파도타기 하다

But the Republican candidate did more than just surf on an anti-Biden wave.

② (인터넷) 서핑하다

ⓓ crowdsurf ⓥ (많은 사람이 모인 곳에서) 청중의 머리 위로 엎드린 자세로 지나가다

Videos of concertgoers screaming, "Stop the show!" to no avail circulated widely on social media;other clips showed individuals being crowdsurfed to safety.

콘서트 압사사고

- surface ⓥ 수면으로 오르다, 표면화되다

For most Americans, "gun violence" surfaces only when there is a mass shooting, as was tragically the case in Atlanta and Boulder, Col.

surface ⓝ 표면

scum, skim

- scum ⓝ

① (액체 표면에 더러운 성분이 모인) 거품

② 인간쓰레기

Pyongyang responded by calling Balton "human scum" and a "blood sucker."

북한 문제
Balton : 트럼프 정부의 국무부 관리

- skim

① (액체 위에 뜬 기름기 등을) 걷어 내다

As the scum rises, skim it off.

② (돈을 어느 정도의 기간에 걸쳐) 조금씩 훔치다(빼내다)

Despite the threats from her madam, Jane escaped as soon as she was able to skim a few hundred euros from her daily earnings.

scroll, stroll

- scroll ⓥ (컴퓨터에서) 스크롤하다

Just past midnight on Sept. 6, a Cornell University freshman was scrolling through Snapchat in her dorm.

- stroll ⓥ 거닐다, 산책하다

stroller ⓝ 유모차

"Demons stroll the hallways," Jack wrote of the prison.

sociable, social, societal

- **sociable** ⓐ 사람들과 어울리기 좋아하는, 사교적인

They are sociable people who enjoy having parties.

- **social** ⓐ 사회의(societal)

For many Koreans, economic dissatisfaction is exacerbated by the country's conservative social codes and notorious sexism.

cf **socialize** ⓥ 사귀다

Before Kabul fell, a usual day for Jack would include visiting the gym after a day at the office, or meeting friends for coffee inside one of the country's trendy cafes, pockets of calm and sanctuary where young women could freely socialize. — 아프간

- **societal** ⓐ 사회의(society or social relations 혹은 a particular society)

Masks have relieved many South Koreans of the societal pressure to maintain a level of facial beauty.

social distancing, social media, social mobility

- **social distancing** ⓝ 사회적 거리 두기

Social-distancing is really about the common good. — 코로나 관련

- **social-media** ⓝ 소셜 미디어

Activists deleted social-media accounts. — 홍콩 보안법

- **social mobility** ⓝ 사회적 유동성 — 개천에서 용 날 때 사용

In a survey of 21,000 South Koreans last year, 88% of respondents said they were considering emigrating to another country because of a sluggish economy, distrust in the government and a lack of social mobility.

slew, stew

- **slew** ⓝ 많음, 다수(a slew of)

And for much of this country's history, a slew of race-based immigration laws, like the Chinese Exclusion Act, prevented most immigrants from outside Western Europe from coming to the US or claiming US citizenship.

- **stew** ⓝ

① 스튜(고기와 채소를 넣고 국물이 좀 있게 해서 천천히 끓인 요리)

② 혼란 상태

War gaming suggests a dangerous stew of violence, refugees and a race to control those nuclear weapons would ensue. — 한반도 전쟁

steak, streak

- steak ⓝ (음식) 스테이크
- streak ⓝ ① 바탕을 이루는 부분과 색깔이 다른 기다란 줄 모양의 것 ② 티, 기미

There's a streak of insanity in his family.

splash, sprinkle

- splash ⓥ 물을 끼얹다

The most recent missile passed over Japan on Sept. 15, following an earlier one on Aug. 29. Both went over the northern island of Hokkaido before splashing into the Pacific Ocean.

- sprinkle ⓥ 뿌리다, 간간이 섞다

Sixty-something Jack, who sports a red cap sprinkled with tiny winking mirrors in the traditional Sindhi style, recommends taking frequent rests under a tree.

'sp~' 중에는 물과 관련된 단어들이 있다(spit, splatter, spatter, spill, spigot)
북한 미사일

지구온난화

stationary, stationery

- stationary ⓐ 정지된, 움직이지 않는

Jack's wife eventfully purchased a stationary bike.

- station ⓥ (특히 군인을) 주둔시키다, 배치하다

Some 28,500 American troops are stationed in South Korea.

- stationery ⓝ 문구류(Writing and other office materials)

sane, sanitary

- sane ⓐ 정신이 온전한

Occasionally he uses the jungle gym in his local park to do pull-ups. His routine is nothing fancy, he says, but "it keeps my sanity."

- insane ⓐ 제정신이 아닌

NGRI(not guilty by reason of insanity) : 미친 사람의 행동은 죄가 되지 않음

- sanitary ⓐ 위생적인

Fans had temperatures taken, and their hands were kept as sanitized as the atmosphere : Seating was spread out, everyone wore masks, and cheering was banned.

sanity ⓝ
올림픽 참가선수가 코로나로 훈련을 못 한 상황

insanity ⓝ

sanitize ⓥ
도쿄올림픽

span, spin

- **span** Ⓥ 가로지르다

Just 35 miles from the demilitarized zone, the metropolitan area of 25 million, with its fashionable, upscale entertainment bars, globe-spanning banks and new 123-story Lotte Group building, could be wiped off the map in any conflict by North Korea's artillery, let alone its ever improving nuclear arsenal.

ⓓ **span** Ⓝ (어떤 일이 지속되는) 기간

After that test, Mr. Kim urged his engineers to build a solid-fuel ICBM "in the shortest span of time."

- **spin** Ⓥ (휙) 돌다, 돌아서다

spin-spun-spun

Now, a pair of mechanical engineers have unraveled why these ancient Tupperware, made of mud slapped and pressed by hand and spun on a pottery wheel, are exquisitely suited to fostering the growth of probiotic microbes that transform humble cabbage into a culinary superstar.

김치가 수퍼푸드 (superfood)가 된 이유

salve, savior, savor

- **salve** Ⓝ (상처 등에 바르는) 연고

salve Ⓥ 연고를 바르다

To the Japanese, South Korea has often been an untrustworthy neighbor that has broken several promises, including treaty agreements that were designed to salve historical wounds.

- **savior** Ⓝ 구세주, 구조자

Lincoln is often depicted as either a secular saint, the savior of Union, and the Great Emancipator, or as a calculating political creature imprisoned by public opinion and white prejudice.

ⓓ **save** Ⓥ ① 구하다 ② 저축하다

Now the archdiocese is seeking help to save Notre Dame from yielding to the ravage of time.

archdiocese Ⓝ 대주교의 관할 구

ⓓ **salvation** Ⓝ 구조(deliverance)

salvation army : 구세군

- **savor** Ⓥ 맛보다

They learn how to savor the taste of a mint until it dissolves on their tongue.

stoke, strike, stroke

● stoke ⓥ

① 연료를 더 넣다

I stoked the furnace for the night.

② (감정을) 더 부추기다

Such calls have gained momentum in recent months, as North Korea has stoked nuclear jitters in the South by testing a series of what it called nuclear-capable short-range ballistic missiles.

such calls : 자체 핵무장론

● strike ⓥ

① 공격하다

It began to sink, and capsized when the ninth and final torpedo struck.

② (질병 등이) 갑자기 닥치다

Even before the pandemic struck, Tokyo 2020 was becoming known as "the most jinxed Olympics," says Jane.

③ 파업하다

hunger strike : 단식투쟁

An attempt to insert a "national education" into the school curriculum was jettisoned only after hunger strikes and demonstrations in 2012.

④ (결론이나 타협 따위에) 이르다

The situation obliges the government to strike a delicate balance.

⑤ 인상을 주다

I was struck on a round of bureaucratic visits to government offices last summer by how casually and liberally young women dressed in even these traditionally austere official outposts.

히잡을 벗고자 하는 이란 소요사태

● stroke ⓝ

① (수영·조정에서 팔·노를) 젓기, 스트로크

② (손으로) 쓰다듬기, 어루만지기

③ 뇌졸증

④ (연속 동작의) 한번 (each of a series of movements)

One stroke brought 100 to 150 milliliters of water ; for food and tea, they needed 150 liters.

우물에서 두레박질

ⓓ stroke ⓥ (동물의 털을) 쓰다듬다, (수염이나 머리카락을) 어루만지다

He put his hand on her hair and stroked it.

ⓓ a stroke of genius : 천재적인 솜씨, 천재적인 아이디어

A cynic might call this a stroke of marketing genius.

signify, signal

- **signify** ⓥ 의미하다(mean)

But for many Russians, the annexation signified that Russia, for the first time since the dissolution of the Soviet Union, was once again a real superpower.

- **signal** ⓥ 신호를 보내다(to notify by a motion, action, movement, or sound)

Masks signal respect for others' well-being.

cf **signal** ⓝ 신호

Although the ministry gave no specific date for dropping those restrictions, it was yet another signal that the two countries, which have been at odds over history and territory for years, are now willing to cooperate to face rising threats from North Korea's advancing nuclear program and China's growing military ambitions in the region.

cf **signals intelligence** ⓝ 신호 정보

The secret report was based on signals intelligence, which meant that the United States has been spying on one of its major allies in Asia.

signification ⓝ

윤석열 대통령의 일본방문
the ministry : (일본) 정부 부처

미국의 도청 사건
the secret report : 미국 정부의 비밀문서

significance, signification

- **significance** ⓝ 중요성, 중대성

ⓓ **significant** ⓐ 중요한, 의미있는(meaningful)

More than 3,000 US and allied dead, tens of thousands with significant wounds and a few trillion dollars expended — to say nothing of hundreds of thousands of Afghans killed and wounded as well.

- **signification** ⓝ 의미

You should assume that the author is using the word in its ordinary signification.

숫자로 표시한 아프간 전쟁

stallion, stellar

- **stallion** ⓝ 종마(being used for breeding)

Winter had frozen over the Apache-Sitgreaves National Forests in late January 2019 when Jack saw the dead stallion, known to locals as Raven.

- **stellar** ⓐ ① 별의(relating to the stars) ② 뛰어난(outstanding)

In this poll, unlike normal Australian elections, voting isn't compulsory and anything less than a stellar turnout could strengthen opponents of same-sex marriage in the parliament.

statue, statute

• **statue** ⓝ 조각상

During the French Revolution, mobs of people carted off or smashed some of its paintings and statues.

파리의 노틀 담(Notre Dame) 대성당 이야기

• **statute** ⓝ 법률

We also know that some laws, like the segregation statute, contravene basic principles of the Constitution.

stature, status

• **stature** ⓝ

① 키, 신장(natural height)
② 지명도, 위상(the degree to which someone is admired or regarded as important)

Her replacement, probably Socialist Party leader Jack, will try the same approach, but with less stature on the European stage.

• **status** ⓝ 지위, 자격

Since six-party denuclearization talks were suspended in 2009, Pyongyang's pariah status has only deepened, even as its nuclear-weapons program has matured.

solidarity, solitary

• **solidarity** ⓝ 단결, 연대, 결속

At the World Cup, Iran's team stood silently during the national anthem, signaling their solidarity with the protesters.

이란 사태

cf **solidify** ⓥ 굳어지다, 굳히다

solidification ⓝ

Each of these upbeat, dance-ready singles, released strategically over the course of two years, became record-breaking hits and solidified BTS's place in the pop firmament.

these : BTS 곡

• **solitary** ⓐ 혼자 있는

The 24-minute film he produced, Leaving Fear Behind, landed him six years in a squalid prison, where he was "tortured day and night and kept in solitary confinement for over 86 days,"

cf **solitude** ⓝ 고독

In reality, although she romanticizes the solitude she had in Gombe, she acknowledges that connecting with people gives her energy.

침팬지 대모 제인 구달(Jane Goodall)
Gombe : 탄자니아의 국립공원

sprint, spurt, squirt

- sprinter ⓝ 단거리 주자

Those who take a knee in Tokyo may face the same sanctions as US sprinters Smith and Carlos, who were expelled from the 1968 Mexico Olympics for raising a fist on the podium to protest racism.

sprint ⓥ (짧은 거리를) 전력 질주하다

- spurt ⓥ

① (갑자기) 전속력으로 달리다

ⓒ 마라톤 중계에서 결승점을 앞두고 'spurt 하기 시작했습니다' 라고 중계하곤 함

② 뿜어져 나오다, 솟구치다

The old man saw flying fish spurt out of the water and sail desperately over the surface.

- squirt ⓥ (액체를) 찍 뿜어내다(in a thin fast stream)

sea squirt : 멍게(우렁쉥이)

ⓒ 멍게가 머금은 물을 찍 뿜어내곤 합니다

splint, splinter

- splint ⓝ 부목(아픈 팔다리를 고정하기 위하여 일시적으로 대는 나무)

Son wears a splint on one of his fingers from a recent injury.

손흥민

- splinter ⓝ 조각, 가시

Despite the antipathy to Park, the main opposition Democratic Party only polls an approval rating of 31%, with Park's ruling Saenuri Party at 15% and the splinter People's Party at 14%.

박근혜 탄핵

the splinter People's party : main 당에서 분리된 당

scar, scare

- scar ⓝ 상처, 흉터

SARS-scarred populations : SARS의 상흔이 있는, SARS를 겪은

A scar runs along the inside of his forearm, which he broke last year helping South Korea qualify for the World Cup.

scarry ⓐ

손흥민

- scare ⓥ 겁먹다, 무서워하다

With dozens of people killed so far in mass shootings in the US in 2019, thousands of Americans killed like Jack are seeking security through an influx of products marketed to those scared of being shot or of losing loved ones to gun violence.

총기사고

ⓒ scary ⓐ 겁먹은

How sharks become so scary

기사 제목

sparrow, swallow

- sparrow ⓝ 참새
- swallow ⓝ 제비

One swallow does not make a summer. 　　속담

- swallow ⓥ

① 삼키다

Did he really believe that the whale swallowed Jonah, that Joshua made the sun stand still and that Adam and Eve were the first people? 　　성서

② 견디다

That budget-tightening measures will be introduced by a millionaire may make them particularly hard for ordinary people to swallow. 　　a millionaire : 영국 신임 총리

sallow, shallow

- sallow ⓐ (얼굴이나 피부에서) 병색이 보이는

Her timid, sallow aspect told me all I needed to know.

- shallow ⓐ 얕은

sightings of great white sharks in shallow waters

strafe, strife

- strafe ⓥ 비행기에서 공격하다, 폭격을 가하다

The *Oklahoma*'s crew tried to fight back, but it was hit with eight torpedoes in the first 10 minutes of the attack, and repeatedly strafed. 　　태평양전쟁

- strife ⓝ 다툼, 불화(angry or bitter disagreement over fundamental issues)

Italy may be drawn to an authoritative figure in times of economic strife. 　　총리선출

spangle, sparkle

- spangle ⓥ 스팽글(옷에 장식으로 붙이는, 반짝거리는 얇은 조각)로 장식하다

At the war's end, NFL commissioner Layden called for all of the league's teams to continue to play "The Star-Spangled Banner" at every game, arguing that the tradition was just as important as it had been during the war. 　　NFL : National Football League

ⓓ The Star-Spangled Banner : ① (미국) 국기 ② (미국) 애국가

- sparkle ⓥ 반짝이다, 반짝반짝 빛나다 　　sparkly ⓐ

It was morning, and the new sun sparkled gold across the ripples of a gentle sea.

spark, spike

- spark ⓥ 촉발하다, 유발시키다

Research suggests that it sparks energy, boosts brainpower, improves immunity, curbs stress, and improves mood.

it : humor

- spike ⓥ 급등하다(it increases quickly and by a large amount)

In 2016, the year Jack set out from Nigeria, the number of migrants arriving in Italy from Libya spiked to 163,000, prompting a political backlash and a determination to stanch the flow at all costs.

spike ⓝ

shade, shadow

- shade ⓝ 그늘, 음영

Residents gathered under the shade of a large tree to air their frustrations over the slow pace of development.

- shadow ⓝ 그림자, 어둠

George Floyd's death brings into full view the terror and trauma that shadow Black people's experiences in this country.

five o'clock shadow : (아침에 깎은 뒤) 저녁 무렵 거뭇거뭇 자란 수염

foreshadow, overshadow

- foreshadow ⓥ 전조가 되다, 조짐을 나타내다

In a country of hidden agendas, historical and current events foreshadow her purpose and fate.

her : 김정은의 딸 김주애, 김정은의 후계구도

- overshadow ⓥ 그늘을 드리우다

But the run-up to the 2018 Winter Olympics threatened to overshadow anything set to take place on the snow and ice in Pyeong Chang, South Korea.

한반도의 불안한 정세

shifty, shitty

- shifty ⓐ 부정직해 보이는, 속일수로 보이는 (looking dishonest, deceitful)

He looks a bit shifty to me.

- shitty ⓐ 형편없는(of poor quality)

a shitty job

secondary, secondly

• secondary ⓐ (중요도에서) 이차적인, 부차적인

But Putin was insulted by Bush's attitude toward Russia, feeling that the American President treated it merely as a large, secondary European country.

• secondly ⓐᵈᵛ 두 번째로

Yet continued Chinese support for North Korea has never really been in doubt, for two key reasons : Pyongyang's fall would rob Beijing of a buffer against a US-allied united Korea. And secondly, the collapse send a ruinous flood of millions of refugees north into China.

superiority, supremacy

• superiority ⓝ 우월, 우월   superior ⓐ

She suffered the double bind of race and gender. The first pitted her against white superiority, while the latter made her inferior in the eyes of men of all races.

• supremacy ⓝ 지고(至高), 최고   supreme ⓐ 최고의

white supremacist

squall, squeal

• squall ⓝ (눈과 비를 동반한) 돌풍

• squeal ⓝ (길고 큰) 꽥 소리를 지름   squeal ⓥ

Cincinnati police responded to a squeal of a call Wednesday afternoon.

solace, solicit

• solace ⓝ 위안, 위로

Raising her four daughters and young son by dint of loans, limited family legacies and hand-me-downs, Alice of Greece would eventually find solace in religion and become a nun.

• solicit ⓥ 간청하다, 요청하다   solicitation ⓝ

She took care to solicit artifacts from previous Presidents, as well as   She : 미국 제35대 대통령
redesigning rooms to reflect different eras of American history.   케네디 부인 재클린

shove, shovel

- **shove** ⓥ 아무렇게나 넣다(push)

On March 3, nearly a year after he found the diamond, he shoved all his belongings into a suitcase for what he thought would be a brief stop to pick up a visa at the Canadian High Commission in Ghana before booking an onward flight to Canada.

가나(Ghana)에서 다이아몬드를 발견한 젊은이의 캐나다 유학

- **shovel** ⓝ 삽

So he kept shoveling gravel until nightfall, pausing occasionally to grip the heavy stone in his fist.

shovel ⓥ 삽질하다
다이아몬드 광산

spiral, sprawl

- **spiral** ⓥ 나선형으로 움직이다, 급등하다

Youth unemployment is above 30%, while spiraling inflation has made life unaffordable for many people.

- **sprawl** ⓥ 큰 대자로 눕다, 널브러지다

He rushed his son to the hospital, then secreted his whole family to another part of the sprawling capital, always fearing the tap on the shoulder that meant he'd been found.

탈레반

showdown, slowdown

- **showdown** ⓝ 마지막 결전(a decisive confrontation or contest)

Late one Wednesday night at the end of May, Trump's national security team told him a North Korean official had called Pence a "political dummy" and threatened a nuclear "showdown."

slow down ⓥ

- **slowdown** ⓝ 둔화

European politicians have begun bracing for auto tariffs from Washington, which look poised to hit as the global economy begins slowing down.

static, statistic

- **static** ⓐ 정적인

Encouraging cultural differences would not mean a static world.

statics ⓝ 정역학

- **statistic** ⓐ 통계적인

Statistically, sharks have far more to fear from us than we do from them—fisheries wipe out an estimated 100 million each year.

statistics ⓝ 통계학

suspend, sustain

• suspend ⓥ

① 매달다, 걸다

Just six miles(10km) from Dandong, a new $350 suspension bridge spans the Yalu River.

suspension bridge : 현수교
Yalu River : 압록강

② 유보하다, 연기하다

More crucially, Beijing could suspend the half-a-million tons of crude oil that flows each year through the pipe-line located near Dandong.

ⓓ suspension ⓝ

① 유보, 연기

Kim demands the complete suspension of South Korea-U.S. joint military exercises as a condition for dialogues with both countries, which is a nonstarter for Washington.

② 정학

There, school harassment is frequently grounds for suspension or expulsion, while many South Korean schools just impose community service or a restraining order.

학교폭력
There : 미국

• sustain ⓥ

① 살아가게 하다, 지속시키다

Flat island is too hot, too salty and too small to sustain human life.

② (피해를) 입다, 당하다

He benefited himself from the advice of his father Son Wong-jung, a player in the domestic K-league before he sustained a career-ending injury at age 28.

He : 손흥민

sustainability, sustenance

• sustainability ⓝ 지속 가능성

sustainable ⓐ

But if the US is interested in a long-terms, sustainable solution with North Korea, many experts say demanding denuclearization from a regime that sees nuclear weapons as its only life-line is folly.

• sustenance ⓝ 생명력을 유지시켜주는 음식

Also now I have gained on him in the question of sustenance.

I : 어부
him : 고기(생선)

straight, straightforward

- straight ⓐ 이성애자의

At one point, he had as many as seven establishments – spaces where queer and straight people could mingle – but he lost customers during the pandemic and closed his last remaining restaurant in August 2020.

he : 홍석천

ⓓ go straight : 곧장 가다

For negotiations to go straight to sanctions relief would be a mistake.

한반도

- straightforward ⓐ 단순한, 간단명료한

The meals were usually simple and straightforward, a plate of steak and baked potatoes or a hamburger and fries.

squawk, squeak

- squawk ⓥ

① (짧고 날카로운) 소리 내다

The geese flew upriver, squawking.

② 불평하다

The customers squawked about the high prices.

- squeak ⓥ

① (그렇게 크지도 길지도 않게) 끽소리 내다

A rat squeaked and ran into the bushes.

② (간신히 어려움을) 넘기다, 이겨내다

Plants that squeak past an early overnight frost can last for another month of warm autumn weather.

stink, stint

- stink ⓥ 악취가 나다, 구린내가 나다(stench)

Money does not stink.

유럽에서는 화장실 사용료를 받음

- stint ⓝ 잠시 활동한 일(직업)

Bolton, born in Baltimore and educated at Yale, has worked for every Republican President since Reagan, including a stint as US ambassador to the UN under George Bush.

skiff, skip

- **skiff** ⓝ 작은 보트

Jack's damaged and overturned skiff was found around 2:30 PM on Friday.

- **skip** ⓥ (일을) 거르다, 빼먹다

She let her kids skip school, she didn't insist that they finish college, and she took Jack to get his lip pierced at age 15, to the shock and dismay of other mothers in the grocery store.

자녀 교육

spot, spy

- **spot** ⓥ 알아차리다

If you slip out for dinner, who's going to spot you?

cf **spot** ⓝ

① (특정의) 장소, 위치, 자리

When~, so rack up extra steps by choosing a distant spot.

먼 곳에 주차하여 걷기 운동 권고

cf **blind-spot** ⓝ 사각지대, 맹점

Her single-minded pursuit of that objective of political reform inside of Burma has created a very glaring and tragic blind spot.

Her : 미얀마(버마)의 여성 정치인
tragic : 탄압받는 소수 부족

② 지위

India has plummeted in democracy metrics across the board, including the World Press Freedom Index, where it now ranks 142 out of 180 countries, four spots behind South Sudan and three behind Myanmar.

- **spy** ⓥ 발견하다, 찾아내다

General Jack, the former commander of the US Forces Korea, says Pyongyang may spy a "window of opportunity" while there are "two progressive administrations, both in the US and South Korea, which doesn't happen that frequently.

opportunity ⓝ 북한의 핵무기 개발 기회

scam, scan

- **scam** ⓝ 신용 사기

Jane then blamed the prosecution in her 2019 trial and how the media portrayed her as a notorious scam artist.

- **scan** ⓥ (무엇을 찾느라) 유심히 살피다

He used a scanning electron microscope and a CT scan to zoom in and measure the pores.

김치와 장독
scanning electron microscope : 주사형 전자현미경

slay, sly

- slay ⓥ 죽이다

The Baghdad Gate, a brick relic from the 8th century, stands over the skeletons of slain ISIS fighters that lie in the open air, their flesh eaten away by dogs.

- sly ⓐ ① 음흉한 ② (남들은 모르는 비밀을 자기는) 다 알고 있다는 듯한

Putin gave a sly smile.

slay-slew-slain

species, spice

- species ⓝ (생물의) 종

But the most surprising images are of the more than 6,100 species thriving in the DMZ, ranging from reptiles and birds to plants.

- spice ⓝ 양념

variety is the spice of life.

한반도의 DMZ 기사

seasoned, seasonal

- seasonal ⓐ 계절의

They are all desperate for change. But the only change is the seasonal cycle of cease-fires —from the start of the school year to winter holidays to Easter—violated to some degree by both sides.

- seasoned ⓐ 양념을 한

advice seasoned with wit

Easter : 부활절

sanction, sanctuary

- sanction ⓝ

① 제재

Sanctions work best when they are massive, swift, and ruthlessly implemented.

② 허가

He appealed to the bishop for his sanction.

- sanctuary ⓝ 안식처, 피난처

The school's small library was his sanctuary, where he devoured adventure books such as Jules Verne's Twenty Thousand Leagues Under the Sea to escape the harsh reality of going hungry day after day.

이재명 후보

subsequent, subservient

- **subsequent** ⓐ 그다음의

In the 1990s, retail giants like Nike were plagued by reports of workers paid less than $2 a day and subsequently pledged to end child labor.

subsequently ⓐⓓ
subsequence ⓝ

- **subservient** ⓐ 굴종하는

Hong Kong is a town where the ruling class has long comprised either tycoons or bureaucrats subservient to whomever is the overlord-London previously, Beijing today.

subservience ⓝ

salon, saloon

- **salon** ⓝ ① 미용실, 이발소 ② (역사) 살롱

The salon has been able to raise prices twice over the past year, which means higher commissions for workers.

- **saloon** ⓝ 술집(bar)

The Central had a hotel on the upper floors, a saloon on the first floor and a bowling alley in the basement.

string, stringent

- **string** ⓝ

① 줄, 끈

② 현악기(string instrument)

③ 조건, 단서(strings)

In the press conference following the summit, Biden played down a no-strings meeting with Kim so as not to provide him "international recognition as legitimate."

summit : 한국과 미국의 정상회담
no-strings : 조건이 없는

cf a string of : 일련의, 계속되는

An epidemic of sexual harassment has led to a string of high-profile suicides.

- **stringent** ⓐ (규칙 따위의) 엄중한

US ambassador to the UN Jack called it "the most stringent set of sanctions on any country in a generation."

stab, stub

- **stab** ⓝ 시도, 노력(at)

But on the mainland, the topics of the day were a special election in Alabama, the latest GOP stab at repealing Obamacare and a fight President Donald Trump had picked with the NFL.

트럼프와 NFL(National Football League)의 갈등. mainland : 미국, GOP : 미국 공화당

- cf **stab** ⓥ (칼) 찌르다

Most of the victims, shot or stabbed with bayonets, were women and children who were "murdered" as they pleaded for their lives.

베트남전

- cf **backstabbing** ⓝ 뒤통수 때리기, 교묘하게 험담하기

The move validated Jack's view of the US as "deceitful, untrustworthy and backstabbing."

- **stub** ⓝ (연필이나 담배의) 몽땅
- cf **stub out** : (담배를) 비벼 끄다

So if you do smoke, there has to be a safe place to stub it out.

scoff, scofflaw

- **scoff** ⓥ
  ① 경멸하다, 조롱하다
  ② (많은 양을) 급히 먹다

scoff ⓝ

On their journey, they have pilfered from grain stores, scoffed mountains of corn and pineapples, and caused over $1 million of damages as they amble slowly through farmland and villages.

코끼리의 집단 이동

- **scofflaw** ⓝ 법을 자주 어기는 사람

Sure, there was some early resistance, and even now you see a few scofflaws on the subway.

마스크 착용

- cf scofflaw는 law를 scoff 함을 뜻함

schema, scheme

- **schema** ⓝ 개요(an outline of a plan or theory)

This blueprint, called a schema, keeps data entry reliable, search efficient, and the system parsimonious.

- **scheme** ⓝ 계획

Putin will now start devising a complicated scheme for ruling the country in the future.

stool, stoop

- stool ⓝ (등받이와 팔걸이가 없는) 의자
- stoop ⓥ

① (상체를) 구부리다, 앞으로 숙이다 (forward and down)

he stooped down and reached towards the coin.

② 몸을 낮추어 치사스러운 짓까지 하다

Jack wouldn't stoop to thieving.

stalk, stall

- stall ⓝ ① 마구간 (ox-stall) ② (시장의) 가판대, 좌판
- stall ⓥ

① 지연시키다

Moon traveled to Washington in May to attempt to persuade the new occupant of the White House to re-energize a stalled peace process.

② (엔진 등) 시동이 꺼지다, 일이 제대로 진행되지 않다

By the 1980s, it was apparent that the Cuban revolution had stalled.

- stalk ⓥ 몰래 접근하다

Yet the Orwellian fear that began stalking Cuba after Fidel took power in 1959,

> Moon : 문재인 대통령
> the new occupant of the White House : 바이든 대통령
>
> stalker ⓝ 스토커

scald, scold

- scald ⓥ (뜨거운 물에) 데이다, 데치다

Scald the tomatoes in boiling water so that you can peel them more easily.

ⓓ scalding ⓐ 델 정도로 뜨거운(더운)

on a scalding June afternoon

- scold ⓥ 비난하다, 꾸짖다

Republicans used the attacks to scold and chasten mainstream environmentalists.

script, scripture

- script ⓝ 대본

The best moments in sports come when the script gets thrown out.

- scripture ⓝ 성경

He taught me that prayer is not an escape from real life, but a passage to it. And his understanding of scripture demanded he afflict the comfortable as surely as he comforted the afflicted.

> He : 남아공의 투투(Tutu) 대주교

skylight, skyrocket

- skylight ⓝ (건물) 채광창

"We have the most valuable thing in politics besides a boatload of money, which is time," Jack says, looking up to the skylight in the atrium of the Hart Senate building.

- skyrocket ⓥ 급등하다

However, relations have deteriorated since then, with tensions skyrocketing in 2022 as North Korea fired a record number of missiles, and as a new South Korean president took office.

윤석열 정부 이후의 한반도 정세

score, scorn

- score ⓥ 득점을 올리다, 득점하다

As a forward for the English Premier League's Tottenham Hotspur Club, he has become the top Asian goal scorer in the elite's league's history.

scorer ⓝ 득점을 올리는 선수
he : 손흥민

- scorn ⓥ 경멸하다

That Park has done little to soften South Korea's patriarchal culture only heightens a sense of betrayal. "Park spoiled it for us," says 17-year-old high school student Jack, scrawling a scornful message to Park on a protest wall in central Seoul.

scornful ⓐ 경멸하는 (contemptuous)
박근혜 대통령

sober, somber

- sober ⓐ 술 취하지 않은, 맑은 정신의

Police arrested the woman for disorderly conduct while intoxicated and released her to a sober friend.

ⓓ sobering ⓐ 정신 차리게 하는 (a more serious, sensible, or solemn mood)

But these games also offer a sobering preview of another future, one in which the kinds of record-breaking heat waves that roasted Asia, Europe, and North America this summer are no longer extreme events but seasonal norms brought about by a changing climate.

ⓓ event에는 스포츠 종목이라는 뜻도 있음. 따라서 예문에서는 중의적으로 쓰임
Qatar 월드컵 기사

- somber ⓐ ① 어둠침침한 ② 심각한

Moon insists Kim somberly told him that "he wants to pass down a better future for his children, and that he did not want them to carry the burden of nuclear weapons."

Moon : 문재인 대통령
Kim : 김정은

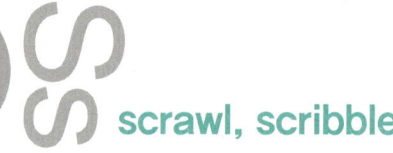

scrawl, scribble

- scrawl ⓥ 갈겨 쓰다(careless, untidy)

They have confronted armed members of the Taliban and demanded their hard-won gains be preserved, holding up handwritten messages scrawled on sheets of paper and chanting, "Work, education and political participation is our right!"

- scribble ⓥ 갈겨 쓰다(quickly, untidy)

Between calls, Arden began to scribble thoughts on scraps of paper.

동의어

scrap, scrape

- scrap ⓝ (종이나 옷감 따위의) 조각(a small piece of paper, cloth etc)

The insurgents still hold scraps of territory, but they have no hope of challenging Assad's hold on power.

Assad : 시리아 독재자

ⓓ scrap ⓥ 폐기하다

The original logo had to be scrapped following accusations it was plagiarized from a theater in Beligium.

- scrape ⓝ 긁힌 상처

I came away from the accident with only cuts and scrapes.

ⓓ scrape ⓥ

① 간신히 하다

By early 2016, Jack and his wife had scraped together enough money to pay a smuggler to get the family to Greece.

② (무엇을 떼어내기 위해) 긁다

She scraped the mud off her shoes.

ⓓ skyscraper ⓝ 마천루

sky+scrape

Birds were shot for food, but those who escaped did not choke on air pollution or crash fatally into urban skyscrapers, whose lights entice them.

sheen, shin

- sheen ⓝ 윤, 광택

sheenful ⓐ

Her hair had a lovely coppery sheen.

- shin ⓝ 정강이(shank)

The police determined that Mr. An, then 17, had hit three younger students in the head with a baseball, a cellphone and a belt buckle, and a fourth student on the shin with a bat.

학폭

scrappy, scrubby

- **scrappy** ⓐ 결기있는(determined, argumentative or pugnacious)

The World Baseball Classic is a battle of the game's top professional players. A scrappy Czech Republic team, full of guys with regular jobs, just might win your heart.   *WBC 야구 대회*

- **scrubby** ⓐ ① 보잘것없는 ② 관목이 우거진

But gradually the pebbles were shoveled out and the hole filled with scrubby sand, weeds and rocks.

- ⓓ **scrub** ⓝ 관목, 덤불(low bushes and trees that grow in very dry soil)
- ⓓ **scrub** ⓥ 문질러 씻다(청소하다)

Sportswomen are burning their jerseys, journalists are scrubbing their social media presence, and Kabul's streets are increasingly devoid of women.

scrabble, scramble

- **scrabble** ⓥ (무엇을 하기 위해) 굉장히 노력하다

Now, airports from New Zealand to Canada are scrabbling for public support in a bid to remain open.

- **scramble** ⓥ

① (항공기를) 급히 이륙시키다

Beijing responded by scrambling fighter jets, protesting that the US warship had "illegally entered waters near the relevant reef … and jeopardized regional peace and stability.

② (서로 밀치며) 앞다투다, 앞다투어 하다

In response, women — mostly from the rural states of Punjab — scrambled onto stages, took hold of microphones and roared back a unanimous "No!"   *파키스탄*

③ 급하게 하다, 서두르다, 허둥지둥하다

Many gyms are scrambling to add cheaper online options to retain members.   *코로나로 영업손실을 겪는 Gym들*

sleeper, slipper

- **sleeper** ⓝ 침실용 기차(기차의 침대차)
- **slipper** ⓝ 실내화

His clothing usually consists of dull robes and cheap slippers.

sleeper hit, sleepover

- sleeper hit ⓝ 모두의 예상을 깨고 흥행에 성공한 영화

As more and more flights got canceled and more and more international borders closed to foreigners, road trips became the sleeper hit of 2020. — 비유적 표현

- sleepover ⓝ (남의 집에서) 자고 가기

The kids weren't allowed to have sleepovers, they couldn't go to a friend's home unless their mother Jane had met the parents, and one bad grade could lead to the confiscation of beloved toys. — 자식 교육

sleepy, slippage, slippery

- sleepy ⓐ 잠이 오는

The wine had made her sleepy.

- slippage ⓝ 불이행

Slippage on any job will entail slippage on the overall project.

- slippery ⓐ

① 미끄러운

The townpath was slippy with mud. — slippy ⓐ 같이 씀

② 파악하기 힘든, 이해하기 힘든

Jane has proved herself equally adept in the slippery world of Chinese politics

saw, sow

- saw ⓥ 톱질하다

This blade is too dull for sawing. — saw ⓝ 톱

- sow ⓥ 씨를 뿌리다

Hate incidents sow fear across US. — 미국의 혐오 범죄

spout, sprout

- spout ⓥ (액체를) 내뿜다, 분출하다

The result is sewer backups that spout polluted water into basements and onto city streets.

- sprout ⓥ (식물의) 싹이 나다, 발아하다

The first summit between US President Biden and China's Xi Jinping showed that the recent climate-change talks could sprout green shoots in other parts of their relationship. — 비유적 표현

stenographer, stereotype

- stenographer ⓝ 속기사

She rose from abject family — working once as a stenographer and a milk-booth vendor to support her family.

steno~ : 작은, 좁은, ~graph : 쓰다

- stereotype ⓝ 정형화된 생각, 고정 관념

There is a stereotype that Asian Americans have class privilege and have 'succeeded' in this country.

spare, spear

- spare ⓥ

① (불편한 일을) 모면하다

The nose of American Airlines Flight 77 hit the first floor. I was about 150 ft. away on the fourth floor, and was spared.

9·11 테러

② (노력이나 경비를) 아끼다

They didn't have an unfair head start, but they were spared some of the most difficult obstacles faced by less fortunate kids.

cf spare ⓐ 여분의, 예비의

Few people had spare cash for inessentials.

inessential ⓝ 없어도 되는 것

- spear ⓝ 창(lance)

Guam is the Asian spear tip of the world's biggest military, and consequently a natural target.

미국령 괌

spar, sparse

- spar ⓥ 말다툼하다(to argue with someone but not in an unpleasant way)

Police and protesters sparred over three consecutive days.

- sparse ⓐ 드문, 희박한(of few and scattered elements)

And yet, her athletic opportunities proved sparse.

sequel, sequence

- sequel ⓝ (영화나 연극 등의) 속편

According to the leak, Fan declared $1.5 million for work on the sequel to her 2003 movie *Cell Phone* but actually pocketed $7.5 million.

Fan : 중국의 영화배우 판빙빙, declare ⓥ (세금 당국에 소득을) 신고하다

- sequence ⓝ 순서, 배열

The content of the program should follow a logical sequence.

sequester, sequestrate

- sequester ⓥ 격리시키다   sequestration ⓝ

Consumed by paranoia about the rampaging virus, North Korea completely sequestered itself from the world, even turning down food aid.

ⓒⓕ carbon sequestration ⓝ 탄소 격리(대기 중 이산화탄소를 담체에 고정하여 저장하는 과정)

- sequestrate ⓥ (법률) 가압류하다   sequestration ⓝ

the power of courts to sequestrate the assets of union

stamp, stomp

- stamp ⓝ ① 우표 ② 스탬프 ③ (발걸음) 쿵쿵거림

Each park visitors' center has its own unique passport stamp, which includes the date.

- stomp ⓝ (쿵쿵거리며) 걸음, 걷는 소리   stomp ⓥ

From inside, they could hear heavy machinery driving into his yard, stomping, and gunfire.

전쟁 중 지하 대피소

suggestive, suggestible

- suggestible ⓐ 남의 영향을 받기 쉬운

highly suggestible and compliant individuals

- suggestive

① 연상시키는

These headaches were most suggestive of raised blood pressure.

② 외설적인

a suggestive remark.

shimmer, simmer

- shimmer ⓥ 희미하게 빛나다(glimmer)

Those of us who live here now, as the city tries to shimmer back to life amid the seemingly endless COVID crisis, feel that toothache of the heart every time we pass one of our many shuttered storefronts.

here : New York

- simmer ⓥ (액체나 노여움이) 부글부글 끓다

As high-profile perpetrators in the West apologized for their behavior and some lost positions of power, many in Asia saw a chance to reignite long-simmering movements pushing for gender equality.

MeToo

shudder, shutter, stutter

- **shudder** ⓥ 마구 흔들리다, 전율하다

His head bounces inside the cockpit as a wheel shudders over a rumble strip.

- shudder at : ~에 진저리를 치다

Nowadays, reformers have changed their tune : they argue that eliminating long summer vacations could shrink achievement gaps between students. It's an idea backed up by data—but one at which their forebears might shudder.

change one's tune : 의견을 바꾸다
방학의 길고 짧음

- **shutter** ⓥ 문을 잠그다 문을 닫다(shut)

Three days after his death, the official mourning period essentially shuttered the country.

- **stutter** ⓥ ① 말을 더듬다 ② 작동이 원활하지 않다

And Moon himself has seen domestic support wane as South Korea's economy stutters.

shelf, shelve

- **shelf** ⓝ 선반

The cocoa industry, for example, is rife with child slavery, yet there have been few calls to pull chocolate from shelves, even though the profits of Europe's chocolate industry are created, at least in part, by labor exploitation in West Africa.

- **shelve** ⓥ ① 선반에 올려놓다(to place on a shelf) ② 보류하다

Upstairs, a mishmash of snowboarding awards are piled into a box, since Kim and Berle haven't built enough shelving to display all the hardware.

Kim : 미국 스노우보드 선수
Berle : Kim의 남자친구

- mishmash ⓝ 뒤죽박죽(a confused mixture of things)

scoop, scope

- **scoop** ⓝ (아이스크림을 덜 때 쓰는) 숟갈
- scoop ⓥ 재빨리 들어올리다

His mother scooped him out of bed one night to escape a bombing raid on his village.

- **scope** ⓝ 범위(the opportunity to do or develop something)

The health care professionals currently fighting COVID-19 are, in many cases, doing so outside the scope of their normal duties.

straddle, straggle, struggle

- **straddle** ⓥ 양쪽으로 다리를 벌리고 앉다, 이쪽저쪽에 걸치다

When Elizabeth took the throne, the UK was the seat of an empire that straddled the globe.

cf **astride** ㉑ (무엇의) 양쪽으로 두 다리를 벌리고

a photograph of my mother sitting astride a horse

- **straggler** ⓝ (대오 등에서 뒤처진) 낙오자

I picked up only a straggler from the albacore that were feeding.

- **struggle** ⓥ 몸부림치다

Despite South Korea's riches, it is also where even top college graduates struggle to earn enough to get a foot on the housing ladder, and where pensioners must recycle cardboard to make ends meet.

prep : 전치사(preposition)

straggle ⓥ (많은 사람이 움직일 때) 여기, 저기서 소그룹으로 움직이다

cf albacore : (참치의 일종인) 날개다랑어

strip, stripe

- **strip** ⓝ 좁고 기다란 땅

The tree was obscuring the line of sight between UN and North Korean guard towers on the narrow strip of land that has separated the peninsula's communist North from its capitalist South since an armistice effectively ended the 1950-53 Korean War.

cf **strip** ⓥ ① 옷을 벗기다 ② 스트립쇼 하다

The verdant island was stripped of its foliage.

- **stripe** ⓝ 줄무늬

Why is it that all the fast-moving fish of the dark current have purple backs and usually purple stripes or spots?

판문점 상황

savage, salvage, ravage

- **savage** ⓐ 야만적인, 흉포한(very violent or cruel)

"Bobby believed we should work to 'tame the savageness of man and make gentle the life of the world.'

- **salvage** ⓥ 구조하다

European and Chinese attempts to salvage the Iran deal are faltering, and Iran says it will increase its uranium enrichment capacity now that the US has abandoned the pact.

- **ravage** ⓥ 황폐하게 하다, 유린하다

I helped persuade them to have their skinny, cancer-ravaged dog put down.

savageness ⓝ

Bobby : 미국 제35대 대통령 Kennedy 동생
강조문은 그리스 비극 시인 Aeschylus의 말
salvage ⓝ

cf put down : (동물) 안락사시키다

strap, strop

- strap ⓝ 끈, 줄
- strap ⓥ (끈, 줄로) 묶다

Jack, who years later quit his job as a manufacturing engineer to support Jane's career, scooped her up out of bed, carried her to the car and buckled three seat belts on her in the back seat of his Honda Pilot. "I was just like a mummy, strapped down," says Jane. *(Jack과 Jane은 부부 / Jane : 운동선수)*

- strapped ⓐ (돈이나 시간이) 궁한

People who feel strapped for time are more likely to be anxious or depressed. They are less likely to exercise or eat healthy foods.

- strop ⓝ 가죽숫돌(a narrow piece of leather used for making a razor sharp)

staff, stuff

- staff ⓥ 직원을 채우다

He will still need to make sure that the clinic is staffed and stocked, and the teachers for the school are paid.

- understaffed ⓐ 인원이 부족한

Concert medics have also said they were dangerously understaffed. *(콘서트 압사 사고)*

- staff ⓝ
① 직원(crew)

Some CEOs are cutting staff even as the job market booms.

② 긴 막대기(a long thick stick that an official holds in some ceremonies)

③ ~하는 것

Here is the stuff of which fairy tales are made : the Prince and Princess on their wedding day.

- half-staff : 조기를 게양한

"I feel numb," said Jack, 45, who came to pay her respects at the Queen's official residence in the Scottish capital, over which the national flag flew at half-staff. *(엘리자베스 여왕의 죽음)*

- stuff ⓥ (빽빽히) 채워 넣다(채우다)

The incumbent will almost certainly claim victory through a fraudulent election with vote rigging and ballot stuffing, analysts say.

- the stuff of legend ⓝ 전설적인 인물, 전설적인 사례

The Jacks would go on to become the stuff of legend and are often called the Jewish Kennedy. *(이민 가정의 성공적인 자식 교육. Kennedy 역시 이민 가정 출신의 35대 대통령)*

sprain, strain

• sprain ⓥ (몸의 관절 부분에서) 삐다, 접지르다 sprain ⓝ

I fell down the steps and sprained my ankle.

• strain ⓥ

① 안간힘을 쓰다(using all your strength or ability)

the constitutional democrat who strained every sinew after independence from Britain to establish liberal democracy

strain every sinew : 전력을 다하다

② 무리를 주다(by making too much work or too many problems).

First, blood flow to the skin increases, straining the heart.

ⓓ strain ⓝ

① (유전적인) 성질, 기질

America has long been resistant to adequate poverty policies because of its strong strain of thinking that the poor are responsible for their own situations, no matter their suffering, but child poverty is too harmful and punishing to ignore.

② (동식물, 질병 등의) 종류(a type of animal, plant, or disease)

In 1918, a particularly virulent strain of flu managed to spread within a few months to the remotest corners of the world.

스페인 독감

③ 부담, 가중

This long strain on people's mental health could have been exacerbated by isolation, a loss of resources, the death of loved ones and reduced social support.

코로나

④ 특정한 경향(a particular tendency as part of a person's character)

In the strain of her smile, I could see the weight she carried.

she : 우크라이나 대통령 부인

⑤ (음악) 선율

ⓓ strained ⓐ 껄끄러운, 불편한(pushed by antagonism near to open conflict)

Lots of people struggle with the holidays because of strained family relationships.

휴일이 싫은 사람들

stupor, stupa

• stupor ⓝ 멍때림

As the days went on people handled their fear differently. Some sat in a stupor, hugging their pets. Others ran around looking for water and wondering how to survive.

우크라이나-러시아 전쟁

• stupa ⓝ (불교) 사리탑(a dome-shaped building erected as a Buddhist shrine)

swipe, swoop

● swipe ⓥ

① 슬쩍하다(to steal something)

Doting aunts passed babies from lap to lap as a gaggle of toddlers tore through the crowded living room, pausing only to swipe Syrian sweets from a coffee table. — 유럽에 정착한 시리아 난민들의 가정에서의 일상

② 후려치다(to strike or move with a sweeping motion)

She opened the window and swiped at the flies with a rolled-up newspaper to make them go out. — She : 뉴질랜드 총리

③ (신용 카드 등을, 휴대폰 등의 touch screen에) 손가락을 대다, 카드를 삽입하다

For years, Jane has been getting up early and swiping through her phone in the hope that Amazon Flex would drop some delivery shifts and she'd be quick enough to nab one.

● swoop ⓥ 급습하다

She and her husband are dressed casually (she in sneakers, he barefoot in shorts), trying to keep their 19-month-old daughter, also in shorts, from poking all the finger food. They switch off watching over her, with an aide swooping in as needed. — 뉴질랜드 총리(she) 부부

spell, spill

● spell ⓝ

① (특정한 날씨 등이 지속되는) 한동안

It's not yet the longest spell of drought.

cold spell : (평상시보다 기온이 낮은) 한동안의 추위

② 주문, 마법

magic spell

ⓓ spell ⓥ 철자를 말하다

Pupils should know how to spell commonly used words.

● spill ⓥ (액체가) 흐르다 — spill-spilt-spilt

It is no use crying over spilt milk.

ⓓ spillover ⓝ ① 넘침, 과잉 ② 여파

How India handles its internal crisis is already having spillover effects.

secluded, secular

- secluded ⓐ ① 한적한, 외딴 ② 다른 사람과 거의 접촉하지 않는

In the six decades since, the leader of the world's most secluded people has become the most recognizable face of a religion practiced by nearly 500 million people worldwide. 〔달라이라마 망명정부〕

- secular ⓐ 세속적인, 종교와 관계없는

By the 1840s, when a wave of Irish and Scottish immigrants brought the custom to the US, it was basically a secular pastime. 〔the custom : Halloween〕

swig, twig

- swig ⓝ 꿀꺽꿀꺽 들이킴

Jane pauses to slurp down some pho noodles and take a swig of cucumber water, which her husband has brought her.

- twig ⓝ (나무의) 잔가지
- cf twig ⓥ 깨닫다, 이해하다

He seemed confused until he twigged that something was going on.

stubble, stumble

- stubble ⓝ

① (면도를 안 해) 까칠하게 자란 수염(short stiff hairs, scruff)

Both of these razors give me a fantastic and super-easy shave — even after my stubble's grown for five days.

② 그루터기(short stiff pieces left in the fields after wheat, corn etc has been cut)

- stumble ⓥ 발이 걸리다, 휘청하다(trip)

Jack stumbled over the step as he came in.

- cf stumble ⓝ 휘청거림

How exactly does one accomplish world domination? Surely it takes remarkable talent, charm, kindness, altruism and dedication. But you'd still be missing a key component : a devoted community to uplift your efforts, soften your stumbles and shoot light from their eyes into the sky in your name every single night. 〔BTS 이야기〕

- cf stumbling block : 장애물

But this has been a surprisingly tough year for a Chinese leader who has faced few genuine stumbling blocks during his time in power. 〔this : 코로나 사태〕

squad, squadron, squat

• squad ⓝ

① (군대의) 분대

cf 소대(platoon), 중대(company), battalion(대대), brigade(여단), corps(군단)

② (스포츠의) 선수단

It's clear that Son enjoys being an elder statesman for the younger players on the squad. — 손흥민

cf firing squad : 총살형 집행대

the thousands of dissidents who languished in his prisons, some of whom ended up in front of firing squads

• squadron ⓝ (해군) 소함대, (공군) 비행중대

a guided-missile cruiser, two-destroyers and eight aircraft squadrons

• squat ⓝ 쪼그리고 앉음

Jack, a modern pentathlete from Poland, did squats while holding his dog.

squat ⓥ

modern pentathlon : 근대5종

smug, snug, snuggle

• smug ⓐ 의기양양한, 우쭐하는

We saw former Minneapolis police officer Jack sit there, smug, hand in his pocket, with little regard for the man dying underneath his knee. — 백인 경찰의 흑인 목조르기 사망사고

• snug ⓐ 아늑한

Yet the small plot where the sprightly 86-year-old grows corn, beans and cabbages in South Korea's Tongilchon village lies snug against the DMZ and is just a few miles from the likely location of Kim and Trump's summit.

• snuggle ⓥ (옆 사람에게) 파고들다, 달라붙다

For years, I assumed that if we ever got a dog, it would be mainly for my husband and kids, and I would have to let them do most of the snuggling or else suffer constantly red, itchy eyes.

steady, steadfast

• steadfast ⓐ (태도나 목표 따위가) 변함없는

For many North Korea watchers, Moon's steadfast defense of Kim is verging on delusional.

• steady ⓐ 안정된, 균형 잡힌

Normally, uneasiness there would prompt key Asian players to look to the US for steadiness.

steadiness ⓝ — 한반도 상황

T

외신으로 보는
대한민국
VOCABULARY

tweak, twitch

- tweak ⓥ 수정하다, 변경하다

Park President had allowed Choi to tweak speeches and advise on government policy.   박근혜 대통령 / 최순실

- twitch ⓝ

① 씰룩거림, 경련

The involuntary twitch of a lip betrays a rage only barely contained.

② 게임에 특화된 인터넷방송 플랫폼

Twitch, the platform on which that attack was live-streamed, said the footage had been viewed live by five people and then seen by 2,200 others before the company took it down.   총기사고

currents, torrent

- currents ⓝ (물, 공기의) 흐름

Franklin, who sailed for England as a teenage runaway and later measured the temperature of the ocean currents, thereby becoming the first people to chart the Gulf Stream accurately, was ~.

- torrent ⓝ 급류, 마구 쏟아짐

Sitting and watching your insane inner torrent puts you in touch with a fundamental truth : everything changes.   명상

- torrential ⓐ 'torrent'의 성질을 띠는

The death toll following torrential rains in Brazil rose to over 100 with more than 100 still missing.

taboo, tattoo

- taboo ⓝ 금기, 터부

Over the next month, "joyful events" are taboo in Thailand.   태국 국왕의 죽음

- tattoo ⓝ 문신

Air New Zealand dropped a ban on staff tattoos.

tambourine, tangerine

- tambourine ⓝ (악기) 탬버린
- tangerine ⓝ 귤

Tangerines were given to North Korea to be distributed among divided families ; prized matsutake mushrooms were sent the other way.   남북정상회담 때 선물교환

tycoon, typhoon

- tycoon ⓝ (경제계의) 거물

Hong Kong is a town where the ruling class has long comprised either tycoons or bureaucrats subservient to whomever is the overlord — London previously, Beijing today.

- typhoon ⓝ 태풍

cyclone ⓝ 사이클론
hurricane ⓝ 허리케인

tote, tot

- tot ⓝ 어린아이(youngster)

The consensus is that balance bikes are a better way to get your tiny tot ready to take on two-wheeled bikes.

- tote ⓥ 휴대하다, 지니다

Machine-gun-toting troops patrol the main sites, but street crimes remains ever present.

tawny, tony

- tawny ⓐ 황갈색의

a lion's tawny fur

- tony ⓐ 멋진(fashionable and expensive)

Over platters of iced whitefish, kimchi and spiced mackerel at a restaurant in Seoul's tony Gangnam neighbourhood

top-dog, underdog

- top-dog ⓝ 승자 (the person who has the most power in a group)

The South China Sea dispute is about who is going to be top dog in Asia.

- underdog ⓝ 약자, 패자

To millions of underdogs in the developing and developed worlds alike, Fidel was a tropical avenger who stood up to superpowers in the name of social justice.

Fidel : 쿠바의 1인자

ⓓ dog : 영어권에서는 정치인을 가리켜 'dog'(개)라고 많이 씀. 주인(유권자)을 위해 지치지도 않고 일한다는 의미. 'Top dog'는 개들의 치열한 싸움에서의 승자.

trash, tray

• trash ⓝ 쓰레기

But the sea was not always full of plastic trash that can choke them to death.

• tray ⓝ 쟁반

cf in tray : 처리해야 할 일이 있는(holding documents you still have to deal with)

Biden has more urgent issues crowding his in tray : the pandemic, global warming and, crucially, China's rise.

trashy ⓐ
them : fish

ashtray ⓝ 재떨이

turnabout, turnaround

• turnabout ⓝ 반전(reversal)

The turnabout less than two years later comes after a rise in homicides, following a decline from 2016 to 2019.

• turnaround ⓝ (상황의) 호전

it was a remarkable turnaround in his fortunes.

text, textile

• text ⓝ ① (휴대폰) 문자 ② 글, 문자(any written material)

One of the two female assassins, perhaps reflecting Kim's reported sense of humor, wore a T-shirt emblazoned with the text lingo LOL.

• textile ⓝ (옷) 직물, 옷감

Her new museum show reclaims space for women with colorful textile works.

two : 김정남 암살범

LOL : laughing out loud, lingo ⓝ 언어(a language, especially a foreign one)

truculent, turbulent

• truculent ⓐ 쉽게 반항적인

No amount of US carrot or stick has reduced the regime's truculence.

• turbulent ⓐ 격동의, 요동을 치는

The turbulent waters of the Gulf Stream can be treacherous even on a calm, sunny day.

cf turbulence ⓝ (대기) 난류

truculence ⓝ
북한 기사

temperament, temperance, temperature

• temperament ⓝ 기질, 성질

The two women were opposite in temperament.

• temperance ⓝ 금주, 자제

The law's original goal was to allow residents to go around local prosecutors who did not charge saloonkeepers for flouting temperance laws.

• temperature ⓝ ① 온도, 기온 ② (비정상적으로 높은) 열

In general, the new President wants to lower the temperature with China, at least in the near term.   비유적 표현

temper, template

• temper ⓝ (걸핏하면 화를 내는) 성질(성미)(to become angry suddenly or easily)

That temper of hers will get her into trouble one of these days.

ⓓ temper ⓥ 누그러뜨리다, 완화하다

In the early days of the war in 2022, NATO nations, led by the US, proved cautious in their support of Ukraine given concerns of escalation with Russia. However, Ukraine battlefield successes coupled with Russian underperformance tempered those concerns.   우크라이나-러시아 전쟁

• template ⓝ 본보기, 견본

Her childhood became a template for how she brought up her own children.

telling, telltale

• telling ⓐ 효과적인, 강력하게 보여주는(having a great or important effect)

Experts say that it's telling that Kim has put denuclearization on the table for the first time and pledged a moratorium on weapons tests.   김정은

• telltale ⓐ 숨길 수 없는

the telltale bulge of a concealed weapon

tense, terse

• tense ⓐ 팽팽한

They welcomed us in a friendly way, but things felt a bit tense.

• terse ⓐ 간략한, 간결한

His terse reply ended the conversation.

telescope, televise

tele~ : 먼 거리의

- **telescope** ⓝ 망원경

He would gaze from the Potala's roof at Lhasa street life through a telescope.

달라이라마 어린 시절

- **televise** ⓥ 텔레비전으로 방송하다

The First Lady's nationally televised tour of the renovated White House in 1962 drew a record 56 million viewers from around the world.

cf. television set

People stayed glued to television set for news on arcane royal funeral rites.

영국 여왕 장례식

telegram, telegraph

- **telegram** ⓝ 전보

Although she never met her uncles, her family revered Jack and Tom ; photos of them were preserved like relics ; letters and telegrams were sheathed in plastic and stored away.

태평양전쟁에서 수장된 형제 군인의 신원이 밝혀진 기사

- **telegraph** ⓥ

① 전보 치다

Her demonstration that during a crisis it is possible to lead without telegraphing aggression or playing on anxieties was a beacon in a world where the kinds of principles Arden champions seem to be on the wane.

Her, Arden : 뉴질랜드 총리
champion은 동사로 쓰임

② 은연중에 의향을 드러내다

Even the White House has telegraphed its concerns, with a spokesperson commenting that there's "no need for the Italian government to lend legitimacy to China's infrastructure vanity project."

tenure, tenuous

- **tenure** ⓝ

① 재직 기간, 재임

During her government tenure, she fought for integration and against segregation, discrimination and lynching.

② (대학의) 종신 교수직

- **tenuous** ⓐ 극도로 허약한, 보잘것없는

But the pandemic has all but severed the city's already tenuous link to the outside world.

thick-skinned, thin-skinned

• thick-skinned ⓐ 쉽게 동요하지 않는, 둔감한(impervious to criticism)

He was thick-skinned enough to cope with her taunts.

• thin-skinned ⓐ 민감한(too easily offended or upset by criticism)

If the Saudis admit to killing him and are not held to account, then it will give a green light to any thin-skinned ruler to go ahead and assassinate critics without fear of consequences.

transient, transitory

동의어

• transient ⓐ 일시적인, 순간적인

Attempts to curb its program have been shown as transient and flawed.

북핵

• transitory ⓐ 일시적인

The Federal Reserve, in ways reminiscent of the 1970s, proclaimed inflation was transitory and isolated to a few sectors even as labor shortages became unprecedentedly severe and pervasive.

transit, transitional

• transit ⓝ 수송, 운송

Even if masks aren't worn 24/7, Jack says, mask wearing is easy and safe enough to recommend it in high-infection settings like public transit, long-term-care facilities and hospitals.

• transitional ⓐ 과도기적인

transition ⓝ

Under the agreement, the leaders accused of massacres and kidnappings could avoid prison by confessing to their crimes before a special tribunal that was to be set up under a so-called transitional justice system.

taunt, taut, tout

• taunt ⓥ 놀리다, 비웃다

taunt ⓝ

If Trump's "Rocket Man" taunts are supposed to bring Kim to the negotiating table, they aren't working.

김정은

• taut ⓐ 팽팽한(stretched tight)

The rope was stretched taut.

• tout ⓥ 광고하다, 장점을 내세우다

On May 17, the tourism board launched an ad campaign, "Barcelona like never before," touting cleaner and calmer streets.

tenor, terror

- **tenor** ⓝ

① (성악) 테너

② 행로, 방향(course, tone)

But Donald Trump's winning the Republican nomination for the US presidency in 2016 shifted the tenor of bilateral relations. *미국과 중국관계*

- **terror** ⓝ 테러(a feeling of extreme fear)

In fact, terror, trauma and coronavirus are knotted together like a thick briar bush with thorns. *briar : 들장미*

terrible, terrific, traffic

- **terrible** ⓐ 심한, 지독한(very bad, awful)

For months, we've gotten nothing but terrible news — the cancer is everywhere ; it's not responding well to chemotherapy.

- **terrific** ⓐ 아주 멋진, 훌륭한

The same day that Chinese Nobel laureate and human-rights activist Xiaobo died after nearly a decade as a political prisoner, Trump called Chinese President Xi Jinping " a terrific guy" for whom he has "great respect."

- **traffic** ⓝ 교통

ⓓ be stuck in traffic : 교통 정체에 빠지다

While South Koreans may complain that their new, shiny cars are often stuck in traffic, they take pride in them and in the scores of impressive new buildings.

ⓓ trafficking ⓝ 불법 거래, 밀거래

It's very important to differentiate between smuggling and trafficking *traffic ⓥ에 '불법 밀거래하다'라는 뜻이 있음*

terrified, terrifying

- **terrified** ⓐ 겁이 난(very frightend)

But still the Russian political elite waited in horror for the day of the election—not because they had doubts about the result but because they were terrified of what would come next.

- **terrifying** ⓐ 겁나게 하는, 무서운(extremely frightening)

The "Diablo winds," blowing 70 m.p.h. at times, spread the flames with terrifying speed.

trace, trail

● trace ⓥ

① 추적하다(track)

An institution that traces the narrative of African-American life for what may be as many as 4 million visitors a year has to satisfy no end of tricky agendas. | institution ⓝ 흑인 박물관

ⓓ contact tracing ⓝ 동선 추적

Last month a Harvard University study estimated Singapore detects almost three times more cases than the global average because of strong disease surveillance and fastidious contact tracing. | 코로나

② 그리다

The message carried by the military planes wasn't exactly subtle. Scattering flower petals, they traced the colors of India's flag across the sky in saffron, green and white plumes. | tracing paper : tracing에 쓰이는 투명한 종이

ⓓ trace ⓝ 흔적

It was a trace of a history I didn't know existed.

● trail ⓝ

① (특정 목적을 위해 따라 가는) 루트(코스)

First "economic cooperation, then economic integration and finally full reunification" he told TIME matter-of-factly on the campaign trail in April in 2017. | 문재인 대통령 인터뷰

② 계속되는 것들(something that follows or moves along as if being drawn along)

The pandemic is worse among the migration trail.

③ (길게 연이어 나 있는 좋지 않은 것들) 자국(흔적)

Each firearm-related injury and death leaves a trail of destruction, posttraumatic stress, future injury and lost wages.

④ (시골의) 오솔길, 시골길, 산길(a rough path across countryside or through a forest)

trail bike

ⓓ trail ⓥ (경기에서) 뒤쫓아가다, 뒤지고 있다

In the aftermath of the Korean War, South Korea trailed the North in military and economic power.

trope, trove

- **trope** ⓝ 비유, 비유적 용법(used for an unusual or interesting effect)

Jack is resorting to the racist trope of blaming immigrants for the spread of disease.

- **trove** ⓝ 발견물(treasure trove)

Spearheaded by political consultant Jack, the grassroots effort has brought a trove of information that could be invaluable to Macron should he choose to run.

thermometer, thermogenesis

therm~ : 열(heat)

- **thermometer** ⓝ 온도계

The digital thermometer I had been carrying around with me registered 41.1℃ at 10 p.m.

- **thermogenesis** ⓝ (생리작용에 의한) 열 발생

Studies show that these easy activities — known scientifically as non-exercise activity thermogenesis, or NEAT — are associated with lower body weight, better overall health and increased life span.

생활 속 신체활동

tract, traction

- **tract** ⓝ 관, 계(a system of body parts or organs that has a particular purpose)

소화계, 호흡계의 '계'

- cf **urinary tract** ⓝ 요도

I had an educated guess that he was going to get a life-threatening infection this winter : either a urinary tract infection, pneumonia, or COVID-19.

- **traction** ⓝ

① (부러진 뼈의) 견인

He was in traction for weeks after the accident.

② 끌기, 견인, 영향력

But even as K-pop matured to a nearly $5 billion industry with fans around the world, its biggest stars—Rain, Girl's Generation and Big Bang—largely failed to gain traction in Western markets.

gain traction 형식으로 많이 씀

③ (차량 바퀴 등의) 마찰력(the type of power needed to make a vehicle move)

The tires were bald and lost traction on the wet road.

tack, tick, tuck

- tack ⓝ

① 압정

② 방침, 방향

Surely the US President could be persuaded to take a different tack.

cf tack ⓥ 부가하다, 덧붙이다

I've planned to be there for six weeks, including two spent in Japan's strict hotel quarantine. Even after tacking a few weeks on the end, I could hear the clock ticking.

일본(there)의 부모님 방문 결과적으로 시간에 쫓긴다는 내용

- tick ⓥ

① 째깍거리다

The clock is ticking for the policymakers to deliver.

② 체크 표시(v)하다

Yet many measures seem like little more than box ticking

cf box ticking : 형식적인 조건은 충족되어 체크하다(the process of satisfying bureaucratic administrative requirements rather than assessing the actual merit of something)

- tuck ⓥ (옷등의 끝부분을 단정하게) 밀어넣다

"Just being able to let those things out that you just tuck in your little secret part of your heart helps a lot," she says. "I feel much more at peace now."

those things : 마음속에 숨겨놓은 감정들

transpacific, transparent, translucent

- transpacific ⓐ 태평양을 가로지르는

This epic passage established a transpacific link and, and no other shipping route has been more successful or lasted longer.

cf Pacific ⓝ 태평양, Atlantic ⓝ 대서양, Indian ⓝ 인도양

trans~ : '횡단', '초월'의 뜻

epic ⓐ 방대한

- transparent ⓐ 투명한

There is new pressure on the UN this year to make the election process more transparent.

transparency ⓝ

- translucent ⓐ 반투명한

Irradiated Marshallese mothers had borne "jellyfish babies" with translucent skin and no bones.

태평양에서의 핵실험
irradiated ⓐ 방사능에 노출되었던
Marshallese ⓝ 마샬 군도 주민

UVWXYZ

외신으로 보는
대한민국
VOCABULARY

unwell, wellness

• **unwell** ⓐ 건강하지 않는, 몸이 편치않는

People seen as unclean or unwell are at risk of being shunned — which in the state of nature could mean death.

• **wellness** ⓝ 건강함

We've been doing a lot of wellness checks, probably annoying them with attempts at probing heart-to-hearts, watching them for signs of anxiety and depression.

upcoming, up and coming

• **upcoming** ⓐ 곧 있을, 다가오는(forthcoming)

Secretary Pompeo is on his way to North Korea in preparation for my upcoming meeting with Kim Jong Un.

Pompeo : 미국 국무장관
my : Trump

• **up and coming** ⓐ 전도가 유망한(likely to become successful or popular)

an up-and-coming young actor

underlie, underline

• **underlie** ⓥ 기저를 이루다

But it amounts to treating symptoms rather than the underlying disease of climate change, which will likely cause wider, systemic detriments to the farming industry.

the underlying disease : 기저질환
systemic : 전체의

• **underline** ⓥ 밑줄 긋다, 강조하다(underscore)

Two new reports underscore the scale of the challenge.

undercut, undermine

• **undercut** ⓥ

① (다른 제품이나 회사에 비해) 저렴하게 팔다(undersell)

② 약화시키다(weaker or less effective)(undermine)

But to reject the movies themselves amounts to punishing the victim. It undercuts the fine work that so many women — and decent men — have put into Weinstein-produced movies over the years.

Weinstein : 미투(Me Too)의 대상인 영화 제작자
victim : 성희롱 피해자인 여배우

• **undermine** ⓥ (기반을) 붕괴하다, 약화시키다(undercut)

This unpopularity could undermine his agenda.

his : 윤석열 대통령

understanding, understandable

- understanding ⓐ 이해심이 있는

For example, an empathetic leader is likely to be more understanding and give employees greater flexibility.

- understandable ⓐ 이해할 만한

it is understandable that mistakes occur sometimes.

unknowable, unknowing, unknown

- unknowable ⓐ 알 수 없는

Unlike her heirs, however, she remains virtually unknowable, having never allowed the media access to her private thoughts or opinions. 〔영국 여왕〕

- unknowing ⓐ 자신도 모르는, 알아채지 못하는

She was unknowingly in the early stages of pregnancy with Jack.

- unknown ⓝ 무명, 알려지지 않은 사람

The remains were buried as unknowns in the National Memorial Cemetery of the Pacific in Hawaii by 1950. 〔무명용사 묘지〕

union, unison

uni~ : '하나로'의 접두사.
USA : United States of America

- union ⓝ

① 결혼 (marriage)

In rural Japan, one of my mother's relatives, a priest in the native Shinto faith, refused to bless my parents' union. 〔ⓓ Shinto faith : (신도) 일본의 전통적 종교〕

② 노동조합(trade union)

Between their mother's civil rights work, their pediatrician father's campaign against lead paint and their grandfather's union loyalties, the three rowdy youngsters couldn't escape political awareness even if they tried.

③ 미국(특히 남북 전쟁 당시의 북부 주들)

Vermont and Maine, the two whitest states in the union

④ the State of the Union : 연두교서

- unison ⓝ 일치단결, 화합

Besides the sirens, smartphones beeped in unison and television stations suddenly cut to an ominous black screen with bold white script warning of a possible missile attack. 〔민방공 훈련〕

vibrant, vital

같은 의미로 쓰임
vib~ = vigor
시진핑 연설문

- **vibrant** ⓐ 활기찬, 생기 넘치는

"Our party shows strong, firm, and vibrant leadership. Our social system demonstrates great strength and vitality," the 64-year-old said.

ⓓ vibrate ⓥ 떨다, 진동하다

vibration ⓝ 떨림, 진동
vit~ = life
vitality ⓝ

- **vital** ⓐ 활력 넘치는

American leadership is still seen as vital to the stability and prosperity of the entire region, the cockpit of the global economy.

ⓓ vitamin ⓝ 비타민

vegetarian, veterinarian

- **vegetarian** ⓝ 채식주의자(veggie)

A lifelong vegetarian, she had never tried real shrimp, but she sampled it the week she registered the company.

ⓓ vegan ⓝ 우유조차 안 먹는 엄격한 채식주의자

- **veterinarian** ⓝ 수의사(vet)

In another study, though, cats were also evaluated by a veterinarian.

vat, vet

- **vat** ⓝ 그릇, 통(a very large container for storing liquids in)

a vat of grain alcohol

- **vet** ⓝ 수의사

ⓓ vet ⓥ (어떤 직책을 맡게 될 사람에 대해) 조사(심사)하다

vetting ⓝ
Yoon : 윤석열 대통령

On many occasions Mr Yoon has skipped conventional vetting procedures.

ⓓ background checks for private gun sales : (미국) 총기류를 판매하면서 구매자의 범죄 전력 등을 알아보는 것

variable, variant

- **variable** ⓝ 변수

constant ⓝ 상수

The biggest unknown variable is whether Russia goes ahead and takes military action against Ukraine and how the U.S. and its European allies would then respond.

- **variant** ⓝ 변형

Dangerous variants of the virus are circulating.

vassal, vessel

• vassal ⓝ 속국(a country that is controlled by another country)

Korea is nobody's vassal.

• vessel ⓝ

① (액체를 담는) 그릇

blood vessel : vein(정맥), artery(동맥)

② 배(a ship or large boat)

US military vessels and aircraft frequently carry out reconnaissance in Chinese coastal waters.

vincible, vulnerable

• vincible ⓐ 이길 수 있는(capable of being overcome or subdued)

Castro warned there would be "an invincible resistance" to any US interference in Cuban affairs.

invincible ⊗

Castro : 쿠바(Cuba)의 1인자

• vulnerable ⓐ 취약한, 연약한(can be easily harmed or hurt)

Weakened by heat and thirst, sheep and cattle become vulnerable.

ⓓ be vulnerable to : 취약하다

Throughout history, health care personnel have been vulnerable to the infectious agents that afflict their patients.

invulnerable ⊗

가뭄

vagabond, vanguard

• vagabond ⓝ 방랑자(no home and travels from place to place)

• vanguard ⓝ 선봉(leading the way in new developments or ideas)

the student activist who was in the vanguard of the Occupy movement

ⓓ forefront ⓝ 중심, 맨 앞, 선두

The company has always been at the forefront of science and technology.

velocity, veracity

• velocity ⓝ 속도(speed)

THAAD batteries have no payload but destroy enemy missiles by colliding with them at high velocity.

우리나라에 설치된 사드 (THAAD)

• veracity ⓝ 진실성(the fact of being true or correct)

Ultimately, he was confirmed and she encountered public scrutiny as her credibility and veracity were questioned well after the hearing.

he : 공직 후보자
she : 후보자의 과거 성추행을 고발한 자

venal, venial, vernal

- **venal** ⓐ 부패한(in a dishonest way in return for money)

But to Castro, the higher villain was the US, whose interventionist policies he increasingly blamed for the venal rot not just in Cuba but the rest of Latin America.

- **venial** ⓐ 용서할 수 있는, 경미한(not very serious and can be forgiven)

They committed all the venial sins of American teenagers, and some of the cardinal ones as well.

- **vernal** ⓐ 봄의 (spring)

the vernal freshness of the land

vantage, vestige, vintage

- **vantage** ⓝ 유리한 점(vantage point)(a good position from which you can see something)

Or perhaps it's because I'm an immigrant, whose vantage point grants the privilege to look at the country from the inside and the outside.

- **vestige** ⓝ 자취, 흔적

The military bases maintained by Washington for nearly a century were seen to be a vestige of American colonialism.

- **vintage** ⓝ

vin~ : 포도주의

① (특정한 연도·지역에서 생산된) 포도주. 또는 그런 포도주가 생산된 연도

the 2017 vintage here will most likely be unaffected.

포도밭 화재

② 빈티지(old, but high quality)

a piano of 1845 vintage

cf **vintner** ⓝ 포도주 상(someone who buys and sells wines)

vice, virtue

- **vice** ⓝ

vicious ⓐ

① (접두어, 직책상) 부(2번째)

As a former vice president of the influential Agricultural Bank of China,

② 악덕, 범죄

a mobile phone network is being used to peddle vice.

- **virtue** ⓝ 선, 미덕

virtuous ⓐ

If the 40 million Americans in poverty have one common characteristic, it's vulnerability. If they have one common virtue, it's resilience.

virtual, virtuous

- **virtual** ⓐ
① 사실상의
But virtually nobody in the bureaucratic elite in Russia believes Putin will step down in 2024.
② (컴퓨터를 이용한) 가상의
Their triumphs this year weren't just about the music. In October, they put on perhaps the biggest virtual ticketed show of all time, selling nearly a million tickets to the two-night event.

- **virtuous** ⓐ 도덕적인, 고결한
They are, rather, innate characteristics that must be shaped, molded and channeled to virtuous ends.

virtually(adv)

BTS 기사

virtue ⓝ

verifiable, veritable

- **verifiable** ⓐ 검증 가능한
He added that regime officials who are "meticulously planning" for the summit are perturbed by Secretary of State Mike Pompeo's talk of "permanent, verifiable, irreversible" disarmament, which appears to go further than the UN definition.

- **veritable** ⓐ 진정한, 참된
USCRI has rented every uint in the building. Soon it will become a veritable UN in America's Corn Belt.

verify ⓥ
verification ⓝ
북핵
the summit : 북한과 미국의 정상회담

USCRI : US Committee for Refugees and Immigrants
시리아 난민의 미국 정착

virulent, virility

- **virulent** ⓐ 치명적인, 맹독성의
virulently homophobic refrains that reflect widespread Ugandan prejudices

- **virility** ⓝ 정력, 힘
Beef, especially became bound to ideas of white, all-American virility.

refrain ⓐ (음악) 후렴

virile ⓐ

viable, vial

- **viable** ⓐ 성공 가능한, 실행 가능한
Spending hundreds of dollars on a hoodie or backpack is not a viable option for many people.

- **vial** ⓝ 유리병, 물약 병

미국의 총기 사고

vile, vilify, vitriol

- vile Ⓐ 도덕적으로 혐오스러운 (morally despicable or abhorrent)

Angry men and women screamed vile and racist slogans.

- vilify Ⓥ 비난하다, 비방하다

Kim is routinely vilified in the media here, but ~.

Kim : 김정은, here : 일본

- vitriol Ⓝ 독설

vitriolic Ⓐ

The vitriol was so great that state media outlets soon called for such personal attacks to stop.

vent, ventilate

- vent Ⓥ

① (환풍구 따위로) 배출시키다.

Windows should be opened to vent the fumes.

② (감정이나 기분을) 터뜨리다

She vented her frustrations by kicking the car.

- ventilate Ⓥ 환기시키다

ventilation Ⓝ

And in an era before AC, experts worried that poorly ventilated school buildings compound the risks.

AC : air conditioning

vain, vein, artery

- vanity Ⓝ 허영심, 자만

vain Ⓐ ① 허영심의 ② 헛된, 소용없는

Even the White House has telegraphed its concerns, with a spokesperson commenting that there's "no need for the Italian government to lend legitimacy to China's infrastructure vanity project."

cf in vain : 허사가 되어

Police searched in vain for the missing gunman.

- vein Ⓝ 정맥

BTS serves up a mania-inducing mix of heartthrob good looks and earworm choruses, alongside dance moves in the vein of New Kids on the Block and NSYNC.

cf artery Ⓝ 동맥

As the world watched the large container ship *Ever Given* block the vital shipping artery of the Suez Canal, I thought back to my own trips through the canal as a US Navy captain and admiral.

vegetable, vegetation

- vegetable ⓝ 야채
- vegetation ⓝ 초목(plants in general)

Instead, the study found, the forest is more likely to be replaced by smaller, shrublike vegetation that is adapted to warmer, drier conditions.

venerate, venereal

- venerate ⓥ 존경하다

veneration ⓝ
her : 박근혜 대통령

Her presidential campaign capitalized on the support of older conservatives, who still venerate her father for spearheading the nation's miraculous transformation into a world-leading economy in the 1960s and '70s, despite his trampling of human rights.

- venereal ⓐ 성병의(relating to venereal disease)

Instead, the U.S. military focused on protecting troops from contracting venereal disease.

vindicate, vindictive

- vindictive ⓐ 앙심을 품은

vindictiveness ⓝ

In 1968, a group of priests in San Antonio wrote to Pope Paul and asked him to remove their autocratic, vindictive archbishop, Jack.

- vindicate ⓥ (~의) 정당성을 입증하다

vindication ⓝ

But lately Trump has become increasingly energized by the idea that he's shattering precedent, and feels vindicated by the results of his risky moves.

vocal, vociferous

동의어

- vocal ⓐ 소리높여 말하는

Macron has become the most vocal proponent of an economic overhaul of the country, and the most visible target for the anger it is generating.

Macron 대통령의 재무장관 시절

- vociferous ⓐ 소리높여 말하는

Despite such a vociferous defense of the policy, its costs are becoming more apparent.

viral, visceral, eviscerate

- viral ⓐ 바이러스의

The outlier was Psy, a South Korean rapper whose "Gangnam Style" became a viral hit in 2012, though his comic, outlandish persona was an unlikely (some critics argue, problematic) herald for the genre

virus ⓝ
Psy : 가수 싸이
viral hit : 히트

- visceral ⓐ 강한 감정에 따른(조심스러운 심사숙고의 결과가 아니라는 뜻), 본능적인

The experience was raw and very, very visceral. And on the back of it, better systems were put in place.

코로나 이전 SARS를 겪었던 홍콩, 싱가포르, 타이완

ⓓ viscera ⓝ 내장(such as your heart, lungs, and stomach)

- eviscerate ⓥ 내장을 제거하다, (비유적으로) 중요한 부분을 제거하다

one trader describes how his business importing North Korean coal and minerals and exporting building materials has been eviscerated by the sanctions.

vicinity, vicissitude

- vicinity ⓝ 근처, 부근

The deaths occurred in the vicinity of Highway 99, a major north-south route for the Central Valley, which was flooded by the storm.

ⓓ in the vicinity of 형식으로 쓰임

- vicissitude ⓝ 변화, 변천

The problem, of course, is that government is not a business. The public sphere is far less accountable to market measures than it is to the amorphous but real incentives and vicissitudes of politics.

기업인을 장관에 임명

vacuous, vinous, viscous

- vacuous ⓐ 천박한, 멍청한(no intelligence, lack of thought)

Their ceaseless quest for distraction ends up exposing them to the vacuous truth of normal life.

- vinous ⓐ 포도주의

vine ⓝ 포도나무

Some people believe pairing wine with chocolate is a vinous sin.

- viscous ⓐ 끈적거리는, 점성이 있는

The gin too is different, slightly viscous due to the spirit's evaporation and concentration across the decades, yet still floral and expressive.

vacation, vocation

• vacation ⓝ 방학

A common theory holds that summer vacation was created for farm kids who needed to work.

• vocation ⓝ 직업(occupation)

For many Christians, it is seen as prefiguring the vocation of missionaries to promote the Gospel.

vacancy, vacate

• vacancy ⓝ 결원, 공석

Under state law, the governor calls a special election to fill the vacancy when a member of the House of Representative dies or resigns.

• vacate ⓥ 떠나게 하다

The notices to vacate are just the first step in the eviction process.

vacation ⓝ

vanquish, varnish

• vanquish ⓥ (경쟁·전쟁 등에서) 완파하다(conquer)

After vanquishing fellow American Keys in the US Open final on Sept. 9, Jane shared an emotional, extended hug with her longtime pal at the net.

• varnish ⓝ 광택제

The process involves spraying on a durable varnish, rather than paint.

validate, vandalize

• validate ⓥ 인정하다, 승인하다

If we award delinquents and validate their violence as a way to advance in negotiations with the government, we will only be sowing more violence.

• vandalize ⓥ (공공 기물을) 파손하다

Dozens of Jewish tombstones were vandalized in Philadelphia on Feb. 27.

validation ⓝ

voluble, volume

• voluble ⓐ 열변을 토하는

Jack was extremely voluble on the subject of good manners.

• volume ⓝ ① 용량 ② (TV의) 볼륨

After an initial strategy of quiet wrangling to free Jane, the US government has raised its volume on her case.

Jane : 러시아에 불법 억류된 미국 여자 농구선수

wrath, wreath

- wrath ⓝ 분노 ('화'보다 더 '심한 화', extreme anger)

There is no way that the Granite State will escape the wrath of the party.

cf Granite State : 미국 뉴햄프셔(New Hampshire)주의 속칭

- wreath ⓝ 조화 (장례식이나 묘지에 바치는 꽃)

By laying a wreath at a cenotaph for the 140,000 victims of a bomb codenamed Little Boy,

cf 리틀 보이(Little Boy) : 히로시마에 투하된 원자 폭탄의 별명, 암호명에서 따옴

whirlwind, windswept

- whirlwind ⓝ ① 회오리바람 ② 많은 일이 정신없이 이어지는 상황

For a few weeks, I was a whirlwind of fixing-ness.

- windswept ⓐ 바람이 많이 부는

Their brothers sent photos back home showing their delight with island life : wearing leis, balancing pineapples in their hands, standing atop a windswept mountain.

cf lei ⓝ 남태평양 섬에서 흔히 볼 수 있는 목에 건 화환

외국에서 오래 살다가 부모님을 방문한 자식이 부모님을 챙겨주는 내용
태평양 전쟁의 미군 형제

wishful, wistful

- wishful ⓐ 갈망하는, 소망하는

I had heard the same wishful tone over the phone.

cf wishful thinking : 희망 사항

I think she rather likes me. But maybe that's just wishful thinking.

- wistful ⓐ 애석해하는

He speaks wistfully of Taiwan, where conscription and civilian service are both set at just 12 months.

wistfully(adv)

He : 양심적 병역거부자

watershed, watertight

- watershed ⓝ 분수령

It looked like a watershed moment.

- watertight ⓐ 물이 새지 않는, 빈틈없는

The cooler bag also features a watertight zipper to make sure nothing leaks or spills throughout the day.

wander, wonder

- **wander** ⓥ 방황하다, 이리저리 돌아다니다

China's herd of wandering elephants may be climate-change migrants.   중국에서 떼 지어 움직이는 코끼리

- **wonder** ⓥ 궁금해하다

He fingered the cheap rubber and wondered how it would last the journey.   지중해를 건너는 아프리카 난민

cf **wonder** ⓝ 경탄, 경이

Making life fairer and safer for women would work wonders toward reducing the country's existential threat.   우리나라의 저출산 / work wonders : (어떤 문제를 푸는데) 효율적이다

will, wilt

- **will** ⓝ ① 의지 ② 유언장

The absence of change is not, for them, an absence of information. It's an absence of will.

- **wilt** ⓥ 시들다 풀이 죽다

He threatens, he blusters, he used the word nuclear, and the West wilts.   He : 푸틴

willful, woeful

- **willful** ⓐ 계획적인   will ⓝ

Jack was facing up to 20 years in prison after pleading guilty to voluntary manslaughter and willful injury.

- **woeful** ⓐ 통탄할, 비통한   woe ⓝ

This car may well be benefiting from easily improving on a design that was generally woeful.

wad, wade

- **wad** ⓝ (종이돈의) 뭉치

She threw some clothes into a bag, along with her passport, two mobile phones and a wad of cash, before climbing into a taxi with her brother and father.   a wade of 형식으로 씀

- **wade** ⓥ (특히 물·진흙 속을 힘겹게) 헤치며 걷다   wader ⓝ (비 올 때 신는) 장화

Travelers wade through crowds of antigovernment protesters at Hong Kong International airport.

whim, whip

- **whim** ⓝ 변덕 (a sudden feeling that you would like to do or have something)

China's President is on the cusp of a third term. Never before has the globe been so dependent on one man's whims.

- **whip** ⓥ

① 채찍질하다

whip ⓝ 채찍

"Sometimes my tutor kept a whip to threaten me," the Dalai Lama recalls, smiling. "The whip was yellow in color, as it was for a holy person, the Dalai Lama. But I knew that if the whip was used, it made no difference — holy pain.

② (커피) 휘핑하다 (whipping)

ⓓ whipping boy : 남 대신 벌을 받는 사람 (for someone else's mistakes)

wok, woke

- **wok** ⓝ 웍 (중국 음식을 볶거나 요리할 때 쓰는 우묵하게 큰 냄비)
- **woke** ⓐ (gender 및 인종, 성 소수자 이슈에) 이해도를 갖고 관련 행동을 하는 깨어있는

Several have criticized "woke" cultural attitudes.

영국의 보수당

walkaway, walkway

- **walkaway** ⓝ 쉬운 경기 (an easily won contest)

The game was one-sided, but was by no means a walkaway for the victors.

- **walkway** ⓝ (흔히 옥외에 지면보다 높게 만든) 통로

Beneath the walkways and the grass and the squirrels — all the things that make a park — is most of what makes a library.

weigh, wreak

- **weigh**

① 저울질하다, 따져보다

And if North Korea fields a deliverable nuclear weapon that could reach the US in the next four years, would President Trump want to face the American people with the explanation that he weighed the options and decided that doing nothing was best?

② 부담되다, 책임을 떠안다

How do you weigh such an enormous health risk, one that isn't solely or even primarily your own?

암 치료 중인 엄마를 면회 갔다가 자신 때문에 코로나로 전염되면 난감하다는 내용

cf. weigh A against B 형식으로도 많이 씀
Disease quarantines forces us to weigh the needs of others against our own. And the outcome can be ugly.

- **wreak** ⓥ (큰 피해 등을) 입히다, 초래하다

Of all the drastic changes the new coronavirus has wrought, this is the hardest for me to accept.

this : 코로나로 부모님이 일찍 돌아가시는 것

cf. wreak havoc on : 피해 등을 입히다
The virus wreaked havoc on my computer.

weight, heavyweight, lightweight

- **weight**

① (역기의) 웨이트
Bottles of laundry detergent — and beer — have subbed in as weights.

② 중요성, 영향력
We put a lot of weight on the exercise part.

③ (책임감 같은) 짐
Son Heung-Min does not look like a man burdened by the weight of national expectation as he strides into a studio in Seoul's Gangnam neighborhood.

- **heavyweight** ⓝ 영향력이 있는 사람(혹은 조직)

Their company is one of the industry's heavyweights.

- **lightweight** ⓝ 별 볼일 없는 사람

One possibility to succeed to Park is Bank Ki-moon, who shortly ends his term as UN Secretary-General, but he is seen as a political lightweight.

warfare, warlike, wartime

- **warfare** ⓝ 전쟁

What would be the role of the 7th Fleet in nuclear warfare?

- **warlike** ⓐ 호전적인(bellicose)

A trumpeter marched into battle in the van of the army and put courage into his comrades by his warlike tunes.

이솝 우화

- **wartime** ⓐ 전시의

In 2000 in South Korea, Vietnam War veterans attacked the office of a newsmagazine that reported wartime civilian massacres.

wartime ⓝ

waive, wave, waver

- **waive** ⓥ 포기하다

The heir to the Dutch throne, 17-year-old Princess Jane, requested on June 14 that her nearly $2 million annual income be waived while she remains a student and cannot perform royal duties, saying the stipend makes her "uncomfortable."

- **wave** ⓥ (무엇을 손에 들고) 흔들다

In the breezy evening some wore red attire and waved the national flag. 우리나라 축구팀 응원

- **waver** ⓥ 왔다 갔다 하다, 흔들리다

The US-North Korea relationship has long wavered between delicate and dangerous.

wax, wane

- **wax** ⓥ

① 점점 커지다(강해지다)(become larger or stronger)

In the immediate aftermath, the world waxed nostalgic about the younger, 20th century Fidel — the torrid icon who did perhaps more than any other figure in human history to define "the revolutionary."

aftermath : 쿠바(Cuba)의 일인자 Fidel의 사망

② (달이) 점점 커지다

- **wane** ⓥ

① (힘, 세력 등이) 쇠락하다

There are also signs that vaccine skepticism is starting to wane as the outbreaks intensify.

② (달이) 이지러지다

wan, wand

- **wan** ⓐ 창백한, 파리한(pale, weak, tired, exhausted)

she answered with a wan smile.

- **wand** ⓝ

① (마술사의) 지팡이
② 막대기 모양의 것(a tool that looks like a thin stick)

mascara wand

ⓒf magic wand : 요술 지팡이

The new law is not a magic wand that will solve all our problems.

wildfire, wildlife

• wildfire ⓝ (대규모, 파괴적, 급속히 번져가는) 들불

Over the next few hours seven wildfires broke out in Northern California's wine region.

• wildlife ⓝ 야생동물

Traditional Chinese medicine is killing the world's wildlife.

wallow, willow

• wallow ⓥ

① (동물) 물에서 놀다(to roll oneself about in a lazy, relaxed, or ungainly manner)

② 무기력하게 빠져 있다

Centuries of grazing had denuded the land of all vegetation, and the region's 740,000 people were wallowing in isolated poverty.

wallow in 형식으로 많이 사용

• willow ⓝ 버드나무

withhold, withstand

• withhold ⓥ 주지 않다

Lee left school in his early teens, lying about his age to work in factories, where he was frequently hostage to unscrupulous bosses' withholding wages.

Lee : 이재명

• withstand ⓥ 견뎌 내다

The manufacturer says it can withstand 15 tons of crushing force.

wannabe, would-be, soon-to-be

• wannabe ⓝ (누구처럼) 되고자 하는 사람

wannabe와 would-be는 동의어

I recently took a road trip across America, with the goal of meeting wannabe meditators and helping them get over the hump.

over the hump : 고비를 넘다

• would-be ⓐ 되려고 하는(desiring, intending, professing, or having the potential to be)

tips for would-be mothers and fathers

cf soon-to-be ⓐ 곧 있을 예정인

The soon-to-be king is purging opponents, real and potential, and firing a warning shot at would-be troublemakers.

withdraw, withdrawn

- withdraw ⓥ 철수하다

Recently, though, Tokyo and Seoul agreed to withdraw those export controls, and Seoul withdrew its W.T.O. complaint..

ⓓ withdrawl symptoms ⓝ 금단증세

withdrawl ⓝ

- withdrawn ⓐ 내성적인

Students were noticeably more withdrawn and unsure of their environment when classes started.

wink, wrinkle

- wink ⓥ ① 윙크하다 ② 반짝거리다

The airplane's landing lights winked on and off.

- wrinkle ⓝ

① (얼굴의) 주름.

Beside each wrinkle on the face of this old queen of our cathedrals. you will find a scar.

파리의 Notre Dame 대성당

② 기발한 생각(a change in a customary procedure or method)

Trump's new wrinkle brings promise and risk.

북핵

ⓓ 기발한 생각을 하려면 주름이 생김

weld, welt, wield

- weld ⓥ 용접하다

His style of painting welds impressionism with surrealism.

- welt ⓝ (맞거나 쓸려서 피부가) 부푼(부은) 자국

In recent days, Afghan social media has swirled with photos of men and women, showing fresh welts from being beaten by Taliban mobs for not dressing according to Islamic custom.

- wield ⓥ 행사하다, 휘두르다

Instead, North Korean leader Kim Jong Un has launched more missiles this year, 43, than any time since 2011, when he took power — apparently replaying the strategy he wielded in 2017 with Donald Trump.

wag, wage

- **wag** ⓥ (개가 꼬리를) 흔들다 흔들다

it's (a case of) the tail wagging the dog.   주객이 전도된 상황

⑪ finger-wag ⓥ 삿대질하다

And when they do behave badly — like breaking quarantine — there's a social reason too for the tongue-clucking and finger-wagging that follow.

- **wage** ⓥ (전쟁을) 벌이다

When the Taliban seized power in 1996, it waged a war against Afghan women.

waggle, wiggle

- **waggle** ⓥ 흔들다(up and down or from side to side using short quick movements)

Listeners are instructed to waggle their tongues, raise their arms to the ceiling or simply lie back and relax.

- **wiggle** ⓥ (꼼지락꼼지락) 움직이다

his sister, who was much younger — only a Seven — wiggling with impatience in her chair.

xenophilia, xenophobia

- **xenophilia** ⓝ 외국인(문화, 풍습)에 매료되기

Xenophilia is the opposite of xenophobia. Broadly speaking, it describes openness to the immense human diversity of the world.

- **xenophobia** ⓝ 외국인을 싫어함.

In recent years the Dominican Republic has stepped up efforts to expel undocumented Haitian migrants amid rising xenophobia.

xeno~ : 외국의(alien)
philia : 좋아함
phobia : 싫어함

yang, yin

- yang ⓝ (동양 철학에서의) 양

Nadal is on the verge of equaling Federer, his longtime tennis yang who has become a very friendly rival.

- yin ⓝ (동양 철학에서의) 음

Some speculate that Fan is in hiding, but most agree her disappearance seems tied to leaks on Chinese social media in late May of "yin yang" contracts under her name — in which one contract is disclosed for tax purposes and a larger one is discreetly paid to the star.

ⓓ yin-yang contract : commonly used in Chinese showbiz which conceal the actor's real salary showing a different pay on paper.

Nadal, Federer : 테니스 선수

Fan : (중국) 판빙빙 영화 배우

yoke, yolk

- yoke ⓝ 멍에

ⓓ yoke ⓥ (두 사람의 생각 등을) 얽어매다

Instead she split her party, yoking a tide of pro-poor populism to storm to a massive election victory in 1971.

- yolk ⓝ (계란) 노른자

The yolk contains choline, which is essential for brain development and may help with memory.

zeitgeist, zenith

- zeitgeist ⓝ 시대정신

There he announced a $2.5 billion investment in South Korean content over the next four years and noted that stories created in the country "are now at the heart of the global cultural zeitgeist."

he : 넷플릭스 최고경영진

- zenith ⓝ 최고, 정점

At its zenith, FTX soared to a valuation of $40 billion.

FTX : 암호화폐 거래소

색인

10
- amble, ample
- amber, ember
- accomplish, achieve
- affordable, available

11
- affix, annex
- addiction, addition
- assign, assuage

12
- affidavit, affiliate
- alley, ally
- able, capable

13
- allay, alloy
- alternate, alternative
- audible, audit, audition
- aristocrat, autocrat

14
- aptitude, attitude
- affinity, affront
- argue, assert
- autonomous, automatic

15
- argument, augment
- acid, acrid
- accredit, credit

16
- air, aircraft, airlift
- aghast, angst
- affection, affectation

17
- affect, effect
- airpower, airspace
- append, upend

18
- abstract, abstracted
- amass, assess
- attire, attrition
- amnesia, anemia

19
- authoritarian, authoritative
- asset, assist
- acrimony, acronym
- astrology, astronomy

20
- anecdote, antidote
- assassinate, assimilate
- absolve, absorb
- adore, adorn

21
- AI
- adapt, adept, adopt
- aggravate, aggregate
- assail, assault

22
- agitate, agony
- adulterate, adultery
- accrue, accurate

23
- ax, axis
- acquire, acquit
- affable, agreeable, amenable
- ambient, ambiguous

24
- acclimate, accumulate
- accident, incident
- accede, concede
- accelerate, decelerate

25
- abolition, abortion
- anathema, anatomy
- appropriate, approximate
- abysmal, abyss

26
- article, articulate
- absence, abstinence
- acumen, acupuncture
- allude, allure

27
- acute, blunt
- administer, admonish

28
- apartheid, apathy
- access, accession
- aid, aide

29
- adjacent, nascent
- amity, enmity
- amiable, amicable, animosity
- alien, alienable

30
- abide, abode
- armament, armistice
- attach, attaché

31
- ardent, arduous
- annals, annual
- antipathy, sympathy
- apparatchik, apparatus

34
- bump, pump
- fist bump, fist pump
- base, bias

35
- boom, boon
- bigwig, wig
- bruise, cruise
- bamboo, bamboozle

36
- budge, dodge, nudge
- browbeat, drumbeat
- bandage, bondage

37
- breastfeed, breathtaking
- bunt, butt, buttress
- bald, bold

38
- behemoth, behest
- batter, battery
- brigade, brigadier

39
- better, bitter
- buffer, buffet
- backwater, backward
- bemoan, moan

40
- backstab, backstop
- bog, bogus
- beam, seam

41
- burnish, furnish

41	breeze, freeze	59	unclean, unclear
	balk, bulk		cadet, cadre
42	belonging, belongings		clarify, classify
	bereaved, bereft	60	criticize, critique
	breadbasket, breadline, breadwinner		critical mass, critical point
	burro, burrow		chore, core
43	breakout, breakthrough	61	circle, cycle
	bunch, bundle		circuitous, circulate,
44	bellicose, belligerent		captive, captor
	bluff, buff	62	commute, telecommute
	barely, barley		castrate, castigate
	bookmark, earmark		civic, civil
45	belie, betray	63	carcass, corpse
	benefactor, beneficiary		couch, crouch
	breach, broach		copper, corpulent
46	bellow, billow		commodity, commonality
	blue-blooded, full-blooded	64	crackle, crinkle
	cold-blood, warm-blood		chart, charter
	befall, befit		collide, collude
47	bail, bill	65	classic, classical, classified
	blur, slur		culinary, cutlery
	bay, bray		accord, cord
48	brass, brazen		cucumber, sea cucumber
	barb, barber	66	corridor, corrode
	boo, coo, moo, woo		cardinal, cordial
	bob, sob		considerable, considerate
49	bacon, beacon		carriage, coach
	bazaar, bizarre	67	cement, cemetery
	breed, brood		component, composure
50	blizzard, buzzard		correlate, corrugate
	banquet, bouquet		coda, coma
	beau, beauty	68	convey, convoy
	bait, bite		canvas, canvass
51	barrel, barren		capitulate, catapult
	burst, bust		carton, cartoon
	blacklist, whitelist	69	crowdfund, crowdsource
52	bit, bitt		collective, collectible
	blind, blink		collaborate, corroborate
	breadth, breath		communicable, communicative
	baggy, buggy	70	clatter, clutter
53	brim, brink		communicate, communique
	buddy, bully		console, consolidate
	burden, burdensome, overburdened		clomp, clump
		71	constable, constant
			contend, content
56	charisma, chasm		bone of contention, point of contention
	consecrate, desecrate	72	clash, crash, crush
	calligraphy, chemotherapy, choreography	73	crashing, crushing
	clot, clout, cot		cereal, cerebral
57	crude, cruel		contagious, contiguous
	cannon, canon	74	contain, contaminate
	crucial, crucible		conscience, prescience
58	clean, clear		conscientious, conscious
	clean-cut, clear-cut		click, clock

75	cloak, cluck, croak	92	dairy, diary
	carry, miscarry	93	detain, deter
	ceiling, cellar		detergent, deterrent
76	complex, compound		detriment, detritus
	connection, connectivity		dip, drip
76	claim, clamor	94	dim, dime
77	cornerstone, millstone, milestone, touchstone		dire, dour
			destiny, destination
	comparable, comparative, compatible		den, din
78	clamp, cramp	95	defang, default
	cram, cramped		device, devise
	cause, clause		dramatic, drastic
	calamity, catastrophe	96	dynamic, dynamo
79	celebrate, celestial		deadline, deadlock
	chalk, choke		domestic, domesticated
	crass, cross	97	delude, deluge
80	confab, confide		drab, drag
	chafe, chaff		dinghy, dingy
	clench, clinch	98	demean, demeanor
81	capital, capitol		dismal, dismay
	crotch, crutch		deferment, deference
	condolence, condone		dab, dub
82	credence, credential	99	dud, dude
	credible, credulous		dearth, death
	costume, custom		depart, deport
	competition, competitiveness		depot, despot
83	center, centralize	100	dressage, dressing
	crawl, creep		dessert, desert
	creeping, creepy		despoil, spoil
	cant, canter	101	defuse, diffuse
84	crumble, crumple		delinquency, relinquish
	confess, profess		demagogue, demography
	commission, commitment	102	dimple, pimple, wimple
85	construct, deconstruct		disinformation, misinformation
86	confidant, confident		drawback, drawdown
	clang, clank		despair, desperate
	clink, clunk	103	downmarket, upmarket
	coalesce, coarse		disparage, disparate
87	comprise, compromise		dividend, divine
	compassion, compensate		downtime, uptime
	commensurate, commiserate	104	downtick, uptick
			downsize, upsize
			downside, upside
90	don, doff		downbeat, upbeat
	distract, distraught	105	dialect dialectic
	detract, retract		discreet, discrete
	de facto, de jure		discriminate, incriminate
91	discus, discuss		deduce, deduct
	déjà vu, de rigueur	106	diverse, divert
	de-mine, demise		deliberate, deliberative, debilitate
	dandle, dangle	107	deprave, deprive
92	dawdle, doodle, dwindle		doubt, suspect
	drawl, drool	108	dibs, digs
	detonate, donate		defunct, defund

108	digit, digital	125	expand, expanse
109	daze, doze		expend, expense
	dissect, disseminate		expendable, expensive
	dole, sole	126	exploit, explore
110	degenerate, denigrate		expatriate, expatiate, repatriate
	decisive, decided, divisive	127	existent, existential
	diagonal, diagnose		entitle, entity
	devolve, dissolve		emphasis, empathy
111	devoted, devotional, devout	128	exalt, extol
	delete, delve		exhort, extort
			extricate, intricate
			equestrian, pedestrian
114	elegy, eulogy	129	enjoin, enjoy
	enclave, exclave		eclipse, elapse
	endonym, exonym		embargo, embark
	excoriate excruciating		
	egalitarian, egregious		
115	ennoble, noble	132	formative, formidable
	excommunicate, incommunicado		flax, flex
	endemic, epidemic, pandemic		fluke, flux
116	en masse, en route		fester, foster
	enlist, enroll	133	disfigure, prefigure
	engine, engineer		fraught, freight, fright
	enfold, unfold		fatigue, fatigues
	exhale, inhale	134	fisherman, fishmonger
117	explicit, implicit		fruiter, fruiterer
	exuberant, exude		ferment, foment
	exit, exodus		forge, forgo
118	emergence, emergency		fauna, flora
	endanger, engender	135	fault line, front line
	evoke, invoke, revoke		flag, flog
	erratic, erroneous		forceful, forcible
119	high-end, low-end		fairway, faraway
	eradicate, erase	136	fort, fortress
	embody, embolden		force, forced
	expert, expertise		fickle, flicker
120	eject, evict	137	fungible, fungus
	equivalent, equivocal		afflict, inflict
	evacuate, evaporate		fragile, frail
	ensue, ensure		florid, fluid
121	erode, erupt	138	ferry, fury
	express, expressive		familial, familiar
	exquisite, inquisitive		fervent, feverish
	explode, implode		foothill, foothold
122	entranced, entreat	139	flash, flesh, flush
	electric, electronic		fandom. fathom
	elevate, escalate	140	fallow, fellow
123	ethic, ethnic, ethos		florescent, fluorescent
	extinct, extinguish		fodder, folder
	establishment, antiestablishment	141	flank, flunk
124	elide, elude		filch, filter
	earthy, earthen, earthly		facade, facet
	emigrate, immigrate		fortuitous, fortunate
	envisage, envision	142	a few, few

142	foresight, hindsight	150	glow, glower
	fillet, filly		growl, prowl
	fraction, fractious	161	glimmer, glimpse
143	fertile, futile		genesis, genius, genus
	funeral, furnace		genealogy, geology
	flaunt, flout	162	governess, governor
144	flatline, flatten, headline		glory, gory
	farther, further		grievance, grieve
	flagrant, fragrant	163	gleam, glean
145	faction, fiction, friction		graft, grift
	faint, feint		gasp, grasp
	ferocious, fierce		
146	feast, feat	166	haven, heaven
	foggy, fogy		hyperbola, hyperbole
	flay, fray		hurl, hurtle
147	fluster, flutter		huddle, hurdle
	face value, stone-faced		harbinger, harbor
	forage, foray	167	hardly, hardy
	forestall, foretell		hub, hubris
148	feather, feature		hangry, hanker, hungry
	flair, flare	168	heterogenous, homogeneous
149	fix, fixer		hone, honk
			harass, harness
152	gruff, guff	169	habit, habitat
	gorge, gorgeous		hot air, hot spot
	gaff, gaffe	170	initial, initiative
	gook, goon		ICU, IUD, DUI
153	gaggle, giggle		interfere, intervene
	gargle, gurgle		irony, ivory
	grandee, guarantee	171	irrigate, irritate
	grace, grand		inter, intra
154	graceful, gracious		icon, idol, scion
	grim, grime	172	idea, ideal
	gatekeeper, goalkeeper		inhabit, inhibit
	ghastly, ghost		isle, islet
155	ghost kitchen, ghost write	173	incubate, intubate
	gut, gutter		inmate, innate
	gut feeling, gut reaction, gut wrenching		inchoate, incoherent
156	governance, government		inappropriate, misappropriate
	globe, glove	174	inherent, inherit
	globalization, glocalization		incite, indict
	gauge, gauze		interlock, interlude
157	garish, garnish		impassable, impasse
	grid, grit	175	impassive, impressive
	gill, grill		infest, infidelity
158	grade, degrade		implicate, imply
	downgrade, upgrade		impart, impartial
159	gravel, grovel	176	inculcate, inoculate
	grave, gravity		inundate, inured
	gravitas, gravitate		implacable, implausible
	garlic, ginger		ill-conceived, ill-equipped, ill-gotten
160	goods, goody	177	impeachment, impediment
	gargantuan, gregarious		impinge, impish

177	impracticable, impractical	193	liter, litter
	imperil, imperial		
178	imperious, impervious		
	impending, imposing	196	mangle, mingle
	impertinent, imperturbability		mislead, misread
179	improbable, impromptu		mediate, meditate
	improvise, extemporize, extemporaneous	197	medicine, medication
	intense, intensive		medical, medicinal
180	ignoble, ignominious		mussel, muzzle
	incalculable, incurable		mantle, mental
	incarcerate, incantation, incarnate	198	mass, landmass, massive
181	irascible, ire		mess, morass
	indigenous, indignant, indignity	199	mean, means
	install, instate		moderate, modest
		200	metabolism, metastasize
			mandate, mandatory
182	jug, jut		morbid, moribund
	jet lag, jetway		matchmaking, matchup
	jangle, jingle	201	memorialize, memorize
	jungle, jumble		manhandle, mishandle
183	jubilation, jubilee		misfire, surefire
	jiggle, juggle		militant, militia
	jaw, maw, paw	202	mutual, mutate
184	jump-start, kick-start		major, minor
	ajar, jar, jarring		majority, minority
	jaunty, jumpy		maximum, maximize
		203	miniature, minimum
			mound, mount
185	knock out, knockout		mechanical, methodical
	knee, kneel, knell	204	muddle, muffle
	kite, kitten		mob, mobster
	kennel, kernel		module, modulate, mold
		205	mute, mutter
			marrow, mellow
188	lockdown, lockstep		mercenary, mercurial
	loyal, royal		marital, martial
	ludicrous, lugubrious	206	malinger, malice
	lascivious, luscious		mobile, mobilize
189	lewd, lurid		metrics. meteoric
	liquid, liquidation	207	marine, maritime
	leech, lurch		mode, model
	limelight, limestone		magnanimous, magnificent, magnify
	legacy, legend		maize, maze
190	lore, lure	208	melt, smelt
	lift, list		margin, marshal
	livid, vivid	209	moon, moot
191	landscape, moonscape, seascape		million, millennial
	ladder, lard, larder		
	laboratory, lavatory		
192	lull, lullaby	210	nebulous, nefarious
	log, logo		needle, noodle
	limb, limbo, limp		navel, novel
193	facelift, powerlift, uplift		nonage, nonbinary
	loop, loophole	211	nuance, nuisance

211	nevertheless, nonetheless	230	prior, priority
	nada, nadir		pull-up, push-up
	nibble, nimble	231	puppet, puppy
212	normalcy, normality		propensity, prosperity
	normal, abnormal		personable, presentable
	negligence, negotiate		preclude, prelude
	nozzle, nuzzle		PDA
213	natural, nurture	232	pamper, pepper
	neuter, neutral		penetrate, perpetrate
	naturalist, naturalize, neutralize		pronounce, pronouncement, pronunciation
		233	pinch, punch
			produce, productivity, production
216	omnipotent, omnipresent		patent, patient
	order, ordor	234	parcel, particle
217	outage, outrage		pack, pact, peck
	oppression, opprobrium	235	persist, pester
	overwhelm, underwhelm		package, packet
218	overstate, understate		pock, pocket
	outmaneuver, outnumber	236	pregnant, progeny
	outride, override		primal, primary
	ongoing, outgoing		preeminent, prominent
219	officer, official, officious		peach, preach
	outlier, outlandish	237	pallet, pellet, pullet
220	onset, outset		praise, prize
	out, outing, ouster		press, pressure
	overhead, overhear		prospect, prospectus
221	offline, online	238	parlor, parole, patrol
	outpost, outpouring		pageantry, peasant, pheasant
	orient, disorientate, reorient		proliferate, prolific
222	oversee, overseas	239	persecute, prosecute
	overtone, overture, overtures		precipitate, precipitous, propitiate
	outlaw, outlay		pane, panel
223	outreach, overreach	240	proceedings, proceeds
	outbreak, outburst		process, procedure
	outflank, out-flatter	241	precede, proceed
	outtalk, out-touch		precedence, precedent
			potent, potential
		242	punishing punitive
226	pertinacity, pertinent		proactive, provocative
	phenom, phenomenon		pretence, pretension
	peddle, puddle		portion, potion
	pad, paddy	243	passel, tassel
227	permanent, perma-smile		proportion, proposition
	paradox, paragon		pure, purge
	perk, perky	244	propaganda, propagate
228	peek, peep		pat, pet, pot
	plague, plaque		pip, pit
	pain, painstaking	245	physiology, psychology
229	plait, plate		prone, prune
	protein, protean		principal, principle
	peal, peel		presumptive, presumptuous
	periodic, periodical	246	pantheon, pathogen
230	prologue, prolong		precursor, procure
	prostate, prostrate		porter, portal

246	protocol, protract	264	resource, resourcefulness, resourcing
247	pinpoint, pinprick		rake, rock
	parameter, barometer, paramedic	265	rack, racket
	predate, predator		reprisal, reproach
	premier, premiere		retail, retaliate, wholesale
248	quarry, quarter	268	sag, shag
	quality, quantity		sure-footed, underfoot
249	qualitative, quantitative		scrutiny, security
	quack, whack	269	sap, seep
	quadruple, quadriplegia, quadrennial		stiff, steep
			swell, swelter
		270	surge, swarm
252	rapport, rapprochement		systematic, systemic
	rickets, rickety		ship, sip
	reconnaissance, renaissance		spat, spate
	raze, razor	271	schism, schtick
253	reckless, ruthless		spit, spite, split
	render, rendition		stoned, stony
254	evolve revolt, revolution	272	surf, surface
	resident, residual		scum, skim
255	rabid, rabies		scroll, stroll
	rural, urban	273	sociable, social, societal
	resolve, resolute, solve		social distancing, social media, social mobility
256	renegade, renege		slew, stew
	runaway, runway	274	steak, streak
	rash, rush		splash, sprinkle
257	rag, rig		stationary, stationery
	remission, remittance		sane, sanitary
	ramble, rumble, rumple	275	span, spin
258	rife, ripe		salve, savior, savor
	raft, rift	276	stoke, strike, stroke
	run down, rundown	277	signify, signal
259	resurge, resurrect		significance, signification
	reinstall, reinstate		stallion, stellar
	rage, enrage	278	statue, statute
	rot, rug, rut		stature, status
260	respectable, respectful		solidarity, solitary
	respective, irrespective	279	sprint, spurt, squirt
	raid, rail		splint, splinter
	resume, résumé		scar, scare
261	rambunctious, rowdy	280	sparrow, swallow
	responsible, responsive		sallow, shallow
	riffle, ripple		strafe, strife
	resilience, resistance		spangle, sparkle
262	rile, roil	281	spark, spike
	rankle, rattle		shade, shadow
	refer, referee		foreshadow, overshadow
263	retrograde, retrospect	281	shifty, shitty
	relax, relay		secondary, secondly
	raven, ravenous, ravine		superiority, supremacy
	road hog, road rage		squall, squeal
264	retake, retain		solace, solicit

283	shove, shovel	299	staff, stuff
	spiral, sprawl	300	sprain, strain
	showdown, slowdown		stupor, stupa
	static, statistic	301	swipe, swoop
284	suspend, sustain		spell, spill
	sustainability, sustenance	302	secluded, secular
285	straight, straightforward		swig, twig
	squawk, squeak		stubble, stumble
	stink, stint	303	squad, squadron, squat
286	skiff, skip		smug, snug, snuggle
	spot, spy		steady, steadfast
	scam, scan		
287	slay, sly		
	species, spice	306	tweak, twitch
	seasoned, seasonal		currents, torrent
	sanction, sanctuary		taboo, tattoo
288	subsequent, subservient		tambourine, tangerine
	salon, saloon	307	tycoon, typhoon
	string, stringent		tote, tot
289	stab, stub		tawny, tony
	scoff, scofflaw		top-dog, underdog
	schema, scheme	308	trash, tray
290	stool, stoop		turnabout, turnaround
	stalk, stall		text, textile
	scald, scold		truculent, turbulent
	script, scripture	309	temperament, temperance, temperature
291	skylight, skyrocket		temper, template
	score, scorn		telling, telltale
	sober, somber		tense, terse
292	scrawl, scribble	310	telescope, televise
	scrap, scrape		telegram, telegraph
	sheen, shin		tenure, tenuous
293	scrappy, scrubby	311	thick-skinned, thin-skinned
	scrabble, scramble		transient, transitory
	sleeper, slipper		transit, transitional
294	sleeper hit, sleepover		taunt, taut, tout
	sleepy, slippage, slippery	312	tenor, terror
	saw, sow		terrible, terrific, traffic
	spout, sprout		terrified, terrifying
295	stenographer, stereotype	313	trace, trail
	spare, spear	314	trope, trove
	spar, sparse		thermometer, thermogenesis
	sequel, sequence		tract, traction
296	sequester, sequestrate	315	tack, tick, tuck
	stamp, stomp		transpacific, transparent, translucent
	suggestive, suggestible		
	shimmer, simmer		
297	shudder, shutter, stutter	318	unwell, wellness
	shelf, shelve		upcoming, up and coming
	scoop, scope		underlie, underline
298	straddle, straggle, struggle		undercut, undermine
	strip, stripe	319	understanding, understandable
	savage, salvage, ravage		unknowable, unknowing, unknown
299	strap, strop		union, unison

320 vibrant, vital
     vegetarian, veterinarian
     vat, vet
     variable, variant
321 vassal, vessel
     vincible, vulnerable
     vagabond, vanguard
     velocity, veracity
322 venal, venial, vernal
     vantage, vestige, vintage
     vice, virtue
323 virtual, virtuous
     verifiable, veritable
     virulent, virility
     viable, vial
324 vile, vilify, vitriol
     vent, ventilate
     vain, vein, artery
325 vegetable, vegetation
     venerate, venereal
     vindicate, vindictive
     vocal, vociferous
326 viral, visceral, eviscerate
     vicinity, vicissitude
     vacuous, vinous, viscous
327 vacation, vocation
     vacancy, vacate
     vanquish, varnish
     validate, vandalize
     voluble, volume

328 wrath, wreath
     whirlwind, windswept
     wishful, wistful
     watershed, watertight
329 wander, wonder
     will, wilt
     willful, woeful
     wad, wade
330 whim, whip
     wok, woke
     walkaway, walkway
     weigh, wreak
331 weight, heavyweight, lightweight
     warfare, warlike, wartime
332 waive, wave, waver
     wax, wane
     wan, wand
333 wildfire, wildlife
     wallow, willow
     withhold, withstand
     wannabe, would-be, soon-to-be
334 withdraw, withdrawn

334 wink, wrinkle
     weld, welt, wield
335 wag, wage
     waggle, wiggle

336 xenophilia, xenophobia

337 yang, yin
     yoke, yolk

338 zeitgeist, zenith

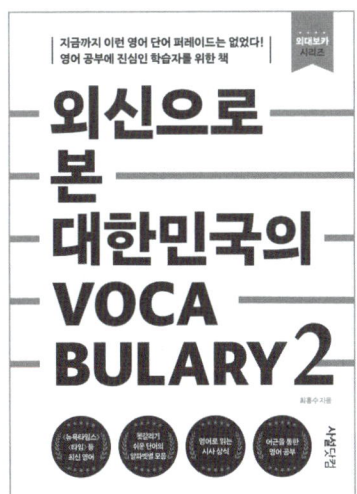

근간 예정

《외신으로 본 대한민국의 VOCABULARY 2》
《외신으로 본 대한민국의 Phrases와 Phrasal verb》

영어를 배우면서 접하는 문장의 출처는 매우 중요합니다.
사설닷컴에서 출간하는 영어책 속 문장들을 통하여 〈Time〉과 〈The New York Times〉 등 기라성(綺羅星) 같은 언론 매체를 마주할 수 있습니다.
우리나라의 높아진 국제적 위상에 맞추어 대한민국에 관한 기사가 쏟아지고 있습니다. 이런 기사를 통해 영어를 공부한다면 영어단어를 좀 더 쉽고 생생하게 익힐 수 있습니다.
《외신으로 본 대한민국의 VOCABULARY 2》는 《외신으로 본 대한민국의 VOCABULARY 1》과 동일하게 구성하였습니다.
《외신으로 보는 대한민국의 Phrases와 Phrasal verb》에도 외신에서 다룬 대한민국에 관한 내용 중 관용구, 숙어가 들어간 문장들을 정리했습니다.

외신으로 본
대한민국의
VOCABULARY 1

초판 1쇄 발행 2023년 8월 15일
지은이 | 최홍수
펴낸곳 | 사설닷컴
전   화 | 010-7498-5559
팩   스 | 031-906-7539
메   일 | hsyjjw@hanmail.net
주   소 | 경기도 고양시 일산동구 강촌로 191
ISBN | 979-11-85203-51-5 (13740)

* 잘못 만들어진 책은 구입처에서 교환 가능합니다.